I.B.TAURIS SHORT HISTORIES

I.B.Tauris Short Histories is an authoritative and elegantly written new series which puts a fresh perspective on the way history is taught and understood in the twenty-first century. Designed to have strong appeal to university students and their teachers, as well as to general readers and history enthusiasts, *I.B.Tauris Short Histories* comprises a novel attempt to bring informed interpretation, as well as factual reportage, to historical debate. Addressing key subjects and topics in the fields of history, the history of ideas, religion, classical studies, politics, philosophy and Middle East studies, the series seeks intentionally to move beyond the bland, neutral 'introduction' that so often serves as the primary undergraduate teaching tool. While always providing students and generalists with the core facts that they need to get to grips with the essentials of any particular subject, *I.B.Tauris Short Histories* goes further. It offers new insights into how a topic has been understood in the past, and what different social and cultural factors might have been at work. It brings original perspectives to bear on manner of its current interpretation. It raises questions and – in its extensive further reading lists – points to further study, even as it suggests answers. Addressing a variety of subjects in a greater degree of depth than is often found in comparable series, yet at the same time in concise and compact handbook form, *I.B.Tauris Short Histories* aims to be 'introductions with an edge'. In combining questioning and searching analysis with informed history writing, it brings history up-to-date for an increasingly complex and globalised digital age.

www.short-histories.com

'Stephen Conway's *A Short History of the American Revolutionary War* offers proof that big things come in small packages. In lucid prose, without a whiff of cant, Conway cuts through a century-long scholarly logjam about whether the American Revolution is best seen as a war about home rule, or about who should rule at home (as Carl Becker famously posed the question). Instead, Conway gives us a global American Revolution with multiple causes and ambiguous and far-reaching consequences. Conway's *A Short History of the American Revolutionary War* locates the conflict's deep roots early in the colonial period, and traces its broad branches from Boston to Bengal, Philadelphia to the Philippines. His tight narrative tracks the war's many fronts in North America, the Caribbean, West Africa, South Asia, and beyond. Conway explores multiple wars as well as multiple continents: here unfolds a brutal civil war as well as a heroic struggle of colonial liberation, a European and ultimately a global conflict as well as the war that made the United States. A political and cultural conflict, Conway's *Revolution* is first and foremost a shooting war, with all the attendant drama and contingency of the finest military history. A diverse cast of characters – ranging from ministers in London; to generals in far-flung fields; to African-Americans fighting for freedom, Native Americans demanding alliance, and women seeking safety and stability – gives a human face to bloody insurrection and grand strategy. This is the work of a master historian at the height of his powers. I know of nothing like it.'
  – Jane Kamensky, Harry S Truman Professor of History, Brandeis University

'A major scholar of the Revolutionary War, Stephen Conway has written an outstanding introduction for both students and laymen. He excels in placing the war in a global context including Europe, the Caribbean, the Mediterranean and India. He has demonstrated better than anyone the diffusion of British troops and ships throughout the world, and the extent to which military demands in the Caribbean deflected much-needed resources from winning the war in the American colonies. Transcending the narrow national focus of so many accounts, he reveals this to have been a war in which Britain was more isolated than at any other time in its modern history and in which it was threatened with serious attempts of invasion for the first time since the Spanish Armada. Conway offers a compelling explanation of why Britain lost America. At the same time, his broader perspective shows that it was a war that the British did not entirely lose, since they won major victories against the Bourbons in 1782 and succeeded in bankrupting France.'
  – Andrew O'Shaughnessy, Professor of History, University of Virginia and Saunders
  Director, Robert H Smith International Center for Jefferson Studies, Monticello

'Stephen Conway's *Short History* takes a remarkably enlarged view of the American Revolutionary War: from a rebellion in the British colonies of North America to the intervention of European powers, to fighting that spread round the globe, to a postwar settlement in which Britain fared unexpectedly well. Conway has told this sprawling story with authority and clarity. He has shown that while the British were unable to keep thirteen of their American colonies, they did have the fiscal and naval resources to survive the war and fare better than their enemies in the late eighteenth and early nineteenth century. This *Short History* is just the place to begin to understand the American Revolutionary War.'
  – Ira D Gruber, Harris Masterson, Jr Professor Emeritus of History, Rice University

A SHORT HISTORY OF THE AMERICAN REVOLUTIONARY WAR

STEPHEN CONWAY

I.B. TAURIS
LONDON · NEW YORK

Published in 2013 by I.B.Tauris & Co Ltd
6 Salem Road, London W2 4BU
175 Fifth Avenue, New York NY 10010
www.ibtauris.com

Distributed in the United States and Canada Exclusively by Palgrave
Macmillan, 175 Fifth Avenue, New York NY 10010

ISBN: 978 1 84885 812 1 (hb)
ISBN: 978 1 84885 813 8 (pb)

A full CIP record for this book is available from the British Library
A full CIP record is available from the Library of Congress

Library of Congress Catalog Card Number: available

Typeset in Sabon by Ellipsis Digital Limited, Glasgow
Printed and bound by T.J. International, Padstow, Cornwall

Contents

Preface

All authors incur heavy debts in writing a book; I am no exception. Over many years of studying the American Revolution, my understanding has been enriched by reading the work of a large number of other historians. I have not been able to do justice to their contribution to my thinking in the Notes to this book, but another indication of the extent of my appreciation comes in the form of the 'Further Reading' section at the end. One particular debt merits highlighting. I have benefited greatly from the new perspectives opened up by the work of the Contractor State Group – a network of scholars in many different countries that has been studying the impact of war-related spending on various European states in the eighteenth century. The Contractor State Group is already responsible for several volumes of essays, all of which I found very helpful. More importantly, perhaps, members of the Contractor State Group have been generous in their willingness to share ideas not yet in print. My colleagues and friends Rafael Torres Sánchez of the University of Navarra at Pamplona and Joël Felix of the University of Reading have talked to me extensively about their respective interests in Spain and France in the American Revolutionary War. The three of us hope, one day, to write a book together that considers the war from the vantage points of its principal European participants; I hope they will consider this slim volume as helping us to reach that goal.

I have also learned a lot from my contact with the historians involved in the *Oxford Handbook on the American Revolution*, edited by Jane Kamensky and Edward Gray. I attended a conference run by the editors in a snowbound Chicago in February 2011, at which I was able to talk with many leading American historians of the Revolution; more recently Jane and Ed kindly invited me to a conference on 'Britain's American War', in the very congenial setting of the Huntington Library in California, which stimulated me to think in new ways about a conflict with which I was already very familiar. I am grateful to all who contributed to those two conferences, both established historians and newcomers; the presence of so many of the latter emphatically demonstrated that a talented new generation of scholars is looking afresh at the American Revolution and its war.

Unusually for a brief and synoptic study of this kind, I have drawn extensively on archival material. Much of it had been consulted years ago, as part of my research for earlier books, but some has been examined specifically for this work. I am greatly indebted to the archivists at the following institutions: the Bedfordshire Record Office, Bedford; Boston Public Library, Boston, Massachusetts; Birmingham City Archives; the British Library, London; the Centre for Buckinghamshire Studies, Aylesbury; the Centre for Kentish Studies, Maidstone; Dr Williams' Library, London; the Historical Society of Pennsylvania, Philadelphia; Hull University Library; the Huntington Library, San Marino, California; Leicestershire Record Office, Leicester; Library of Congress, Washington, DC; the National Archives of Scotland, Edinburgh; the National Archives of the United Kingdom, Kew; the National Army Museum, Chelsea; the National Library of Ireland, Dublin; the National Library of Scotland, Edinburgh; the National Library of Wales, Aberystwyth; the National Maritime Museum, Greenwich; the New-York Historical Society, New York City; the New York State Library, Albany; Nottingham University Library; the Public Record Office of Northern Ireland, Belfast; the Royal Artillery Institution, Woolwich; Sheffield Archives; the Somerset Record Office, Taunton; the Staffordshire Record Office, Stafford; the Surrey Record Office, Guildford; the West Suffolk Record Office, Bury St Edmunds; the West Yorkshire Archives Service, Leeds; the William L. Clements Library, Ann Arbor, Michigan. I am also grateful to the owners of private collections, particularly the Marquess of Bath for access to his papers at Longleat; Lady Elizabeth Godsal, who allowed me to examine the Colleton, Garth and Godsal Family

Papers at Haines Hill; the Duke of Northumberland, who gave me permission to use the Percy Papers in Alnwick Castle; and Mr Oliver Russell, who arranged for me to see the Macpherson Grant Papers at Ballindalloch Castle.

I should like to record three further debts. The first is to the History Department at University College London. I am fortunate to work with such marvellous colleagues, whose work always inspires me to further efforts with my own. The students I have taught over the years have also stimulated me to think afresh about many issues that had been settled in my mind; imagining how they might react to what I was writing helped me greatly to decide on the structure and content of the current work. My second debt is to Alex Wright of I.B.Tauris, who asked me to write the book and persisted even when I doubted whether I had the time to undertake the task. Despite my early reservations, I have enjoyed revisiting the American Revolution and its war, and I thank Alex for his encouragement and support. Finally, I want to express my gratitude to my family, especially my wife and son, who for many years have put up with my absorption in the War of Independence with remarkable patience and good nature.

Introduction

The conflict that began as a rebellion of most of Britain's North American colonies in 1775, and ended with the British acknowledgement of the independence of the United States in 1783, will be familiar to most readers, if only as a result of its various cultural manifestations. The war has been prominent in novels such as James Fenimore Cooper's *The Spy* (1821) and *Lionel Lincoln* (1825); in writings that blend fact and fiction, such as Kenneth Roberts's *Rabble in Arms* (1939); in plays like George Bernard Shaw's *Devil's Disciple* (1897); and in films, notably Robert Dillon and Hugh Hudson's *Revolution* (1985), in which Al Pacino takes the lead as New York fur-trapper Tom Dobb, and Roland Emmerich and Robert Rodat's controversial and much criticized *The Patriot* (2000), starring the Australian actor Mel Gibson as the all-American hero Benjamin Martin.

Nor has the war lacked for more serious historical treatment. From the moment it concluded, the flow of publications has been steady; though only on the western side of the North Atlantic has it ever truly turned into a torrent. The years surrounding the bicentennial of American Independence in 1976 inspired a great wave of writing, some of it merely repeating what was already known, but most opening up new perspectives, particularly on the role of women and African–Americans. More recently, historians have again focused on the war and tried to understand it afresh, not least because, as the United States changes demographically, those marginalized in, or even omitted from, the established narrative – be they Native Americans, African–Americans or Hispanic–Americans – are finally receiving proper attention. For many Americans, the subject has been perennially interesting for obvious reasons; the war saw the birth and survival, in difficult and trying circumstances, of their nation. As that nation has, in the last century or more, played a vital role in shaping the world, we should not be surprised that non-Americans have also wanted to know more about an important conflict.

Given the very substantial literature that already exists on the war, and the appearance recently of a similarly short volume,[1] some justification for a further study seems necessary. In my case, justification is doubly required, as in the mid-1990s I published a general history of the war and then went on to write a detailed study of its impact on Britain and Ireland.[2] Why should I want to return to the war now? In my many years of research, writing and teaching on different aspects of eighteenth-century history since I first published on the subject, I have inevitably come to see the War of Independence in new ways and to appreciate the importance of matters that, in the 1990s, I (and other historians) under-emphasized or even overlooked. Recent studies of Britain as a European power, with important European connections, have encouraged me to re-evaluate and modify my earlier conceptions of the war.[3] So, too, has the emphasis in the scholarship of the last few years on geography; particularly place, landscape and distance.[4] Perhaps above all, I have benefitted from the insights provided by working with an international team of scholars in the Contractor State Group, who have been studying different aspects of European war-making in the eighteenth century. Through the labours of my colleagues, I have learned a good deal in particular about the impact of the War of Independence on Spain.[5] I welcome the opportunity to present my new thinking.

In this account, the subject is placed in a context that most historians chose either to downplay or even ignore. American historians tend to call the struggle the Revolutionary War. They see it either as securing independence, and so as a kind of postscript to the Revolution, or as a transformative experience and so an integral part of the Revolution itself. But whether they see the war as merely confirmative or as an important aspect of the Revolution, American scholars, with very few exceptions, view the conflict as one fought almost entirely in and for America. For those who follow this line, the war's final act was at Yorktown, Virginia, in October 1781, when Lord

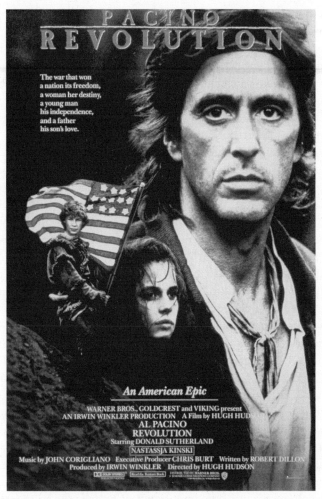

Al Pacino in Hugh Hudson's *Revolution*, a film that helped perpetuate
many of the myths of the War of Independence.

Cornwallis's British army surrendered and military operations in
North America effectively ceased.[6] Many British historians tell the
same story, though usually with more understanding of the difficulties that British military commanders encountered in trying to
win an armed struggle at such a great distance from home.[7] Only

a few historians present the war from a different perspective, and emphasize its global dimensions.[8] I tried to do this back in the 1990s, but now I want to promote the global view more boldly, for it dramatically changes the war's appearance, and even challenges the conventional wisdom that it was simply an American triumph and a British defeat. The current work places the conflict in a very broad context, and argues that it was a world war as much as a struggle for America's future.

From 1778, when the French turned out to be belligerent, the War of Independence became much more than a war for America. It spread to all areas of Anglo–French contact and competition: to the Caribbean, West Africa and Asia. Britain and Ireland faced the threat of invasion. In the summer of 1779, the Spanish entry into the war increased the danger of an enemy landing in the British Isles, as the combined Bourbon fleets outnumbered the Royal Navy. Spanish intervention also broadened the war's geographical range still further; now Central America became a military theatre, and the British government was soon hatching ambitious plans to extend the war into the Pacific. At the same time, British ministers were compelled to think defensively; the Mediterranean outposts of Gibraltar and Minorca became exposed to enemy attack. The Dutch joined the war at the end of 1780, extending the conflict yet again, as their scattered bases in the West Indies, West Africa, the Cape and southern Asia became targets for the British armed forces. This global war, furthermore, continued after Yorktown. Admiral Rodney's victory at the Saintes in April 1782 saved Jamaica from Franco–Spanish invasion; to this day, John Bacon's classically clothed statue of Rodney, gazing out over Spanish Town Square like a Roman emperor, reminds us of the importance of his triumph to the island's planter elite. In the same year as Rodney's ships preserved Jamaica, British troops seized Dutch slave-trading stations in western Africa. The siege of Gibraltar was still underway when the peace preliminaries were signed. In faraway India, the war went on for months after the negotiators in Paris had finally agreed terms.

The global perspective is, of course, a British one; it was the British who fought in all the widely scattered military and naval theatres; it was for them that the war was truly a worldwide conflict.

John Bacon's statue at Spanish Town, Jamaica, of Admiral Sir George Brydges Rodney, victor of the Battle of the Saintes in April 1782.

But my intention is not to counter too American-centric a view of the war with a purely British one. If the book appears simply as an apology for British politicians, admirals and generals, then it has failed in its purpose.[9] My aim is to persuade readers to see the war not just as the British government would have seen it (though that perspective is a valuable one, giving some sense of unity to an otherwise diverse set of conflicts), but also from the viewpoint of the continental European powers. For the European enemies of the British, as well as for the British themselves, the war became a great deal more than a struggle for and in America. For the French government, it was an opportunity to reduce British power, which had been boosted considerably by the Seven Years War (1756–63), and to restore lost French territory and prestige. If Britain could be stripped of its North American colonies, its strength would surely be undermined. French minsters were not content with this outcome, however; they also wanted to improve France's position in the West Indies, West Africa and, perhaps above all, in Asia. For the Spanish government, the War of Independence likewise represented an opportunity to regain lost territory. Florida, which had been ceded at the end of the Seven Years War, was at the top of list, but it also included long-lost possessions such as Gibraltar, Minorca and even Jamaica, annexed by the English in 1655. The Dutch entered the war reluctantly, because the British forced them into it, but they also had global ambitions, albeit of a defensive nature. They held islands in the Caribbean and had a foothold on the South American mainland. Their trading posts stretched in a great arc from the west coast of Africa down to the Cape and across to India, Ceylon and the East Indies. The Dutch objective was to hold on to as many of these scattered stations as they could.

In adopting a global view of the war, I am not ignoring the American one. The war's international dimensions mattered to Americans as well as to the British, French, Spanish and Dutch. The Americans emerged triumphant in the sense that they secured their political independence from the British Crown. While this was not their war aim when the first shots were fired at Lexington and Concord in the spring of 1775, it became their principal objective from July 1776; to have achieved their independence by the time the peace treaties were signed was no mean feat. Yet, to imply that the Americans won the war through their own efforts alone would be highly misleading. Even before the conflict broadened to include the Bourbon powers and the Dutch, the colonial rebels realized that they needed foreign help. At first, assistance came primarily in the form of munitions and money; but for the European powers to provide anything more substantial required evidence that the Americans were not going to come to terms with the British government and secure for themselves an enhanced position within the British Empire. The Declaration of Independence, though usually seen as a straightforward announcement, for domestic consumption, of America's breaking the final ties with Britain, was at least partly about persuading the European powers that America was serious about its rebellion, and would not be returning to the British fold. As soon as the French government was clear that the Americans were in earnest, it began to prepare for full military and naval intervention. That intervention, when it eventually came in the spring of 1778, greatly increased the chances of the Americans sustaining their independence. The fortunes of the new United States, in other words, crucially depended on events far from America itself. Christopher Marshall, a Pennsylvanian enthusiast for the Revolution, was under no illusions about the importance of such distant developments, celebrating in his diary in June 1781 reports (inaccurate, as it turned out) that 'Hyder Aly Kan' of Mysore had retaken all the French posts in India seized by the British earlier in the war.[10] Marshall recognized that the people of the United States were involved in a global conflict, and that the efforts of European states, and even Indian princes such as Haidar Ali, helped to determine how much force British ministers could deploy in America. Even the timing and the terms of the peace treaty, including the striking territorial generosity to the United States, owed much to perceptions amongst the protagonists of the balance of power between the British and their European enemies.

If the conflict became a global struggle from 1778, its Anglo–American aspect can be viewed as a civil war. Its internecine character had two aspects. First, the war divided the transatlantic British nation. The American colonists regarded themselves as Britons, at least until 1776. They were contending, as they saw it, for the rights that they shared with Britons in Britain. Metropolitan Britons, at least in the first months of the war, also tended to view the Americans as part of the extended British family. To those Britons who sympathized with the colonists, they were brothers or cousins across the ocean with legitimate grievances against an authoritarian government in London. Even metropolitan Britons who objected to the conduct of the colonies and supported coercion tended to view Americans as 'rebels', a designation that was hardly positive, but at least implied that they were still the king's subjects. The Declaration of Independence, somewhat surprisingly, did not fundamentally alter British attitudes; partly because it was long expected, and therefore came as no surprise, and partly because news of the Declaration was soon followed by reports of British success in the New York campaign of 1776, which persuaded many Britons that American resistance would soon be at an end. From the British perspective, the decisive parting of the ways came not in 1776, but in 1778. When the Americans allied with the French, the long-running enemy, they finally put themselves outside the British fold.[11]

The conflict was a civil war in another sense. It not only split the transatlantic British nation; it also spilt both Britain and America internally. In Britain, opinion was bitterly divided. What proportion of Britons supported Lord North's policy of coercion is difficult to say; it was almost certainly a larger segment at the beginning of the war than it was by its end. But throughout the conflict, a sizeable part of the British political nation sympathized with the American rebels. To call these Britons pro-Americans would be misleading. Many of them were not pro-Americans in any meaningful sense of the term; they were opponents of the government, who feared that if the North ministry succeeded in subduing the colonists, then the British people would be next on the list.[12] America was also riven by the war. Very few colonists had any sense of allegiance to the British Parliament, and so long as the dispute was about Parliament's rights it makes little sense to refer to American loyalism. But once the issue became the colonies' connection with the Crown, a sizeable loyalist party emerged. John Adams famously reckoned that one third of Americans were hostile to independence.[13] Modern scholarship puts the proportion somewhat lower (perhaps one fifth) but, as in all civil wars, allegiances were fluid – many people understandably tried to avoid too close an identification with either side – and the number of loyalists, and for that matter revolutionaries, ebbed and flowed according to the fortunes of war.[14] As a civil contest, the conflict had a complex character. Awareness of a common background may have inhibited participants from treating their enemies as they would have done full-blown outsiders;[15] on the other hand, we have much evidence to suggest that the struggle in America, both between Britons and Americans and between Americans and Americans, was sometimes fought out with the kind of fratricidal fury we tend to associate with internecine wars. Decorous and restrained though the conflict was in certain respects, it was also shockingly violent and brutal.[16]

Revolutionary War, War of Independence, global conflict and civil war; all these labels could easily be applied to the struggle that took place between 1775 and 1783. To capture its complexity and range in a short study is no easy undertaking. For any author attempting such a task, selectivity is unavoidable. With limited space, some interesting aspects of the war have had to be considered only briefly; others have had to be omitted altogether.

The book proceeds in a broadly chronological fashion, though not as a continuous narrative. It starts with the background to the war, particularly the long- and short-term explanations for the breakdown in the relationship between Britain and its North American colonies. The next chapter looks at the conflict's first phase from the spring of 1775 until the end of 1777. During this time, the war was truly a war for America; even so, the two sides made strenuous efforts to convince other states, as well as their own peoples, of the justness of their cause. British attempts to persuade the French and Spanish that they had an interest in seeing the American rebellion crushed, as they too were imperial powers, ultimately came to nothing; the defeat and surrender of a major British field army at Saratoga, in upper New York, in October 1777, convinced the French government that it should accelerate its plans to intervene formally in the war in support of the Americans, who had sent their own emissaries to Paris in 1776. Even before the Franco–American alliance was unveiled in February 1778, ministers in London could see the writing on the wall. From December 1777 they began to prepare for a much wider and more demanding war against Britain's Bourbon rivals: France and Spain. That wider war is the subject of the third chapter. It carries forward the story of the conflict in America but also examines the broadening of the war to take in new parts of the globe. Although the British were, in some senses, thrown on the defensive by Bourbon and then Dutch involvement, and the dramatic escalation of the war, they also, as we will see, took the opportunity to advance their worldwide presence wherever possible; at one point the government in London was even preparing ambitious plans to take the war into the Pacific Ocean, with the aim of attacking vulnerable Spanish possessions in South America and the Philippines.

The fourth chapter focuses on the impact of the war on those we would now describe as civilians – the people not directly involved in the fighting. The struggle's imprint varied greatly, of course, depending on where one looks. In this chapter we follow a geographical approach, examining first the inhabitants living in the fighting zones, then the non-combatants in those areas exposed to attack but not actually the scene of fighting and finally those places remote from the conflict. Some locations might find themselves in one category at one time and another at a different time, and each of the three zones had things in common. But this concentric view reveals much about the intensity of the experience for the people of the different places examined. The fifth chapter looks at the peace-making between the British and the Americans and the British and their European enemies in 1782–3, and more generally tries to explain why the British lost the war in America but preserved much of the rest of their empire in the post-Yorktown phase of the struggle. The final chapter explores the legacy of the war for the different belligerents. The conflict's consequences, as we will see, were in some areas surprisingly modest, but in others truly momentous.

The editors of the *Short History* series envisage their volumes as providing 'an introduction with an edge'. I have taken their injunctions to heart, and written a book that reflects my own view of the Revolutionary War. While I have, of course, been influenced by the work of others, and have incorporated their insights into my own account, I have not attempted to synthesize the existing scholarship in a neutral manner. As a result, I have tried to avoid overburdening the reader with extensive footnotes identifying the publications of those many writers who have produced their own histories of the war. Citations are confined, for the most part, to sources for quotations or for numerical data. The main exception to this self-imposed rule is my acknowledgement of particularly novel ideas that are not my own, or references to specialist works that cover in much more detail matters I can mention only briefly. To guide readers who want to know more, or wish to consider my interpretation alongside alternatives (a highly recommended course of action), a select list of important books and articles is included at the end. I have also drawn up an outline chronology, to enable readers to see at a glance the course of the war in its various settings, and a *dramatis personae*, designed to introduce the principal characters in the story. In the firm belief that spatial awareness is as important as temporal knowledge, a number of maps appear at appropriate points in the text to aid geographical orientation. Illustrations are also included, not because I think they provide us with objective images of the past but to give an impression of how contemporaries, or near-contemporaries, chose to represent the war.

Dramatis Personae

Adams, John (1735–1826), American politician. A Boston lawyer and Massachusetts representative at the Continental Congress, Adams later became second president of the United States.

André, John (1750–80), British army officer. André was executed as a spy by the Americans when he was implicated in the plot to persuade **Benedict Arnold** to hand over the strategically important fort at West Point, New York, to British forces.

Arnold, Benedict (1741–1801), American general whose early achievements as a commander were overshadowed by his changing sides in 1780. Arnold served in the Continental forces in Canada and at Saratoga, but fled to the British army when the Americans discovered his plan to surrender West Point to Sir **Henry Clinton**.

Barrington, William Wildman (1717–93), 2nd Viscount. British secretary at war (minister responsible for the army) until December 1778. He doubted the wisdom of trying to defeat the American rebellion by military means, preferring a naval blockade.

Burgoyne, John (1723–92), British general. He served in America from 1775, when he arrived in besieged Boston with **William Howe** and **Henry Clinton**. He is best known as the commander of the army that surrendered at Saratoga in October 1777. He went on to support the parliamentary opposition.

Burke, Edmund (1729–97), Irish-born British politician. He was a member of the political party led by the Marquess of Rockingham and an opponent of the war against the Americans. He proposed a plan of reconciliation before the fighting started that, had Parliament supported it, may well have avoided the outbreak of hostilities.

Campbell, Archibald (1739–91), commander of the British forces that captured Savannah, Georgia, at the end of 1778. Campbell was later lieutenant governor of Jamaica and governor of Madras.

Carleton, Guy (1724–1808), British soldier and colonial governor. He successfully defended Quebec in December 1775, and was knighted in 1776. Carleton succeeded Sir **Henry Clinton** as commander-in-chief of British forces in North America in 1782, oversaw the British evacuation of New York, 1783, and became 1st Lord Dorchester in 1786.

Carlisle, Frederick Howard (1748–1825), 5th Earl of, British diplomat. In 1778 he led the commission appointed by **Lord North**'s government to negotiate a compromise peace with the Americans. Congress refused to see him.

Catherine II known as the Great (1729–96), Empress of Russia from 1762. Catherine was German by birth. She refused to hire troops to the British government in 1775, and in 1780 formed the League of Armed Neutrality to protect neutral shipping from seizure by the Royal Navy.

Chatham see **Pitt**.

Clinton, Henry (1730–95), British general. A veteran of the Seven Years War in Germany, he served in America from 1775, was knighted in 1776 and became commander-in-chief in North America in succession to Sir **William Howe** in 1778.

Coote, Sir Eyre (1726–83), British general. After having served in India during the Seven Years War, he was commander-in-chief in Bengal, 1777–83.

Cornwallis, Charles (1738–1805), 2nd Earl, British general. Cornwallis served in America from 1776 to the end of the war, surrendering at Yorktown in October 1781. His defeat did not stop him from playing a key role in later British imperial activity; he became governor general of Bengal and then lord lieutenant of Ireland.

Dalling, John (c.1731–98), British soldier and colonial administrator. Dalling was governor of Jamaica, 1777–82, later served in India and was made a baronet in 1783.

Dartmouth, William Legge (1731–1801), 2nd Earl of, British politician. Secretary of state for the colonies when the war began,

Dartmouth was replaced in November 1775 by the more energetic Germain.

Dickinson, John (1732–1808), American politician. A Philadelphia lawyer, Dickinson articulated American resistance to parliamentary taxation in his *Letters from a Farmer in Pennsylvania* (1767–8). He was a moderate voice in the Continental Congress, holding out against independence until the end. But, despite his reluctance to break the ties with Britain, he held public office in the new United States.

Dunmore, John Murray (1732–1809), 4th Earl of, colonial governor. As the last royal governor of Virginia, in November 1775 he tried to rally the enslaved of the colony to the royal standard. He was later governor of the Bahamas, where he was again sympathetic to the enslaved population.

Eliott, George Augustus (1717–90), British general. He commanded the garrison of Gibraltar during the Great Siege of 1779–83, which earned him a knighthood in 1783 and led to his being created Baron Heathfield of Gibraltar in 1787.

Estaing, Jean-Baptiste-Charles-Henri (1729–94), Comte d', French admiral. He brought the Toulon fleet across the Atlantic in 1778, arriving off New York in July. He threatened the British garrison of Newport, Rhode Island, later that year and Savannah, Georgia, in 1779.

Floridablanca, José Moñino y Redondo (1728–1808), Conde de, Spanish statesman. He was chief minister from 1777 and during the period of Spanish involvement in the war.

Fox, Charles James (1749–1806), British politician. Fox was a prominent opponent of the war against the Americans; he became foreign secretary in the Rockingham government of 1782.

Franklin, Benjamin (1706–90), American polymath, politician and diplomat. He represented the United States in Paris from late 1776 and was one of the American negotiators in the peace talks of 1782–3.

Frederick II, known as the Great (1712–86), King of Prussia. His war with France's ally Austria in 1778 briefly inspired British hopes of a revival of the British–Prussian alliance of the Seven Years War.

Gage, Thomas (1719–87), British general. He was the commander-in-chief of the British army in North America, 1763–75, and governor of Massachusetts when the war broke out. Gage was suspected by some of his subordinates of too great a reluctance to use force; he was replaced by the far more popular **William Howe.**

Galvéz, Bernardo de Gálvez y Madrid (1746–86), Conde de, Spanish military commander and colonial administrator. In 1779, as governor of Louisiana, he took charge of the Spanish attack on British West Florida; by May 1781 his forces had captured all of the British posts. He later served as viceroy of New Spain.

Gates, Horatio (1727–86), American general. A former British officer, he enjoyed much fame after his victory at Saratoga and was briefly seen by some Americans as a better commander than Washington. However, Gates was himself heavily defeated at Camden, South Carolina, in 1780 by **Cornwallis.**

George III (1738–1820), King of Great Britain and Ireland from 1760. George supported **Lord North**'s government and its prosecution of the war, accepting the Rockingham ministry and American independence with the greatest reluctance. His wartime role is usually overstated, although his German connections were valuable in facilitating negotiations with the princes who provided auxiliary troops for service in America.

Germain, Lord George (1716–85), British politician. He succeeded Dartmouth as secretary of state for the colonies in November 1775, and continued in that office until February 1782, when he became Viscount Sackville. Germain was the British minister chiefly responsible for the running of the war.

Grant, James (1720–1806), British general. He served in America 1775–78, and then commanded the British forces despatched to the Caribbean when France entered the war.

Grasse, François-Joseph-Paul (1722–88), Comte de, French admiral. He bettered the British fleet led by Admiral **Graves** at the Battle of the Chesapeake in September 1781, sealing Cornwallis's fate at Yorktown, but a few months later was defeated by Admiral **Rodney** at the Battle of the Saintes.

Graves, Thomas (1725–1802), British admiral. Commander of the fleet in North American waters in 1781; he was defeated by de Grasse at the Battle of the Chesapeake that September.

Greene, Nathanael (1742–86), American general from Rhode Island. He rose from a militia private when the war began to quartermaster general of the Continental army and commander in the south from 1780.

Grenville, George (1712–70), British politician. First minister in 1763–5, Grenville was responsible for the first attempts to tax the colonies after the Seven Years War. He was particularly committed to his stamp duties scheme, which he believed would be simple to administer and would be accepted by the Americans.

Haider Ali (*c*.1720–82), ruler of Mysore. He defeated the British forces at Pollilur in 1780 but was himself defeated by **Coote** in a series of engagements in 1781.

Howe, Richard (1726–99), 4th Viscount, British admiral. Commander-in-chief of the navy in American waters, February 1776 to July 1778. He was also (with his brother William) a commissioner empowered to accept American surrender; instead he chose to try to negotiate with the rebels, often going beyond his brief.

Howe, William (1729–1814), British general. Commander-in-chief in North America, 1775–8, Howe was knighted on 13 October 1776 for his services in America. He resigned after **Burgoyne's** surrender at Saratoga, and spent the next few years trying to clear his name.

Jay, John (1745–1829), American statesman and diplomat. A New Yorker, Jay served as president of the Continental Congress and was ambassador to Spain; he was involved in the peace negotiations in Paris in 1782.

Lafayette, Marie-Joseph-Paul-Yves-Roch-Gilbert du Motier (1757–1834), Marquis de, French officer who served in the Continental army from 1777. Lafayette commanded American troops in Virginia in 1781 before the arrival of **Washington**.

Lee, Charles (1732–82), American general. Like **Gates** and **Montgomery**, Lee was a former British officer. He was in charge of the American forces that repulsed a British attack on Charleston, South Carolina, in the summer of 1776, but was captured by

British cavalry in New Jersey in December 1776. Exchanged in 1778, he resumed service with the Continental army, but his reputation was damaged by his conduct at the Battle of Monmouth.

Lincoln, Benjamin (1733–1810), American general. He surrendered Charleston to Sir **Henry Clinton** in May 1780, but had the satisfaction of receiving the British surrender at Yorktown in October 1781.

Louis XVI (1754–93), King of France from 1774. He supported (though with reservations) French intervention to sustain the Americans, first with arms, munitions and money, then with military and naval forces.

Montgomery, Richard (1738–75), American general. A former British army officer, Montgomery remained personally committed to the British crown. He was killed leading American troops at Quebec on the last day of 1775.

Morgan, Daniel (1736–1802), American general. He acquired fame for defeating the British and loyalist forces under **Banastre Tarleton** at Cowpens, South Carolina, in January 1781.

Newcastle, Thomas Pelham-Holles (1693–1768), 1st Duke of, British politician. Newcastle was secretary of state under Walpole, and carried forward his belief in the need to avoid a constitutional clash with the colonies. He lived long enough to help campaign for repeal of the Stamp Act in 1765.

North, Frederick, Lord North (1732–92), British politician. Prime minister when the war began, he continued in office until March 1782 when he resigned. 'Lord North' was a courtesy title; he was the son of the 1st Earl of Guilford, and sat in the House of Commons. North was no great war leader, but he organized the funding of Britain's war effort.

Oswald, Richard (1705–84), British merchant and diplomat. Appointed to conduct the Rockingham government's negotiations in Paris in 1782, Oswald played a key role in agreeing terms with the Americans.

Peirson, Francis (1757–81), British army officer. Killed while defending Jersey in 1781, Peirson was immortalized in John Singleton Copley's dramatic painting of the event.

Percy, Hugh, Earl Percy (1742–1817), British general. The son and heir of the Duke of Northumberland, Percy commanded the relief force that rescued the British troops retreating from Concord on 19 April 1775; he later commanded at Rhode Island before resigning and returning home in 1777, after falling out with General **Howe**.

Pitt, William, 'the Elder' (1708–78), 1st Earl of Chatham, British politician. The leading British minister for much of the Seven Years War, Pitt was popular in the colonies; even more so when he spoke in favour of repeal of the Stamp Act. Nevertheless, his ministry of 1766–8 tried to tax the Americans. In 1775 he proposed a plan to settle the disputes between the British government and the colonies.

Pitt, William, 'the Younger' (1759–1806), British politician. Son of **Pitt the Elder**, Pitt the Younger served as Shelburne's Chancellor of the Exchequer in 1782–3 and became first minister, aged only 24, at the end of 1783.

Prevost, Augustine (1723–86), Swiss-born British general. Prevost had joined the Royal American regiment on its foundation in 1756; he commanded British forces in the south in 1779, successfully defending Savannah from Franco–American attack.

Rawdon, Francis (1754–1826), Lord Rawdon, British general. After serving in most of the campaigns in North America, he led the British forces in South Carolina when **Cornwallis** advanced north, defeating **Greene** at Hobkirk's Hill in 1781. He subsequently had a distinguished career in India.

Rochambeau, Jean-Baptiste Donatien de Vimeur (1725–1807), Comte de, French general. Rochambeau commanded the French expeditionary forces sent to the United States in 1780, and brought the French troops down to Yorktown for the siege that effectively ended the fighting in North America.

Rochford, William Henry Nassau de Zuylestein (1717–81), 4th Earl of, British politician. Secretary of state for the southern department when the war broke out, Rochford hoped to keep the Bourbon powers out of the Anglo–American conflict by emphasizing the common interests of the European imperial states in the suppression of colonial rebellion.

Rockingham, Charles Watson-Wentworth (1730–82), 2nd Marquess of, British politician. He formed a brief government in 1765–6, which repealed the American Stamp Act, and, after many years in opposition, came back into power in 1782 in another brief ministry that began to negotiate an end to the war.

Rodney, Sir George Brydges (1719–92), British admiral. His victory at the Battle of the Saintes in April 1782 saved Jamaica from invasion, probably helped the British negotiators at Paris obtain reasonable terms and earned him elevation to the peerage as Baron Rodney.

Rutledge, John (1739–1800), American statesman. As governor of South Carolina in 1779, he appeared to be willing to surrender Charleston to Prevost in return for South Carolina's neutrality for the rest of the war.

Sandwich, John Montagu (1718–92), 4th Earl of, British politician. Sandwich served as first lord of the Admiralty during the war, resigning in 1782. He favoured concentration of British naval strength in home waters to protect the British Isles from invasion, but was forced to compromise with colleagues who wanted the navy deployed in imperial theatres.

Schuyler, Philip (1733–1804), American general. Schuyler was a great New York landowner who received high command in the Continental army in 1775; he was nominally in charge of the invasion of Canada, though in practice American forces were led by Montgomery. Suspected of defeatism, or even sympathy with the enemy, in 1777 he was replaced as commander of the northern army by Gates.

Shelburne, William Petty (1737–1802), 2nd Earl of, British politician. He was colonial secretary in the Rockingham government of 1782 and on Rockingham's death became first minister. His government negotiated the peace with the Americans and their Bourbon allies.

Steuben, Friedrich Wilhelm (1730–94), Baron von, American general. After having served in the Prussian army during the Seven Years War, von Steuben became inspector general of the Continental army, training it in European-style drill. He went on to become chief of staff to **Washington.**

Stuart, James (d. 1793), British general. He succeeded Sir **Eyre Coote** as commander of the British forces in southern India, but was unable to gain the upper hand over the rulers of Mysore or their French allies.

Suffren de Saint-Tropez, Pierre-André de (1729–88), French admiral. Suffren served in many theatres during the war, including North American waters and the Caribbean, but his reputation was established by his daring attack on British ships at Porto Praya in the Cape Verde Islands, and by his engagements with the Royal Navy off India and Ceylon.

Sullivan, Thomas (1740–95), American general from New Hampshire. Sullivan served in the siege of Boston, in the northern theatre and in the New York campaign of 1776; he tried, unsuccessfully, to take Newport from its British garrison in 1778, and led a destructive expedition against native peoples on the frontier in 1779.

Tarleton, Banastre (1754–1833), British soldier. He commanded the loyalist provincial corps the British Legion in the southern campaigns of the war in America, experiencing early success but suffering defeat at the hands of **Daniel Morgan** at the Battle of Cowpens in January 1781. He gained a reputation for ruthlessness, which has been perpetuated in popular accounts of the war in novels and films.

Tipu Sultan (1750–99), succeeded his father Haidar Ali as ruler of Mysore at the end of 1782. Tipu was a formidable soldier – perhaps even more so than his father – who inflicted defeats on the British forces in southern India and continued fighting after the news arrived of the signing of the peace in Paris.

Turgot, Anne-Robert-Jacques (1727–81), Baron de Laune, French politician and political economist. As controller-general of finances 1774–6 he opposed French aid for the American rebels, but lost the battle within the French ministry to the more powerful **Vergennes**.

Vaughan, John (*c.*1731–95), British general. He served in North America and then succeeded James Grant as commander of British troops in the West Indies.

Vergennes, Charles Gravier (1717–87), Comte de, French politician. Louis XVI's foreign minister, Vergennes successfully argued that the French government should take advantage of Britain's American troubles. He was the most powerful French minister of the American war period, and oversaw the French negotiations at Paris in 1782–3.

Walpole, Sir Robert (1676–1745), British politician. While in power long before the American crisis, Walpole is regarded by some historians as at least partly responsible; his loose-reined approach to American affairs allowed the British colonies to develop a substantial degree of local self-government in the 1720s and 1730s, which made them all the more resistant to British attempts to impose greater central control from the 1760s.

Ward, Artemas (1727–1800), American general. A veteran of the Seven Years War, Ward took charge of the New England militia besieging the British army in Boston. He remained in command until **Washington**'s arrival.

Washington, George (1732–1799), commander-in-chief of the Continental army, 1775–83. Washington was a Virginia gentleman, appointed commander-in-chief by Congress, partly due to his military experience in the Seven Years War, and partly because he was a southerner. He later became first president of the United States.

Yorke, Joseph (1724–92), British diplomat. Ambassador at The Hague, he persuaded the British government that the position of the Anglophile *stadhouder* William of Orange would be strengthened by an Anglo–Dutch war.

Timeline

1607   Foundation of first English permanent settlement in North America, at Jamestown, Virginia.

1619   First meeting of the Virginia House of Burgesses.

1620   Plymouth plantation founded in New England by radical Protestant English settlers.

1621   An order of James I's Privy Council in London insists on Virginia tobacco coming to England before being exported elsewhere.

1624   Virginia becomes a royal colony.

1630s   Charles I considers placing Puritan New England colonies under the superintendence of Sir Ferdinando Gorges, an enemy of Puritanism.

1649   Execution of Charles I.

1651   The Westminster Parliament passes a Navigation Ordnance regulating colonial overseas trade.

1660   Restoration of the monarchy; passage of the first of a series of Navigation Acts (others follow in 1663, 1673 and 1696).

1684   Massachusetts loses its charter for persistent refusal to be bound by the Navigation Acts.

1685   James II creates the Dominion of New England.

1688–9   Glorious Revolution in England leads to the overthrow of James and the end of the Dominion of New England.

1696   Formation of the Board of Trade.

1702–13   War of the Spanish Succession increases interest of the London government in the colonies.

1721	Walpole becomes first minister, dominating British politics for the next two decades. His loose-reined approach to colonial affairs means that the colonies acquire a substantial measure of local self-government.
1739–48	Anglo–Spanish conflict develops into the War of the Austrian Succession, which (as in the War of the Spanish Succession) increases the British government's interest in the colonies.
1748	The Earl of Halifax becomes president of the Board of Trade and tries to assert greater control over the colonies.
1754	First clashes between British colonists and the French in the Ohio Valley; the effective beginning of the Seven Years War.
1756	The Seven Years War starts in Europe.
1757	At the end of the year, William Pitt offers the colonies an enhanced status for provincial officers and parliamentary subsidies to help cover the costs of raising provincial regiments.
1758	Colonial assemblies respond to Pitt's new settlement by raising larger number of troops than ever before.
1759	British forces capture Quebec.
1760	Fall of Montreal marks effective end of the Seven Years War in North America.
1763	Peace of Paris concludes the British and Bourbon aspects of the Seven Years War; Royal Proclamation temporarily blocks westward expansion of the colonies to avoid conflict with the Native peoples and to promote Protestant settlement in the new province of Quebec.
1764	Parliament's Revenue Act specifically taxes foreign molasses imported into the North American colonies to raise money to support the British army garrison; Parliament also passes a Currency Act to call in paper money circulating in the colonies.
1765	George Grenville's Stamp Act, intended to raise more money to support the regular army in America, causes vociferous opposition throughout the colonies.

1766	Parliament repeals the Stamp Act but simultaneously passes the American Declaratory Act, asserting its sovereignty over the colonies; the Rockingham government's Revenue Act lowers the duty on molasses entering the North American colonies, but extends it to all molasses, British as well as foreign.
1767	Parliament approves Charles Townshend's duties on a select range of British imports into North America.
1768	Anti-customs rioting encourages the British government to send troops to Boston.
1770	British soldiers open fire on Bostonians in an event soon dubbed 'the Boston Massacre'; Lord North persuades Parliament to repeal all of the Townshend duties except for the one on tea – the only productive duty.
1772	Credit crisis creates major problems for the British East India Company.
1773	Tea Act tries to facilitate dumping of cheap tea in North America; Lord North reveals that he is hoping to increase the revenues created by the Townshend tea duty as well as help the East India Company; widespread resistance to the landing of tea shipments, culminating in the Boston Tea Party in December.
1774	Parliament passes the Coercive (or Intolerable) Acts to punish Boston for the Tea Party and to remodel the government of Massachusetts; a Continental Congress meets to coordinate American opposition.
1775	April: British troops and colonial militiamen clash in Massachusetts. May: American forces capture Ticonderoga. June: Battle of Bunker Hill. July: Congress sends Olive Branch petition to George III. August: Royal proclamation declares the colonies to be in rebellion; French government sends an agent to confer with Congress. November: British garrison at St Johns surrenders to Americans; Parliament passes Prohibitory Act, exposing

colonial merchant shipping to seizure by the Royal Navy; Lord Dunmore tries to recruit enslaved Virginians to the royal cause.

December: American attempt to capture Quebec City repulsed.

1776   March: British troops evacuate Boston.

May: French government decides to provide clandestine aid to the Americans.

June: British forces repulsed in attempt to capture Sullivan's Island, near Charleston, South Carolina; last American soldiers evacuate Canada; British troops land on Staten Island, New York.

July: Congress declares the rebel colonies to be independent states.

August: Washington's Continental army is defeated at the Battle of Long Island.

September: British forces occupy New York City.

October: Battles of Valcour Island and White Plains.

November: British forces capture Fort Washington, New York, and begin an invasion of New Jersey.

December: British forces capture Newport, Rhode Island, and British troops reach the Delaware in pursuit of Washington's army; Washington boldly counterattacks, inflicting a crushing defeat on a Hessian detachment at Trenton, New Jersey.

1777   January: Washington defeats British detachment at Princeton, New Jersey.

July: Burgoyne's army recaptures Ticonderoga and defeats Americans at Hubbardton.

August: Howe's army lands at Head of Elk, Maryland; a detachment of Burgoyne's army is beaten at the Battle of Bennington.

September: Howe defeats Washington at Brandywine Creek; Philadelphia occupied; Battle of Freeman's farm.

October: inconclusive Battle at Germantown; Burgoyne forced to surrender at Saratoga.

1778   February: Franco–American alliance signed.
April: French Mediterranean fleet leaves Toulon to cross the Atlantic.
June: British forces evacuate Philadelphia; Battle of Monmouth, New Jersey.
July: French and British fleets engage off Ushant; French ships appear off New York.
August: Franco–American siege of Newport, Rhode Island.
September: French capture Dominica.
October: Pondicherry falls to the forces of the British East India Company.
December: British capture Savannah, Georgia, and St Lucia.

1779   January: French take St Louis in Senegal.
March: Americans defeated at Briar Creek, South Carolina; French post at Mahé, India, captured by British forces.
April: Franco-Spanish alliance concluded.
May: British expedition raids Virginia.
June: British establish base at Penobscot, in modern-day Maine; French take St Vincent.
July: French capture Grenada.
August: combined Franco–Spanish fleet lies off Plymouth.
September: Franco–American siege of Savannah begins; Spanish capture British forts in West Florida.
October: siege of Savannah lifted; British take Omoa, in modern-day Honduras.

1780   April: British take San Juan Castle, near Lake Nicaragua.
May: British capture Charleston, South Carolina, and defeat Americans at Waxhaws.
July: French expeditionary force lands at Newport, Rhode Island; Haidar Ali begins invasion of the Carnatic.
August: Cornwallis defeats Gates at Camden.

September: British defeated by Haidar Ali at Polliur.

October: American victory at King's Mountain halts British advance into North Carolina.

December: British government declares war on the Dutch Republic.

1781   January: Tarleton defeated by Morgan at Hannah's Cowpens; British repulse French attack on Jersey.

March: Cornwallis wins Pyrrhic victory at Battle of Guilford Court House; British seize Dutch island of St Eustatius.

April: Greene defeated at Hobkirk's Hill, South Carolina.

May: Spanish capture Pensacola, West Florida.

June: French take Tobago.

July: Lafayette defeated by Cornwallis at Green Spring, Virginia; Coote defeats Haidar Ali at Porto Novo.

August: Franco–American forces begin to march south from New York to Virginia; Coote defeats Haidar Ali again at Pollilur; British East India Company seizes Dutch factory at Padang; British and Dutch fleets clash in Battle of Dogger Bank; Franco–Spanish forces begin siege of St Philip's, Minorca.

September: indecisive battle in mouth of Chesapeake Bay between British and French fleets; British retreat to New York to refit; Coote inflicts further defeat on Mysore forces at Sholinghur.

October: Cornwallis surrenders at Yorktown.

November: French recapture St Eustatius.

1782   January: British capture Dutch base at Trincomalee.

February: British garrisons surrender on Minorca and St Kitts; Tipu Sultan defeats British in Tanjore; British fail to capture Dutch post at Elmina, West Africa.

March: Spanish seize British base on Rio Negro, in modern-day Honduras; Lord North's government falls.

April: Rodney defeats de Grasse at the Battle of the Saintes; French take Cuddalore; Rockingham government takes office in London and opens negotiations with the Americans and the French.

June: Coote defeats Mysore troops at Arni.

July: Rockingham dies and Shelburne becomes first minister.

August: French make a surprise attack on bases of the Hudson's Bay Company.

September: British garrison of Gibraltar beats off major attack.

November: preliminary peace terms agreed between Americans, British, French and Spanish at Paris.

1783   January: Anglo–Dutch armistice.

June: French and British forces engage at Cuddalore until they learn of the signing of the preliminary peace.

September: Americans, British, French and Spanish sign definitive treaty of peace.

1784   January: Tipu continues war in India, capturing Mangalore.

March: Tipu negotiates an end to his war with the British.

May: Anglo–Dutch peace settlement signed.

1

THE LONG ROAD TO LEXINGTON

How far back do we need to go to explain why Massachusetts militiamen and British soldiers exchanged shots at Lexington and Concord on 19 April 1775? Most accounts of the coming of the Revolutionary War rightly focus on the years immediately preceding the outbreak of fighting. The destruction at Boston in December 1773 of a large cargo of tea subject to a tax levied by the British Parliament led to a fierce parliamentary reaction, the most important part of which was the Massachusetts Government Act of 1774. By altering the colony's charter to reduce popular involvement, the Act was the trigger for revolt. These events are usually linked to the first attempts by Parliament to tax the colonies in the 1760s, which are commonly seen as the start of a constitutional crisis that was to eventuate in war and American independence.[1] However, our understanding of the Revolution is enhanced if we are willing to look earlier still.

Many historians point to long-term developments dating from the first decades of the eighteenth century. Some emphasize how the social fluidity and opportunity of the early years of settlement gave way to a more rigid and hierarchical order as the best land was occupied and the economy became more commercialized. They also point to the tensions in the urban centres – especially the northern ports of Boston, New York and Philadelphia. Mounting class discontent, according to this interpretation, led Americans to react against both social and political hierarchies, overthrowing British rule in the process.[2] Others focus on the arrival of large numbers of non-English settlers in the eighteenth century, principally Irish Protestants and Scottish Highlanders, but also many Germans. By the eve of the Revolution, about one tenth of the white colonial population was of German origin; in Pennsylvania, one third. These new migrants – Irish, Scots and German – brought greater religious diversity to the colonies and, in the view of some historians, began to create a distinctly American people likely to be resistant to attempts to impose external authority.[3] Still other historians see a link between the evangelical fervour that intermittently gripped the colonies from the 1720s and the challenges to the established order and the popular political participation that were features of the revolutionary era.[4]

Changes in colonial society no doubt played a part in causing the Revolution, and certainly help to account for why it developed in the way that it did. However, the underlying reason for the colonies' rejection of British authority was not their changing nature but their clinging to old ways, particularly their continuing adherence to seventeenth-century English political culture. In the eighteenth century the people of the colonies, reflecting the political orthodoxy of the time of their founding, associated Englishness with largely self-governing communities. They happily acknowledged their allegiance to the Crown – 'our common head and father', as the Massachusetts assembly described George III in 1768 – even as they tried to emasculate the governors it appointed.[5] They never accepted that the Westminster Parliament had the right to pass laws that bound them. For practical purposes, the colonies acquiesced in some parliamentary legislation, so long as they regarded it as mutually beneficial. Nevertheless, despite their occasional tactical flattery of Parliament, they would not recognize its sovereign authority. A crisis would, of course, have been avoided if Parliament had not tried to impose its will and, in particular, had not tried to levy taxes in America, but the colonies' static conception of their autonomy was repeatedly challenged by the desire of dynamic metropolitan authorities for more central control. After the Seven Years War (1756–63), new imperial imperatives meant that British attempts to interfere increased markedly and created a crisis in the relationship between colonies and mother country. In a very real sense, the American Revolution was – or, at least, started as – a conservative defence of the status quo against British innovation.[6] To understand this, we need to go back to the early years of English settlement.

American commitment to self-government rested on the early experience of colonization. English common law was introduced with the first settlers, and each new colony soon had an elected assembly designed to represent and protect the interests of the settler population, acting much like a local equivalent of the Westminster House of Commons. In theory, popular participation in government was balanced by a strong executive, in the person of the governor, supported by an advisory council. But in the first years of settlement, when colonies were sponsored by private companies rather than the Crown, governors and councils were often themselves elected, reinforcing the tendency towards local control. The institutional framework for local self-government was therefore in place from the very beginnings of English America. Furthermore, initially the colonies functioned with very little interference from London. The Crown, apart from issuing the charters that gave the colonies a legal basis, left the work of early settlement to groups of private investors.

Only once the colonies had established themselves, and started to become profitable, did the Crown show an interest. In 1621, James I required Virginia tobacco exports to be sent to England to boost his customs revenues. Three years later he made Virginia a royal colony, with a royally appointed governor, answerable to the king and his ministers in England. James's son Charles I hoped to see 'one uniforme course of Government' across all his dominions,[7] and he wanted to curb the autonomy of the Puritan New England colonies in the 1630s. To limit the expansion of Massachusetts, Charles established a new royal colony of Maine, and appointed as its first governor Sir Ferdinando Gorges, a staunch Episcopalian opponent of the Puritans. Charles even planned to place the whole of New England under Gorges' charge, only for political and military crisis at home – the coming of the English Civil War – to prevent his putting these wishes into practice.[8]

The civil war in England, and the short-lived republic established after the execution of Charles I, reduced London's interference in colonial affairs. Unsurprisingly, domestic events preoccupied English ministers. However, the desire to control the colonies across the Atlantic did not disappear. In 1651, the Westminster Parliament passed a Navigation Ordnance, designed to exclude the Dutch from trade with English America. With the restoration of the Stuarts in 1660, centralizing impulses increased markedly. Charles II and his brother and successor James II launched the most concerted seventeenth-century assault on colonial self-government. More new provinces were established as royal colonies, or as proprietary possessions of the king's relatives and courtiers, with appointed governors answerable to the king and his minsters in England. Local resistance to the Westminster Parliament's regulation of colonial trade through the Navigation Acts of 1660, 1663 and 1673 led to the revocation of the original Massachusetts charter in 1684, and the beginning of a process of remodelling colonial government. From 1685, James II incorporated all of the New England colonies – and eventually New York and New Jersey – in one great Dominion of New England, ruled by a royally appointed Governor General, Sir Edmund Andros, without elected assemblies.[9] The Dominion soon collapsed, but only after James II had himself been effectively deposed in England during the Glorious Revolution of 1688–9. With the fall of the Stuarts, the new regime in London restored the colonial assemblies but, at the same time, continued its efforts to assert greater central control. The Board of Trade was established in 1696 to gather information on the colonies, oversee their development and make policy recommendations to ministers. Another Navigation Act in the same year enhanced metropolitan supervision of colonial overseas trade.

In the first half of the eighteenth century such interventions were rarer. It was true that the wars of 1702–13 and 1739–48 encouraged government in London to value the colonies and their trade, and therefore to make fresh efforts to exert greater control. However, during the long period of peace while Sir Robert Walpole dominated British politics in the 1720s and 1730s, the colonies experienced very little interference. Rather than being the product of neglect and indifference, limited intervention seems to have reflected a deliberate policy. Walpole recognized that the colonies were contributing to national prosperity and so was keen to avoid any disputes that might disrupt a beneficial relationship. When colonial governors found themselves locked in conflict with their local assemblies, Walpole and his secretary of state, the Duke of Newcastle, encouraged accommodation rather than confrontation, even if that meant giving way to the assemblies' demands.[10] Walpole's era saw some legislative interventions, especially to protect British economic interests, but rarely did he seek to enforce restrictive regulations, and during his period of office the colonies enjoyed considerable autonomy. The Earl of Halifax, an active and determined President of the Board of Trade, tried in the late 1740s and early 1750s to claw back the ground lost to the colonial assemblies under Walpole. However, his tangible achievements were few; perhaps his most important innovation was the introduction of a regular packet boat service between Britain and the colonies, which enabled American governors to communicate more easily with ministers in London.[11]

A new conflict with France that began in the mid-1750s brought Britain and the colonies closer than they had ever been before, yet ultimately helped to drive them apart. At first, the British government sought to repel French incursions in the Ohio Valley by a traditional appeal to the various colonies to provide locally raised soldiers, but the response was disappointing. In 1754, an attempt to coordinate colonial military efforts at the Albany Congress produced agreement, only for the different colonial assemblies to reject what they saw as an attempt to usurp their functions.[12] The failure of the Albany plan, the poor performance of colonial military forces in the first clashes in the Ohio Valley and the reluctance of some of the colonial assemblies to respond to the Crown's requests that they vote money to raise regiments of provincial soldiers encouraged the British government to send its own troops across the Atlantic. At first these troops fared no better than the colonists, but the ministerial response to initial setbacks was to pour more and more resources into North America with the intention of removing, once and for all, the French threat from Canada. Never before had so many Americans come into contact with British soldiers.

Historians who claim that the experience of the Seven Years War was a vital part of the background to the Revolution tend to emphasize American resentments at the behaviour of the British regulars.[13] The letters and diaries of locally raised provincial soldiers suggest a cultural gulf between the two armed forces, with Americans viewing the redcoats as haughty and authoritarian and ignorant of the more contractual basis of military service in the colonies.[14] Yet American discomfort was largely confined to the first, distinctly unsuccessful, phase of the war to the end of 1757, and from the beginning of 1758 Americans had good reason to be more positive about the experience of the conflict. In part this was attributable to the recall of Lord Loudoun, the commander-in-chief of the British army whose abrasive criticisms of the colonists caused considerable upset. More important were the other concessions offered by William Pitt, the British Secretary of State responsible for running the war. He boosted provincial officers' status by no longer requiring them to take orders from the lowliest British ensign or lieutenant, and he gave the assemblies a substantial parliamentary subsidy to help cover the costs of paying for a more extensive mobilization of American manpower.[15]

Colonial enthusiasm for Pitt's new settlement was quickly apparent – the various assemblies between them pledged to put 23,000 provincial soldiers in the field for the 1758 campaign.[16] As large numbers of colonial troops joined equally large numbers of British regulars, the French position became increasingly parlous. That year, British and American colonial forces suffered a reverse at Fort Carillon, where the Marquis de Montcalm, the French commander, mounted a skillful defence. However Louisbourg on Cape Breton and Fort Frontenac on Lake Ontario were captured, exposing the French Canadian heartland to attack from east and west. Quebec in the St Lawrence Valley followed in 1759, and Montreal, the capital of New France, in 1760. American discontents in the first phase of the war were now replaced by the warm glow of success. When the war in North America drew to a close, the colonists appeared far from alienated by the experience of fighting alongside British soldiers. On the contrary, they celebrated their Britishness with great enthusiasm; the assemblymen of Massachusetts proclaiming that it was 'our highest Honour to be ranked amongst the foremost of his Majesty's loyal *American* Subjects' and 'exult[ing] in the Blessings of being freeborn Subjects of *Great-Britain*, the leading and most Respectable power in the whole World'.[17]

If we are to establish that the experience of the Seven Years War played a part in the coming of the Revolution, we have to look beyond American resentments. More important, perhaps, was the impact on New Englanders of the anti-Catholic rhetoric used to encourage their recruitment. In a sense, not much encouragement was required. The region's distinctive environmental conditions – poor soils and a short growing season – produced low crop yields and an agricultural sector that was always struggling to produce saleable surpluses; this lack of profitability, combined with large families and many young men with few prospects of inheriting property, meant that a plentiful supply of potential soldiers was available.[18] But in order to inspire them to volunteer for the provincial service, and build community support for their efforts, clergymen and political leaders portrayed the war against the French in Canada as a new crusade against 'popery', a term that referred to more than Catholicism in its religious sense, and encompassed arbitrary and top-down government in all its forms. New Englanders who had their historical animus to popery intensified in the war were likely to be particularly sensitive to anything that seemed redolent of French-style authoritarianism in the years that followed. They seem to have convinced themselves that parliamentary taxes were a sign that the British government had itself embraced popery.[19]

However, the British response to the experience of the Seven Years War was at least as important as the reactions of the Americans. Colonial resentments in the first stage of the war were understandable; British officers did indeed look with disdain on the contribution of the provincial forces. They continued to do so after 1758 – their contempt was perhaps better disguised in the second phase of the war than in the first, but it was still regularly expressed in letters home and private diaries. The slowness of the Americans to take to the field was a frequent complaint.[20] Worse still, the failure in the first years of the war of the traditional requisition system (whereby the Crown requested each colony to raise a quota of soldiers, the governor conveyed this request to his assembly and the assembly decided whether to agree), left a lasting legacy of doubt in British minds about the suitability of the system as a means of organizing imperial defence. Politicians at Westminster were to refer specifically to the uneven response of the colonies to royal requisitions in postwar debates about America – even the New York assembly acknowledged that the system had not worked equitably.[21] Another feature of the war, known to ministers in London during its course but revealed to the wider British public only when it was safely won, was extensive American trading with the enemy. The impression conveyed in the British press was that the colonists, far from working in productive partnership with the British army, had enabled New France to hold out for longer than it should have done.[22] With very few exceptions, British commentators saw the war as a British triumph, secured in spite of the Americans, not due to their help. Britons' sense that the colonists owed them a debt of gratitude was to be very influential in postwar debates about what to do with a greatly enlarged British Empire.

Even so, the outcome of the conflict, rather than any damage done to Anglo–American relations during its course, is the principal reason for seeing the Seven Years War as an important part of the explanation for the coming of the Revolution. The British government's decision to keep Canada may well have been a mistake; in retrospect, we can see that it probably lessened American dependency on Britain by removing a common enemy on the colonies' doorstep.[23] But a more important ingredient of future tensions was perhaps the expansion of the British Empire in general. Its size and nature had dramatically changed. In 1750 the North American colonies of settlement were the most populated part of Britain's overseas possessions. By 1763, the British Crown's territories in North America had increased to take in French Canada, Spanish Florida and the inland wilderness between the Appalachians and the Mississippi. The scale of these acquisitions meant that many people of non-British background came under British jurisdiction. Two years later much larger numbers of non-Britons were put under British rule in India, when the Mughal emperor granted the East India Company the right to administer justice and collect revenues in Bengal, Bihar and Orissa. An important consequence was that British politicians, surveying their new empire and contemplating their new responsibilities, perhaps subcon-

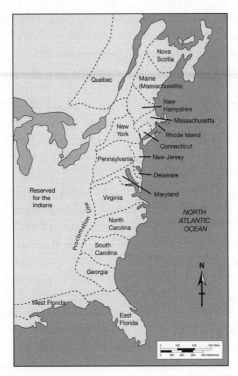

The British colonies in North America in 1763. The Proclamation Line was established by the Royal Proclamation of 7 October 1763, which sought temporarily to stop westward expansion of the old British colonies.

sciously downgraded the colonists. Americans who had enjoyed the special status of fellow-Britons across the Atlantic were now viewed alongside French Canadians, Native Americans and even Bengalis, as just another set of people to be governed.[24]

The centralizing tendencies of ministers in London were further strengthened by their perception that the new empire was vulnerable to French and Spanish attempts to regain lost power and prestige. While the British public was subjected to a good deal of commentary trumpeting the success of the king's army and navy in the war, comparisons made between the new British Empire and the old Roman Empire were not entirely welcome to classically educated politicians and administrators. Anyone who knew their ancient history was aware that the Roman Empire collapsed through overexpansion.[25] The fear of those responsible for the new British Empire was that its outlying provinces would fall prey to the French and Spanish desire for revenge unless the whole empire was bound together more effectively than in the past. The loose-reined approach of the Walpole years was no longer appropriate; much more activity by the central organs of the British state was required. As South Carolina's agent in London reported in January 1764, the Board of Trade planned 'to establish throughout America one uniform system of Government and Policy'.[26]

The British army was expected to feature more prominently in imperial defence than in the past.[27] Parliamentarians, as we have noted, were very well aware of the failure of the old requisition system of raising colonial manpower – or at least its very limited success in the first part of the war. But the ministerial decision to base a force of British troops in North America in peacetime, a decision taken even before the Seven Years War ended, owed more to the immediate need to garrison recently acquired (and potentially mutinous) Canada. The colonial assemblies, which had responded in such a mixed way to royal requests to raise men for war service, were not likely to agree to provide a peacetime occupation force in the St Lawrence Valley. Only regular troops could undertake the task. Ministers also envisaged the army's acting as a frontier police force, preventing settler encroachments on native lands. But the primary reason they wanted a substantial military force in North America was probably for the defence of British interests in the western hemisphere more generally. Rather like the army in Ireland, the army in America was to be available for rapid redeployment overseas in the event of a new war against the Bourbons.[28] It could be sent to the Caribbean or even Central America much more speedily than could troops from Europe. And like the army in Ireland again, it was not to be supported by the hard-pressed British public – who were already protesting at the continuation of wartime levels of taxation – but by the population that it was nominally defending. The stage was set for the British Parliament to play a bigger and more contentious role in the governance of the colonies, for if the Americans were to pay for the army, the only constitutionally proper body to levy the taxes to support such an army was the House of Commons at Westminster.

In the immediate aftermath of the war, then, British and American expectations dangerously diverged. At the moment when the British political elite was inclined to see the colonists as requiring firmer control from London, the Americans anticipated a bright future of imperial cooperation. The colonists celebrated their Britishness with great enthusiasm and looked forward to continuing a successful wartime partnership. Their hope and expectation was that the British government would recognize their key role in the victory and treat them as fully fledged fellow-Britons. A rude awakening was soon to come.

The years following the end of the Seven Years War saw a flurry of British interventions in America. A Royal Proclamation in October 1763 sought to preserve the inland wilderness beyond the Appalachians for the natives and encourage Protestant settlement in newly acquired Canada and Florida. In the same year, the Privy Council ordered the Navigation Acts to be enforced more rigorously. A Currency Act in 1764 aimed to protect British merchants from payment in depreciated money by recalling the paper bills that had been issued in many colonies to help to pay for the war. The American Mutiny Act of 1765 provided for the discipline of the troops forming the new garrison, and instructed the colonial assemblies to compensate owners of property used to provide accommodation for detachments of soldiers on the march. The colonies were expected to make more significant financial contributions to the costs of the army in America through the money raised by the two most controversial pieces of parliamentary legislation of the postwar period. Firstly, the Revenue Act of 1764 reduced a prohibitive duty on foreign molasses entering the mainland colonies and turned it into a revenue-raising tax and, secondly, the famous – or notorious – American Stamp Act of 1765 laid a charge on all legal documents and newspapers.

George Grenville, the British prime minister associated with these measures, was in fact architect of very few of them; historians who write of a 'Grenville Programme' for America overstate his role.[29]

He had no part in the Royal Proclamation, the Order in Council on reform of the customs service or the Mutiny Act, and the Currency Act was a response to mercantile pressure rather than a government initiative. However, Grenville was the driving force behind the taxation; he presented his thinking on what became the Revenue Act of 1764 to the House of Commons that March, and at the same time suggested that he would like to introduce stamp duties the following year. Grenville was convinced that a Stamp Act was the fairest and easiest way to tax the colonies, but, while he appeared willing to consult on the matter, in reality he was prepared to do no more than adjust the rate and scope of the stamp duties to take account of local circumstances.[30]

At first, Grenville justified his American taxes in purely financial terms. The British taxpayer was hard-pressed and the colonists owed a debt of gratitude: 'We have expended much in America', he told MPs, 'Let us now avail ourselves of the fruits of that expense.'[31] Thomas Whately, Grenville's secretary to the Treasury, put it slightly differently when he wrote to an American correspondent in November 1764, but his message was the same: 'burthened as this Country is with Debt and with Expense, some Attention must be had to immediate Revenue, and the Colonies must contribute their Share'.[32] Only when the Americans denied Parliament's right to levy the taxes did Grenville and his supporters present a constitutional case in support of his new duties. He, and the vast majority of MPs, had little doubt that Parliament was competent to tax the colonies. Since the Glorious Revolution, the Westminster legislature had met every year and its power had steadily increased. In 1707, it effectively absorbed the Scottish legislature and became the Parliament of Great Britain. In 1720 it claimed the right to legislate for Ireland, even though Ireland had a Parliament of its own. The sovereign authority of the Westminster Parliament was trumpeted by William Blackstone, one of the leading jurists of the age, in his *Commentaries on the Laws of England*, the first volume of which appeared in 1765. Blackstone was, in truth, expressing no more than received opinion. By the middle of the eighteenth century, a broad consensus existed amongst the British political classes that the legislature at Westminster shared sovereign authority with the Crown, and that all the king's dominions came under its jurisdiction. As the agent of the Connecticut assembly reported after hearing the Commons debate on the stamp duties in March 1765, scarcely any MPs were willing to deny 'ye right of Parliament to tax us'.[33]

Colonial protest began even before the Stamp Act was passed. It was probably intensified by the postwar economic downturn that the Currency Act exacerbated, but American objections were essentially constitutional. Parliament, the colonists argued, could not legitimately tax them as they were not represented in that body; their own assemblies, in which they were represented, were the only legislatures entitled to raise taxes in America. They cited their charters to sustain their position, but based their case on their God-given natural right not to have their property taken from them without their consent, and on the historic English constitution, with its statutory landmarks such as Magna Charta (1215) – 'the great Charter and Fountain of *English* Liberty', as the Pennsylvania Assembly called it in September 1765 – and the Bill of Rights (1689), which they believed protected the Crown's subjects from arbitrary taxation.[34] To demonstrate that they were prepared to contribute to imperial defence, and by inference that a regular British army in America was unnecessary, several colonial assemblies referred proudly to the Americans' record in the recent war; they had responded happily to royal requisitions to raise soldiers, as the decision rested with their own representative assemblies.[35]

Grenville, as a good Whig, did not deny the importance of the link between taxation and representation. He replied that the colonies *were* represented at Westminster, not actually but virtually, in the sense that MPs, as members of the national legislature, took the colonists' interests into account. Whately developed the case for 'virtual representation' in a pamphlet. William Knox and Soame Jenyns, also government supporters, did the same.[36] But such arguments failed to convince Americans, who countered that virtual representation might work within Britain, or even within the colonies, but it could not transcend the great geographical distance that separated the two. To Americans, the 3,000 miles of ocean dividing them from Britain, and the slowness of transatlantic communications, made Westminster MPs poor judges of what level of tax the colonists could bear. Only their own assemblymen, whom they elected and who knew their local circumstances, could be trusted to tax them.[37]

If the dispute had merely taken the form of a polite exchange of views then perhaps the Stamp Act would have survived. But American protest went much farther and took many forms. Besides assembly resolutions, learned pamphlets (often garnished with classical allusions) and essays in newspapers, a majority of the colonial assemblies even agreed to the calling of a congress to present a united front. To British politicians, who had despaired at the seeming impossibility of persuading the different colonies to make common cause during the recent war, the Stamp Act Congress must have seemed alarming – a British fiscal threat had achieved what the French military threat had lamentably failed to do. The serious riots that broke out in many American towns were perhaps more alarming still. The second of Boston's two riots in August 1765 was particularly worrying, as it appeared to go beyond a protest against the Stamp Act and challenge British authority more generally. The rioters attacked the property of customs officials and destroyed the home of the lieutenant governor of Massachusetts. A social dimension was also discerned by some commentators. The governor wrote ominously of a 'war of plunder, of general levelling and taking away the distinction of rich and poor'.[38] What had begun as a conservative challenge to the British Parliament's attempts to change the status quo seemed to be developing into a general attack on the established order, as those at the bottom of American society vented their anger – not just against British encroachments, but at the political and social dispensation within the colonies.

In the end it was not American argument that led to the repeal of the Stamp Act, or even the breakdown in order in several colonial towns, but the determination of American merchants to boycott British goods. A necessary precondition to repeal was Grenville's dismissal by the king in the summer of 1765, an event unconnected with American resistance. The new ministry, headed by the inexperienced Marquess of Rockingham, was not as committed as Grenville was to the stamp duties; by focusing on the damage done to the British economy by colonial non-importation agreements and the threat to employment and social stability at home ('Riots, Mobbs,

& Insurrections' as the elderly Duke of Newcastle put it, when trying to persuade the Archbishop of Canterbury to back the government line),[39] it was able to persuade a sceptical Parliament to support repeal legislation in the spring of 1766. Americans celebrated their victory enthusiastically, but Rockingham's government had made no constitutional concessions; indeed, to sweeten the bitter pill of repeal, Parliament had passed an American Declaratory Act which emphatically asserted its right to legislate for the colonies 'in all cases whatsoever'. And, with Grenville's particular tax gone, Rockingham's Chancellor of the Exchequer, William Dowdeswell, sought to raise money in America by different means. His Revenue Act of 1766 reduced still further the duty on Caribbean molasses entering the mainland colonies, but levied it on all molasses, both from the British and foreign islands. All pretence that the molasses duty was a device to regulate trade was abandoned: it was a tax pure and simple. Its proceeds, furthermore, were to be used for exactly the same purpose as the Stamp Act's – to help pay for the British army in America.[40]

Americans allowed their relief at the repeal of the Stamp Act – and perhaps the very low duty in Dowdeswell's new tax – to disarm them. The Revenue Act of 1766, despite raising far more money than Grenville's taxes, elicited very little American protest. The colonists were also slow to react to the next British tax, which built on the precedent of the 1766 duty. William Pitt, now Earl of Chatham, who succeeded Rockingham, was popular in the colonies, partly because of his willingness to accommodate American sensitivities during the Seven Years War, but also as a result of his more recent spirited support for repeal of the Stamp Act, when he appeared to suggest that Parliament had no right to tax the colonies.[41] But if Americans believed that Chatham's government would not try to tax them, they were much mistaken. In 1767, Charles Townshend, Chancellor of the Exchequer in the new administration, secured parliamentary approval for duties on paper, lead, glass, artists' colours and tea imported into the colonies. Townshend, who had served at the Board of Trade and knew the colonies better than most British politicians, intended to use the proceeds not to support the army, but to pay the salaries of civil officers in America – especially the governors and judges – to free them from financial dependency on the assemblies. His scheme, in other words, was designed to reform colonial government to make it more responsive to instructions from London. In Townshend's view, such a strengthening of executive authority was a vital prerequisite to the raising of further taxes to pay for the army in America.[42]

Townshend's duties did not provoke anything comparable to the storm of protest that greeted the Stamp Act. Perhaps memories of the Stamp Act riots inhibited propertied colonists from launching a rabble-rousing campaign; elite Americans had been shaken by the seeming descent into anarchy and had no wish to repeat the experience. John Dickinson, a Pennsylvanian lawyer who wrote against the Townshend duties, stressed the need for moderate and lawful measures of resistance.[43] Perhaps the state of the economy dampened enthusiasm for vociferous protest; in the later 1760s the postwar downturn was over and had been replaced by a period of buoyant transatlantic trade. Merchants who had been happy to boycott British imports in slack times, when they had large stocks of unsold goods, were much more reluctant to suspend trade when demand was high. Americans may also have been more willing to accept duties on a narrow range of imports – none of which could be described as essential products – than a stamp tax with a wider impact. They may even have accepted the argument put by the Pennsylvanian politician and polymath, Benjamin Franklin, when he was trying to help the Rockingham government secure repeal of the Stamp Act, that the colonists acknowledged Parliament's right to tax their trade.[44] Whatever the explanation, the American campaign against the Townshend duties was a decidedly half-hearted affair; revealingly, no one called for a coordinated response from all the colonies in the manner of the Stamp Act Congress. Only in Massachusetts was there serious and sustained resistance, when an anti-customs riot in Boston in 1768 led the British government to send troops to the town. The presence of British soldiers hardly helped to sooth tensions; Bostonians saw them as agents of despotism and criticised their propensity for vice. Perhaps more importantly, Boston's seafront workers felt threatened by the competition of moonlighting soldiers who offered their services at well below the prevailing wage rates. In March 1770, frightened redcoats fired on a hostile and threatening crowd

Paul Revere's famous engraving of the Boston Massacre, which conveys
the impression – inaccurately – that Captain Thomas Preston, the British
officer in charge, ordered his men to shoot.

in an incident quickly dubbed by local opponents of the army as a
massacre.[45]

Coincidentally, on the very same day as the troops opened fire
in Boston, Lord North, the new prime minister, secured parliamentary support for the repeal of most of the Townshend duties. What
appeared to some as another ministerial retreat on American taxation

was, in fact, nothing of the kind. North continued Townshend's scheme, but on a narrower front. He retained the one duty that was raising significant sums of money – the duty on tea – and by 1772 had accumulated a big enough fund to start paying civil salaries, just as Townshend had envisaged. Most colonists appear to have had no difficulty in consuming the tea, despite the efforts of some of their countrymen to alert them to the danger the duty posed to the power of their assemblies. The relative calm of these years – on 1 January 1771, Samuel Cooper, a Boston clergyman, wrote of 'a Pause in Politics'[46] – was disturbed only by a crisis generated far from America, but which was soon to transform the colonists' views on the one remaining Townshend duty and the tea on which it was levied.

In 1772, the British East India Company faced a major cash flow problem. The credit crisis that hit European financial centres that year left the Company with a vast stockpile of unsold tea in its London warehouses. The Company's directors approached the government for help. They suggested that the tea be dumped on the neighbouring continent, but fears that it would be smuggled back into Britain encouraged the Company and the government to pursue the alternative strategy of selling it at a discount in America. The Tea Act of 1773 remitted all duties on British tea exports to the colonies, apart from the Townshend duty. To reduce the price for American consumers still further the tea was to be sold only through designated agents, cutting out the costs of merchant middlemen. Lord North's motives are difficult to uncover, but he seems primarily to have been focused on the Company's future. He arranged for Parliament to give it a substantial loan and, at the same time, attempted to increase the state's control over the Company's activities through a Regulating Act. Yet North was not blind to the possibilities of killing two birds with one stone. The Tea Act was designed to help the Company but, if it increased American consumption of British tea, it would also boost the revenues produced by the Townshend duty, enabling the payment of colonial civil salaries to be rolled out more speedily. An exchange in the House of Commons, when the bill that would become the Tea Act was being debated, tells us that North was fully aware of the American possibilities offered by the legislation. When Dowdeswell suggested that the Townshend tea duty could be remitted to increase sales in the colonies, North replied that he was 'unwilling to give up that duty'. He went on to explain that 'If the E I Co will export tea to America, they will very much increase that duty, and consequently very much facilitate carrying on government in that part'.[47]

North's hopes for an increase in American revenues were soon dashed. Even though the Tea Act reduced the price of tea in the colonies, and levied no new tax, it provided those who had always been concerned about the Townshend tea duty with the opportunity to inspire their countrymen to new resistance. The purpose of the Townshend duty – to reduce the power of the assemblies and increase that of the governors – was highlighted afresh, and this time Americans listened. It helped that, like the Stamp Act before it, the Tea Act created a large number of powerful losers; the merchants who traded in tea but were not made agents and those who had made substantial profits from selling smuggled Dutch tea, which now lost its commercial advantage in the face of cheaper British tea imports. But it helped even more that tea was a product that could readily be associated with Asiatic despotism and with luxury and all the ills it was believed to bring – dependency, selfishness, effeminacy and a loss of commitment to defending one's community. The Tea Act's enemies depicted it as a 'diabolical plot' to enslave America, and encouraged the colonists to believe that it was their duty to resist the temptation of cheap tea to preserve their own virtue and their country's liberty.[48] Opposition to the landing of the tea was widespread, but it was in Boston, in December 1773, that the most celebrated incident occurred. Large quantities of tea were dumped in the harbour by townspeople disguised as Indian warriors, a piece of symbolism designed, perhaps, to emphasize that the colonists possessed the uncorrupted character of the noble savage.[49]

The Boston Tea Party set Britain and its colonies on a collision course. Perhaps it need not have been so. Perhaps North could have responded in a more measured way in the parliamentary session that began in the spring of 1774. The Boston Port Act, which prohibited the town from trading overseas until it had compensated the East India Company for its lost tea, won near unanimous support in Parliament and was accepted as proportionate even by some of the colonists. North could hardly have done any less; the chances of ever collecting any revenue from the Townsend tea duty, and pursuing the payment of civil salaries that it was designed to support, were very remote unless he could successfully punish Boston's open defiance. But he did not stop at that. Massachusetts generally, and Boston in particular, had been a thorn in the side of British governments for a long time. As North told the House of Commons in March 1774, 'Boston had been upwards of seven years in riot and confusion'.[50] Here was the opportunity to make an example of a persistent troublemaker and encourage more compliant behaviour from the other colonies. He might even have believed that the colonies outside New England would have little sympathy for Massachusetts, given the marked differences between New England's democratic traditions and the more hierarchical social and political systems that operated further south.[51] The Massachusetts Government Act revised the colony's charter to strengthen the hand of the governor and reduce popular participation. A more authoritarian government was to be supported by a strong military presence; not only were more troops to be sent to Boston over the coming months, but the new governor was to be General Thomas Gage, the commander-in-chief of the army in America. Two further pieces of parliamentary legislation designed to facilitate the deployment of troops in the town – the Administration of Justice Act and the Quartering Act – made it clear that North's ministry was prepared to use force.

If North hoped to unite the British political nation behind his punitive policy and divide militant Massachusetts from the more moderate colonies, he achieved the complete opposite. The broad British political consensus over America – all of the ministries since 1763 had supported Parliament's right to tax the colonies and all of them had attempted to exercise that right – broke down once North tried to remodel the Massachusetts charter. Rockingham, leader of the largest opposition group, feared that North was set on an authoritarian course that would destroy the British Empire. Opposition fears were reinforced by the Quebec Act of 1774, which followed hard on the heels of the Massachusetts Government Act. The legislation for Quebec had nothing to do with the older British colonies; it was the product of a long-running attempt to find a suitable system of government for a Catholic population unaccustomed to English political traditions.[52] However, by enshrining government without a representative assembly, and giving a semi-established status to Catholicism, the Quebec Act alarmed North's opponents both inside and beyond Parliament. In the words of Richard Price, a dissenting minister, 'By the government which our ministers *endeavour* to establish in *New*-England, and that which they *have* established in ... *Canada*, we see what sort of Government they wish for in this country'.[53]

Americans reacted with even greater concern. The Massachusetts Government Act, far from isolating the New England colony, united America. The other colonies understandably feared the precedent the act established; if North were allowed to remodel the government of Massachusetts, what would stop him doing the same to them? They viewed the Quebec Act as further evidence of North's malign intentions. Despite its purely Canadian purposes, the older British colonies interpreted it as the blueprint for a more widespread assault on representative institutions. The deputy governor of Pennsylvania wrote in September 1774 of the conviction of people throughout the colonies that there was 'a formed design to enslave America' and that the Quebec Act was 'held up as an irrefragable argument of that intention'.[54] For the first time since the Stamp Act crisis, the colonies came together to coordinate resistance. The Continental Congress, which met at Philadelphia in the autumn of 1774, produced a comprehensive statement of colonial grievances which reiterated the Americans' claims to treatment as English people possessed of English rights and privileges, and called for the repeal of repugnant parliamentary legislation. More importantly, Congress approved a Continental Association, or agreement to suspend trade with Britain. The Association's language made it clear that its purpose was not simply to compel Parliament to retreat, but to immunize the American people from corruption emanating from across the Atlantic.[55] As with the Boston Tea Party, opposition to parliamentary taxation and fear of cultural subversion came together in a potent combination. No less significant were the provisions for the implementation of the Association. A committee was to be formed in every community the length and breadth of the colonies to ensure compliance. These committees were soon to play a big part in the establishment of a revolutionary infrastructure that provided an alternative authority to royal government. They ensured that the Revolution was not simply the work of the largely conservative colonial elite, but a popular uprising with democratic implications.[56]

In Massachusetts, meanwhile, North's attempts to curb popular participation and bolster executive power ran up against overwhelming opposition. The new councillors nominated by the governor were intimidated into resigning their posts: the courts were unable to function. Royal government ceased to exist beyond the confines of Boston, with its British garrison. A provincial congress and local committees exercised authority across most of Massachusetts. Gage had initially been confident that he could manage with the troops at his disposal, but to assert himself outside Boston he called for more regiments. The military build-up on the British side was matched by the preparations of Massachusetts militiamen for open confrontation. Fearful of an imminent attack, they began to drill and stockpile weapons. By the beginning of September 1774 Gage had reached the conclusion that 'conciliating, moderation, reasoning, is over; nothing can be done but by forcible means'.[57] The following month, the provincial congress voted to form an army of observation, made up of 15,000 militiamen, to shadow the British forces in Boston.

With Massachusetts descending into rebellion, North and his parliamentary opponents came forward with last-minute conciliation proposals. North's offering, agreed by Parliament in February 1775, was not so much designed to prevent a war as to prepare the ground for conflict with Massachusetts, and possibly the whole of New England. Parliament made no concession on the vital issue of the right to tax, but would refrain from using its taxing powers in those colonies that made provision for permanent civil salaries and contributed to defence costs. North must have known that Massachusetts would not comply, but he probably hoped to tempt some of the more moderate colonies such as New York. No doubt he also had an eye to domestic opinion; if there were to be a war in New England, the government's position would be strengthened if the New Englanders looked unwilling to compromise.

Chatham, now in opposition, presented his own solution in the House of Lords a few days after North's plan was approved. He recognized that the colonists would never accept Parliament's right to tax, and he was willing to suspend legislation that the Americans found obnoxious, but would only repeal it once they had acknowledged Parliament's right to pass laws for the colonies. To make these laws more acceptable, he suggested that the Continental Congress be made a permanent American legislature, sharing sovereign authority with king and Parliament. Edmund Burke, representing Rockingham's party, proposed his parliamentary motion on conciliation in late March. His plan offered the most generous terms to the Americans. In essence, he suggested that Parliament's right to tax, though theoretically unimpeachable, was impossible to exercise due to American opposition. The only practical way forward, therefore, was for Parliament to agree not to tax the colonies and for the colonies to provide for imperial defence and government in the same way as they had done before 1764 – by the old requisition system. That system had produced very uneven results in the Seven Years War – with some colonial assemblies agreeing to all that was asked of them and others voting only part of the sums required or even no money at all – but to Burke all else had failed, and so a return to the status quo of 1763 was the only possible solution. Simple parliamentary arithmetic meant that neither Chatham's nor Burke's proposals had any chance of becoming official policy, but we should not assume that they were unimportant. Paradoxically, they may well have encouraged Americans to resist in the hope that if, by a show of force, they could topple North's ministry, then other, more sympathetic, British politicians might be able to negotiate a settlement with them.

Very different though the three conciliation proposals were, they had in common the assumption that Parliament's right to legislate for the colonies could not be surrendered. In almost every debate on parliamentary taxation since the Stamp Act crisis, MPs had worried that the Americans, if they succeeded in rejecting Parliament's right to tax, would go on to challenge its right to pass laws for the colonies.[58] What concerned them most was that the Americans would no longer recognize the Navigation Acts (the trade regulations introduced in the seventeenth century) which were widely seen as the foundation of British prosperity and British power; 'of the greatest consequence to this country', in the Attorney General's words in 1766, and 'the cornerstone of the policy of this country with regard to its colonies', according to Burke in 1774.[59] The Navigation Acts directed valuable colonial products to British markets and enabled customs duties to be levied on them. They also excluded many continental European manufactures from the colonies by imposing prohibitive duties on them, thus preserving the colonial market for British goods. Perhaps more importantly, the Navigation Acts stipulated that goods carried by sea between the Crown's possessions must be transported in British ships crewed largely by the Crown's subjects. The aim was to ensure a great reserve of well-trained sailors, who could be conscripted into the Royal Navy in wartime.[60] A great deal, then, depended upon keeping the Americans within the system created by the Navigation Acts. If they broke free of parliamentary trade regulation, British wealth, state revenues and naval supremacy would all be threatened. To both Chatham and Burke, concessions on taxation were a small price to pay if the colonists continued to operate within the Navigation Acts. To North it was no less important that the Americans stay in the system, but he had come to the conclusion that, in the case of Massachusetts, coercion was more likely to achieve that objective than conciliation.

North's hopes of isolating Massachusetts might have made strategic sense, but by the end of 1774 the other New England colonies were clearly preparing for war. That December, Rhode Islanders seized cannons from a royal fort and brought them to Providence, putting it in a state of defence. No doubt the British government accepted that a police action in Massachusetts might well bring the Bay Colony's New England neighbours to its aid. Ministers would have been less sanguine when they discovered that Americans beyond New England were making ready for conflict. Even in the southern provinces, according to a British visitor, the people 'are everywhere learning the exercise as if they were going to be attacked'.[61] But Massachusetts, with its large and growing British military presence, was almost bound to be the place where the first confrontation would occur. 'The People', according to a Virginian doctor who travelled through the province at this time, 'are furious in the cause of liberty'.[62] Only the prudential conduct of the commander of a British detachment sent to search for hidden munitions prevented an open clash with militiamen at Salem in February 1775.[63]

Not many officers in the British garrison could be relied upon to show the same restraint. Gage, married to an American and by temperament reluctant to take precipitate action, faced increasing criticism from subordinates who were itching for a fight. Gage had been awaiting a ministerial response to his request for reinforcements to bring his army up to 20,000 men. On 14 April, he at last received a letter written in late January by Lord Dartmouth, the Secretary of State for the colonies. Dartmouth rejected Gage's judgement that he needed a larger force before he could restore order, arguing that the regiments he had already been sent should be sufficient to overcome a 'rude rabble'. Dartmouth ordered Gage to act without delay to seize the leaders of the provincial congress and put down the rebellion in Massachusetts.[64] The general remained reluctant to arrest provincial congress delegates and decided to concentrate on destroying the militia weapons magazine at Concord.

Late at night on 18 April, some 800 British troops, under the command of Lieutenant Colonel Francis Smith of the Tenth Foot, left Boston heading for Concord. Delayed by the need to await provisions, the British column did not reach Lexington until daybreak the following morning. Here the regulars found their way blocked by the local militia company, which had assembled on the village green. The British commander ordered the militiamen to lay down their muskets and disperse. They refused. A shot rang out – from where remains unclear. The British troops, believing themselves to be under attack, opened fire, killing eight militiamen. The regulars then moved on to Concord, where they destroyed what munitions they could find. A second clash occurred when British light infantrymen, defending a bridge on the outskirts of the town, fired on a large body of militiamen they believed were about to attack them. Unrestrained hostilities immediately commenced.

As the British troops began their return to Boston, they came under sustained attack from a growing number of enraged country people. Smith's detachment, harassed by a largely hidden enemy, taking heavy casualties and running out of ammunition, began to retreat in disorder. Only the timely arrival of a relief force, with artillery support, saved Smith's beleaguered men from destruction. But the British ordeal was not over. For the remainder of the journey back to Boston they were assailed just as fiercely. As a soldier in the relief column put it, 'we received a hot fire from all sides ... every wall lined, and every house filled with wretches, who never dared to Shew their faces'.[65] One report suggests that 'even Weamin' fired on the troops.[66] Earl Percy, who commanded the forces that had rescued Smith's troops, left a vivid description of their march back to Boston. The British regulars, he reported, had 'retired for 15 Miles under an incessant fire which like a moving Circle surrounded & followed us wherever we went'.[67] On the first day of what would prove to be a very long war, British casualties – killed, injured and missing – amounted to 273 men.

2

THE WAR FOR AMERICA

Gage's troops now found themselves besieged by an angry militia army. News of Lexington and Concord spread rapidly, leading to men from the other New England provinces converging on Boston to augment the surrounding forces. The New England mobilization was no doubt furthered by tales of British atrocities on 19 April; although the British made their own accusations about militia barbarities (including the scalping and other mutilation of an injured regular soldier at Concord),[1] the Americans won the first engagement of the propaganda war hands down, showing a keen appreciation of the need to get their side of the story in print before their enemy did.[2] Still smarting from their humiliation, the British troops, cut off from the surrounding countryside, now found fresh provisions running short. Their discomfort was increased by the local topography. High ground to the north and south dominated the town; it would be indefensible if the rebels decided to bombard it from either elevated position. Gage was still reluctant to escalate matters – despite the open fighting on 19 April, it was not until 12 June that he declared martial law – but the arrival from England of Generals John Burgoyne, Henry Clinton and William Howe persuaded him to agree to the occupation of Dorchester Neck, to the south of Boston. The besiegers learned of the British plan, however, and took countermeasures. Artemas Ward, the commander of the New England forces, ordered his troops to fortify the Charlestown peninsula to the north, where they built a redoubt on Breed's Hill on the night of 16–17 June.

The following morning, the rebels announced their presence by firing a few cannonballs into the north end of Boston. British preparations for an advance onto Dorchester Neck were abandoned; troops were instead dispatched to clear the besiegers from Breed's Hill. General Howe, commander of the assault force, assembled most of his men for a frontal attack on the American defences. To his great consternation, their first advance was driven back. After receiving reinforcements, Howe tried again. Reports vary as to whether the regulars took the redoubt at the second or third attempt. But there can be no question that they did so 'with a Great Difficulty', as one officer wrote with nice understatement, and at an appalling cost.[3] In all, 226 British troops were killed and 828 wounded, or about 40 per cent of the attacking force. '[T]he Shocking Carnage of that day never will be erased out of my mind', one stunned officer wrote home.[4] Howe himself may well have been shaken by the experience as he was never again to attempt a frontal assault on prepared American positions. But it was not just the high casualties that disturbed British

The Battle of Bunker Hill. John Trumbull's painting, completed in 1786, captures something of the complicated sentiments of June 1775; a British officer restrains a grenadier from bayoneting the fallen American officer Joseph Warren.

officers; they had not expected such determined American resistance. Gage, reflecting ruefully on the contrast with the Seven Years War, observed that 'In all their wars against the French they never shewed so much Conduct Attention and Perseverance as they do now'.[5]

The heavy casualties inflicted on the British army, at what came to be known (inaccurately) as the Battle of Bunker Hill, made it impossible for Gage to contemplate any further offensive operations in the near future, and an outbreak of dysentery in the town weakened his army still further. But the besiegers, now led by George Washington, the Virginian gentleman whom the reconvened Continental Congress had appointed to take charge of all American forces, were not in a much better state, also suffering from an outbreak of dysentery.

Washington, who had earned his spurs as a provincial officer in the Seven Years War, when he had imposed ferocious punishments on wayward soldiers, was appalled by the New Englanders he now found under his command. He considered the democratic practices of the militiamen who made up his 'Continental army' to be completely inimical to all discipline. The officers of the Massachusetts troops, in particular, he condemned as '*nearly* of the same kidney with the Privates ... there is no such thing as getting of officers of this stamp to exert themselves in carrying orders into execution' as they were elected by their men and wanted to stay in their favour.[6] Washington was reluctant to attempt anything adventurous with such an unreliable force; he was even fearful that the New Englanders would not be able to resist a further British attack.

With neither side seemingly able to take the initiative, the siege settled down to a stalemate. Frustrated officers in the British garrison contemplated ever more extreme solutions to their dilemma. James Grant, as surprised as Gage at the determination of the rebels, longed for the army to escape 'this mortifying and shameful Situation' and urged that the coast of the New England colonies be laid waste, and Philadelphia, the home of the Continental Congress, destroyed.[7] Others looked forward to Native American attacks on the frontier of the rebel provinces, and some even contemplated encouraging the slaves in the south to rise up.[8] Gage recommended to his political masters in London that the army be evacuated from Boston and moved to

George Washington as colonel of the Virginia regiment, 1772.
A painting by Charles Willson Peale.

New York, where he and his senior colleagues assumed that the people were friendly and military operations could be conducted to better effect. By the time the ministry's permission was received in October, Howe had replaced Gage as commander-in-chief. Howe decided that it was too late in the year to organize the evacuation before winter set in, and decided to stay put until the spring.

Meanwhile, the focus of military operations shifted to upper New York and Canada, where the British garrison had been depleted in the months leading up to open fighting by the need to reinforce Gage's army in Boston. The Americans had already captured the great (but barely defended) fortress of Ticonderoga in May. In the middle of September they began a siege of Fort St John, where the British garrison held out until the beginning of November. Their dogged resistance might have saved British Canada by delaying the American advance, though it hardly looked that way in the aftermath of the fall of Fort St John as a few days later the rebel forces

The Death of General Montgomery. John Trumbull's painting (1786)
owes much to the more famous picture by Benjamin West of the
Death of General Wolfe (1770); in both depictions the hero dies
before the walls of Quebec.

entered Montreal. By this time, a second American detachment, which
had advanced through the forests of Maine, arrived in the St Lawrence
Valley and the combined force now advanced on Quebec City, the
last remaining British outpost in the colony. On the final day of the
year, the British garrison succeeded in repelling an American attack,
in which the rebel commander, Richard Montgomery, a former British
officer, was killed. But as 1775 drew to a close, the British position
in North America still looked desperate. All of the old British colonies
were firmly in the hands of the rebels, and even the British army's
hold on Quebec and Boston looked tenuous.

Through the first months of the war, Congress continued to keep
the door open to a settlement. Indeed, early American military
successes may well have encouraged Congress to believe that the
chance of reaching an acceptable agreement had been enhanced.

Surely, after the bloody mauling that their troops had received on 19 April and 17 June, the British government would now be prepared to talk with the Americans? John Dickinson persuaded his fellow delegates to support an Olive Branch petition to the king in July 1775, emphasizing the colonies' continuing loyalty to the Crown and their hope for some accommodation. Congress also sent an address to the British people, offering a possible compromise solution: if Parliament renounced its claim to tax America, the colonies would accept parliamentary regulation of their overseas trade. They were even willing, in return for unrestricted trade, to make a contribution to imperial defence costs. Congress appeared to make the same suggestion when it formally rejected Lord North's conciliation proposal on 31 July.[9]

The British government failed to respond to these American indications of a willingness to come to terms. Instead, the king issued a proclamation in August declaring the colonies to be in a state of rebellion and calling for all his loyal subjects, at home as well as in the colonies, to help put down the insurrection.[10] King George III and his ministers were already trying to assemble a large reinforcement for deployment the next year, along with the British troops that would be withdrawn from Boston, in a concerted effort to crush the rebellion. Lord Barrington, the Secretary at War, or minister responsible for the army, doubted whether a powerful enough force could be raised in time and would have preferred to bring the Americans to submission through a naval blockade of their coast. Some army officers, both at home and in Boston, shared his view.[11] However, the king was adamant that a large army was the only way to end the rebellion speedily. An effective naval blockade, even if it were possible, would take time to bring the colonies to their knees. It also risked provoking the French, who might become nervous about a possible threat to their Caribbean possessions with so many British ships across the Atlantic. In addition, the loyalists had to be considered. Colonial governors, particularly in the south, argued that most Americans were still faithful to the Crown and needed only a British military presence to encourage them to come forward. As the governor of South Carolina put it in August 1775, 'several thousand faithful subjects in the back country ... are ready to take up arms in defence of the constitution, had they the least support'.[12] The governor of North Carolina likewise pointed to the need for only 'a small force' of regular troops to 'lay open the communication with a large body of well affected People who inhabit the interior parts of the Colony'.[13]

But Barrington was right to be pessimistic about the prospects of deploying a substantial army in America for the 1776 campaign. To find the necessary recruits quickly was not easy, especially as the king was reluctant to create new regiments, which was the best way to mobilize large numbers of men rapidly. Rather than go down this route, which he thought would reduce the army's military effectiveness in the short term, George preferred to use well-trained and combat-ready foreign troops. In his capacity as elector of Hanover, he lent his British government more than 2,000 Hanoverians to relieve parts of the British garrisons at Gibraltar and Minorca. His approaches to Catherine the Great for a corps of Russians proved fruitless, and an attempt to secure the Scots Brigade (a military unit in Dutch service in which the officers were all Scottish but the men of mixed nationality) also failed. The king was able, however, to use his German connections to facilitate negotiations with the rulers of Hessen-Kassel, Hessen-Hanau, Waldeck and Brunswick for the hire of a substantial body of German auxiliary troops; around 18,000 men would be sent to America in 1776.

Other aspects of the British government's attempts to Europeanize the American crisis were less successful. Lord North and his colleagues were understandably keen to ensure that the Bourbon powers – France and Spain – refrained from taking advantage of British difficulties. Assurances of friendship from the French and Spanish minsters in London were encouraging and Lord Rochford, one of the secretaries of state, even suggested that their governments might be persuaded to help put down the rebellion, as it was not in the interest of any European imperial power to see the Americans succeed.[14] Rochford had a good point, but he was only too aware that the French, in particular, might be tempted to help the Americans, if only to reduce British power: in September he passed on intelligence to Dartmouth suggesting that the French were already supplying the rebels with arms.[15] In fact, French official opinion was divided; Turgot, the controller general of finances, had no wish for a new war, but Vergennes, the foreign minister, was keen to seize a golden opportunity to humble the British. Indeed, Vergennes had already put out feelers to the Americans, authorizing the sending of an agent to confer with Congress in August. In the spring of the following year Vergennes was finally to triumph in the internal battle with Turgot, and in May 1776 Louis XVI agreed to clandestine French financial aid for the Americans.[16]

Lord North's ministry, on the other hand, rather than negotiate with Congress, appeared determined to ratchet up the conflict. Though the government had decided that the army should be the principal instrument employed against the rebels, it was still intended that the king's fleet play a supporting role. In November 1775, Parliament agreed to an American Prohibitory Act, by which all trading vessels from the rebel colonies were declared fair game for the Royal Navy. Up until this point, many Americans had been able to persuade themselves that their quarrel was with the government and its parliamentary allies, not with the king. As Richard Montgomery had explained to one of his old regimental colleagues at the beginning of July, Britons should 'learn from their sons to resist a wicked ministry – leaving *Majesty sacred*'.[17] Americans described the British troops that they fought, not as the king's soldiers, but as 'the regulars', or even 'the ministerial army'.[18] Their hopes that the king would intervene to save them, perhaps by dismissing North and appointing a new ministry, more willing to compromise with the colonies, took a blow in August, when the king's proclamation declaring them to be in rebellion clearly indicated George's support for his government. Nor did the king's willingness to bring foreign soldiers to America, announced in his speech at the opening of Parliament in October 1775, go down well in the colonies.[19] But it was probably the Prohibitory Act that most weakened colonial faith in George III. By setting the Royal navy – the king's navy – on the Americans, the act undermined the age-old governmental contract, in which the people gave obedience in return for protection. As John Adams of Massachusetts put it 'king, Lords, and Commons have united in sundering this country from that, I think forever'. The act, he concluded, 'makes us independent in spite of our supplications and entreaties'.[20]

*

In the early months of 1776, as the British government continued its preparations for that year's campaign, Americans braced themselves for the onslaught that they knew was coming. The Royal Navy's dominance meant that the whole coastline of the rebellious provinces was exposed; in the evocative words of Charles Lee, another former British army officer serving in the Continental army, 'the enemy (furnished with canvas wings) can fly from one spot to another'.[21] Once the British army landed, Lee was convinced that the only way the Americans could win was by adopting a radical approach. He assumed that it would be impossible for the rebels, as inexperienced soldiers, to match the British troops in a conventional war. Instead, he recommended the Americans' remaining a militia-type force which would not seek to emulate the British army but specialize in partisan fighting, or what would later be called guerrilla warfare. Washington, on the other hand, was determined to create a European-style army and to fight accordingly. He had aspired to be a regular officer earlier in life, and by temperament and social background was averse to a decentred war over which he, and senior officers like him, would have only limited control. Partisan activities would play a part in Washington's campaigns, but only as a supplement to the more conventional operations of the Continental forces. The Revolution and its armed conflict undoubtedly unleashed democratic forces and in important ways changed American society, but so long as members of the elite like Washington remained in charge, the opportunities for a wholesale reordering were greatly reduced.[22]

In March, Howe finally evacuated his army from Boston. As he was obliged to take with him a significant number of loyalist civilians and their property, he decided not to go to New York, as originally intended, but to Halifax, Nova Scotia, a base still firmly in British hands. There he waited for news of the sailing across the Atlantic of the British and German troops who would join him for operations in the lower Hudson Valley. The government in London envisaged Howe's main army advancing northwards to rendezvous with a second force moving south from Canada down the Lake Champlain corridor and into upper New York. This Canadian army would be made up of more British and German soldiers, who would be transported into the St Lawrence Valley to reinforce the belea-guered British forces in Quebec. Once the Americans had been cleared out of the province, they would begin their march towards Howe's army. A third British army was to be sent to the southern provinces to join a small force of troops in North Carolina that had sailed from Boston just before its garrison was evacuated. The expressed aim of the southern operations was to support the numerous loyal-ists in the region. The Scottish Highlanders who had settled in North Carolina were reputed to be especially keen to demonstrate their allegiance to the Crown. Ministers and military commanders may also have been mindful of the large enslaved population of South Carolina. The previous year, Lord Dunmore, the royal governor of Virginia, had already tried to raise black soldiers to support his crumbling authority, and the possibility of South Carolina's slaves' rising in insurrection might be enough to persuade the colony's white settlers to break ranks with the other rebel provinces and sue for terms.

To execute such a plan was to be no easy undertaking. For such a large force of soldiers – the largest any British government had sent abroad – to be supplied effectively was vital, yet no depend-ence could be placed on local resources until British troops had taken control of a significant extent of fertile territory. Enormous quantities of foodstuffs – for both men and horses – had, therefore, to be transported across the Atlantic. Ireland provided 'wet' provi-sions, such as meat and butter, which were assembled at a great depot at Cork, whereas the 'dry' stores, mainly cereals, were procured in England, particularly East Anglia.[23] Lord George Germain, who succeeded Dartmouth as secretary of state for the colonies at the end of 1775, played a major part in ensuring that the British forces were well supplied and equipped. He also oversaw the American campaigns, acting, in effect, as the government's war minister. But Germain, a former soldier, understood only too well that micro-management of operations at 3,000 miles distance was impossible. He set the strategy, but carrying it out was the responsibility of the generals on the spot. In 1776 they had some notable triumphs, yet ultimately failed to deliver the knockout blow that Germain and his colleagues expected.

The least successful operations, from a British point of view, took place in the south. Henry Clinton, the British general commanding the small force sent from Boston that arrived at Cape Fear on 12 March, discovered that he was too late to assist the North Carolina loyalists, who had risen prematurely and been crushed at the Battle of Moore's Creek Bridge in late February. The main British force that had sailed from Ireland under Charles, Earl Cornwallis, joined Clinton in mid-April but, with little prospect of further loyalist activity, the two British generals decided to decamp to South Carolina. There they found local soldiers fortifying the seaward approaches to Charleston but, instead of attacking immediately, they tried to approach the American defences on Sullivan's Island by landing troops on neighbouring Long Island. Poor information about local conditions meant that the British were unable to cross impassable creeks and they were stuck, in the words of one junior officer, 'looking at the Rebbels making Entrenchments opposite us all the time'.[24] By late June Commodore Sir Peter Parker, in charge of the naval support for the expedition, decided that he could wait no longer. His impetuous attack on the American works on Sullivan's Island was a disastrous failure. Parker's ships were unable to silence the rebel guns, which caused much damage to his squadron. Two attempted landings by British troops were repulsed by the defenders. Lee, who had been so doubtful about the ability of American troops to withstand British regulars in conventional operations, was delighted that 'so much coolness and intrepidity' had been shown 'by a collection of raw recruits'.[25] Clinton and Cornwallis, with more and more of their troops succumbing to sickness, decided that their chances of success had gone and re-embarked to join Howe in New York.

In Canada, meanwhile, the British suffered no comparable setbacks but failed to make the most of their opportunities. The ice on the St Lawrence finally melted at the beginning of May, allowing British and German troops led by General John Burgoyne to reach the city of Quebec. There they joined forces with the small British garrison commanded by Guy Carleton, which had withstood an American attack on the last day of 1775. Carleton took charge of the British forces and began to push back the rebels. On 8 June 1776, British troops defeated the Americans at Trois Rivières. Benedict Arnold, the rebel commander, ordered the evacuation of Montreal, and by 18 June the British had reached Fort St John on the border with New York. At this point, however, Carleton squandered the chance to capitalize on his success. Rather than chase the dispirited Americans and recapture the forts at Crown Point and Ticonderoga, he chose to halt and construct a flotilla for operations on Lake Champlain. Not until 11 October did he resume the British advance, defeating Arnold's own small squadron of ships off Valcour Island. Arnold abandoned Crown Point and retreated to Ticonderoga. But again Carleton held back from seizing the advantage. He called upon the garrison of Ticonderoga to surrender, but seemed uncertain what to do when it refused. After some deliberation, and to great American surprise, Carleton concluded that Ticonderoga was too strongly defended to begin a siege so late in the year. He withdrew his forces to winter quarters in Canada, giving up the footholds he had acquired in upper New York.

Howe's army experienced the greatest success, but still could not crush the rebellion. The troops who had left Boston for Halifax sailed for New York in June, arriving off Sandy Hook, to the south of New York harbour, on the twenty-ninth of that month. Washington, who had been waiting for Howe since April, had put the local defences in order. Howe landed his forces on Staten Island at the beginning of July. The island's inhabitants seemed pleased to see the British troops, showing, according to one officer, 'the greatest Satisfaction in our Arrival',[26] which must have increased Howe's confidence that New York's population was well-disposed. But the British commander was still unwilling to begin operations against Washington until he was reinforced by Clinton and Cornwallis's army and the British and German soldiers who were sailing across the Atlantic.

In the eerie calm that preceded the storm, Congress declared the colonies independent states. The decision was not an easy one: Dickinson and other moderates argued against independence till the very end. The basis of the war had now changed dramatically. The Americans were no longer contending for a better deal within the British Empire, but for complete political separation. Independence divided them much more than the first months of the war had done:

many Americans who had enthusiastically resisted parliamentary authority could not accept the final break with the British crown. David Zubly, a Georgia planter, is a good example. Years later he recalled that, in 1775, he had served on a revolutionary committee and borne arms in the militia, but had resigned his commission in April 1776. 'He thought that Great Britain had no right to Tax America, but he did not approve of Opposition by force of Arms neither did he wish for Independence'.[27] The formal Declaration of Independence of 4 July, as if in recognition of the strength of continuing loyalty to George III, set out to destroy the king's reputation by laying all the ills of the past years at his door. George, to whom Congress had pledged its undying loyalty less than a year before, was now denounced as the instigator of a plot to create 'an absolute Tyranny'.[28] Although the Declaration was intended to justify to Americans the rejection of royal authority, its primary purpose was not domestic but international. Congressional leaders knew that they needed foreign help, and that no European power would truly commit to assisting the rebels if Americans appeared to be willing to return to the British fold. The Declaration was an announcement that a new polity – the United States – had arrived on the world stage, a polity capable of making agreements with any European state prepared to offer it support.[29] Congress wasted no time in pursuing possible allies: in September, Benjamin Franklin and Arthur Lee sailed for Paris to present a draft treaty to the French government. However, by the time the congressional commissioners reached the French capital, the Americans must have appeared far from eligible partners to Louis XVI's ministers, as the Continental army had suffered a devastating defeat. Even Vergennes must have wondered whether he had backed the right horse.

Not until the middle of August had all the British forces assembled. Howe's intention was to capture the city of New York, but he also wanted to knock out Washington's army, most of which was stationed on the western end of Long Island where, from defensive works on high ground at Brooklyn, it could command the city on the southern tip of neighbouring Manhattan Island. On 22 August, British troops began to disembark on Long Island. Having probed the American forward defences, about two miles in advance of the

Brooklyn lines, Howe concluded that they were too strong to be taken by frontal assault. He decided to use the Hessian troops to keep the Americans tied down in the centre of their line, while Grant probed the American right and Howe and Clinton took a strong body of British troops to envelop the rebels on their exposed left flank. The different British and German detachments coordinated their activities perfectly and, on the morning of 27 August, the flanking manoeuvre took Washington's forces completely by surprise. The inexperienced American troops retreated in disorder for the safety of the Brooklyn lines, 'reduced', as Clinton described it, 'to a *sauve qui peut*; over bays, marshes, creeks &c'.[30] Large numbers were captured.

By midday the British and German soldiers had reached the fortifications at Brooklyn. At this point, however, the British commander-in-chief called a halt. We can only speculate on what would have happened if he had allowed his troops to press on. It seems likely that if he had seized the moment, while the Americans were still in disarray, Washington's Continentals would have been destroyed as a fighting force. But Howe, perhaps remembering the bloody attack on the defences on Breed's Hill, decided against an immediate assault and opted to open siege works. Washington was at first inclined to stay and fight; he even called for reinforcements from New York City. But on 29 August he heeded the advice of his colleagues that if British ships, commanded by Howe's brother, Richard, Viscount Howe, entered the narrow waters between Long Island and Manhattan, there would be no escape. That night, the battered remnants of Washington's forces crossed over to New York City in a flotilla of small boats.

At this point, Admiral Howe decided that he and his brother should invite the Americans to discuss terms. The Howes had good cause to be better disposed towards their opponents than most British soldiers or sailors, as the Massachusetts assembly had paid for a monument honouring their brother, killed in America in 1758, to be put up in Westminster Abbey. Still, William Howe had shown no particular warmth for the Americans before his brother arrived: in April, while still at Halifax, he had expressed disappointment that the government had not been able to secure the services of Russian troops, whom he believed would act against the rebels with great relish.[31] But the viscount was his elder brother and may well have persuaded the general to adopt a more conciliatory approach. In doing so, the Howes went beyond their remit. Both the general and the admiral had been appointed peace commissioners as well as military and naval commanders, but the government in London envisaged their merely presenting Lord North's conciliation offer to Americans who had submitted. Even before the Battle of Long Island, the admiral had communicated with his old acquaintance Benjamin Franklin, only to be told that a settlement was no longer possible: 'The Time is past', Franklin brusquely responded.[32] Just before the Battle of Long Island, Lord Howe's secretary wrote that the brothers had 'nothing so much at heart as being Instruments of reconciling the two Countries'.[33] Now, after the British had demonstrated their military superiority, the admiral wanted to try again. He offered to meet representatives from Congress and, perhaps influenced by Chatham's conciliation proposal, suggested that American grievances might be redressed, even hinting that Congress would be recognized. After some hesitation, Congress appointed Franklin, John Adams, and Edward Rutledge to talk with Lord Howe. The meeting, as Adams had predicted, led nowhere, with Howe unable to persuade the American representatives to give up their 'System of Independency'.[34]

Military operations therefore resumed. The British troops were feeling confident – perhaps too confident – after their victory on Long Island, which General Howe attributed to his men's use of the bayonet, a weapon that seemed to terrify American soldiers, even when they were fighting in woods.[35] Under the cover of a bombardment from Admiral Howe's ships, a British detachment landed at Kipp's Bay on Manhattan Island. However, by concentrating on securing its foothold, the landing force allowed the Americans to withdraw their garrison from New York City and regroup at the northern end of the island. The next day, British troops experienced a set back at Harlem Heights, which provided a welcome boost for the flagging Americans and perhaps reinforced General Howe's inclination to caution. He and his brother made another attempt to encourage the Americans to come to terms on 19 September, when they issued a proclamation that invited discussion on reconciliation and stated, without authority from

London, that the king would be prepared to allow a significant measure of local self-government. Perhaps the Howes believed that they were doing no more than offering to the rebels the terms contained in North's conciliatory proposal. But we should remember that the government expected talks with the Americans only after they had submitted to British authority, not before. A leading historian of the war has argued that the Howes' attempts to mix fighting with negotiation were a grave error; his judgement that their reluctance to go for the American jugular proved fatal to British hopes of victory is difficult to challenge.[36]

The Americans and British constructed parallel lines across northern Manhattan. To break the deadlock, Howe landed troops on the mainland on 12 October, obliging Washington to take most of his forces to shadow Howe's manoeuvres. Washington's army camped at White Plains, where Howe attacked and captured the far right of the American defences at Chatterton Hill on the twenty-eighth of the month. But, as on Long Island and at Kipp's Bay, the British general failed to press home his advantage. Instead, Howe decided to turn back to deal with the Americans still on Manhattan. The rebel forces were now trapped, with British troops who had been facing them to the south now joined by more to the north and east, and the Royal Navy blocking any possible retreat across the Hudson to New Jersey. On 15 November, Howe demanded that the Americans surrender. They refused and the next day the British launched a coordinated assault from south, east and north. The outer defences quickly succumbed, leaving the remaining American troops crowded into Fort Washington. Recognizing that further resistance was futile, they surrendered. The rebels lost more than 3,000 officers and men, most of them as prisoners, putting their defeat on almost as catastrophic a level as Long Island nearly three months before.

At this point, Howe sent a British force under Clinton and Earl Percy to take Newport, Rhode Island, which could provide a safe anchorage for the navy and a base from which operations might be launched in New England. On 1 December, Clinton achieved his objective and in the process succeeded in blocking most of the fledgling Continental navy in Providence harbour. But Howe's main aim was to secure the west bank of the Hudson in New Jersey and pursue Washington, who had taken part of his army into that state before the fall of the American defensive works on Manhattan. A British contingent led by Cornwallis landed at Closter, New Jersey, on 20 November. Cornwallis immediately began to make headway, chasing Washington's troops hard. A week after coming ashore, the British advanced forces reached Newark, just as the last Americans were leaving. Cornwallis again came close to catching Washington at New Brunswick on 1 December. Morale amongst the retreating Americans was understandably low and now their army began to disintegrate. Soldiers whose enlistments had expired on 30 November started to go home, leaving a desperate Washington begging for help from the militia of New Jersey. The British almost caught up with the bedraggled remnants of Washington's troops once more at Princeton, only for the Americans to cross the Delaware at Trenton and reach the comparative safety of Pennsylvania. Anxious Philadelphians braced themselves for the arrival of Howe's army; Israel Putnam, the local commander, ordered every available soldier and 'all the Inhabitence' to help fortify the city.[37] However, the British general could find no boats and so the pursuit ended.

For the British, the campaign in New York and New Jersey had been brilliantly successful, 'glorious' as one officer described it.[38] As if to put icing on the celebratory cake, on 13 December British light dragoons surprised and captured Charles Lee, who had brought into northern New Jersey the troops that Washington had left in lower New York. The next day, Howe ordered his forces into quarters. But British expectations of 'a quiet winter' were soon dashed.[39] Washington's retreat had been so precipitate that he could not organize local support for his crumbling army; despite this, armed inhabitants began to make life uncomfortable for any British or German soldiers who found themselves isolated from the main body of Howe's forces. Local resistance appears to have been inspired by the behaviour of the invading British and Hessian troops, whose path was marked by extensive destruction and theft, and large numbers of assaults and rapes. As one American source put it, 'the very Quakers declare for taking up arms'; the German auxiliaries, in particular, were accused of having 'stripped every body almost, without distinction – even of all their clothes, and have beat and abused men, women, and children, in the most cruel manner ever heard of'.[40] As early as 12 December, the British commander-in-chief was obliged to threaten summary execution of any Americans 'not drest like solds and without officers' who fired on his troops.[41] Undeterred, local people continued to offer resistance, picking off their enemies, as one British officer noted disapprovingly on 23 December, from the cover of 'woods & bushes'.[42] Buoyed up by victory though they were, British and German troops on the receiving end of such attacks perhaps began to realize that winning battles might not be enough to pacify the rebellious Americans.

The British achievements in the 1776 campaign were undermined much more comprehensively on the night of 25–26 December, when Washington, against all British expectations, boldly recrossed the Delaware and attacked the Hessian brigade quartered at Trenton the following morning. The German garrison, recovering from celebrating Christmas with much gusto, was taken completely by surprise and was in no condition to offer effective resistance. More than a hundred Hessians were killed or injured and nearly a thousand were taken prisoner. American casualties amounted to no more than four men injured. Washington, who had endured defeat after defeat over the previous five months, discovered that nothing succeeds like success. Unable to secure any troops to help him while he was in retreat, he now found that reinforcements were much more readily forthcoming. Rather than retire to Pennsylvania, he decided to strike deeper into New Jersey. Howe ordered Cornwallis, who had chased Washington through New Jersey only a few weeks before, to repel the American incursion. But Washington gave Cornwallis the slip and attacked two British regiments on the march near Princeton. The Americans enjoyed a numerical advantage, but one British regiment, the Seventeenth Foot, bravely fought off Washington's troops and eventually joined Cornwallis at Trenton. The second regiment retreated rapidly to Princeton, from where it and a third regiment, which had remained in the town, attempted to escape to New Brunswick. British losses were heavy, with most of the dead and injured coming from the Seventeenth, and prisoners being taken from the other two regiments.[43]

Eastman Johnson's famous nineteenth-century painting, based on
Emmanuel Leutze's work, of Washington crossing the Delaware to attack
the Hessian garrison at Trenton. The reality must have been very
different, not least because the crossing took place at night.

Washington's victories at Trenton and Princeton ended the long
run of British success and perhaps ensured the survival of the United
States. Prior to the American counterattack, the chances of raising
a new army in 1777 looked remote. Even the normally phlegmatic
Washington had confessed before Trenton that 'the game is pretty
near up'.[44] After his triumphs, American fortunes were transformed.
James Robertson, a British general, ruefully predicted that
Washington would now get the 86 regiments that Congress had
promised.[45] For Howe's army, Trenton and Princeton brought a
more bitter harvest. For the rest of the winter, British troops in
New Jersey were subjected to morale-sapping harassment, 'fired
upon by small sculking parties of the rebels', as one officer put it;[46]
'almost daily molested' in the words of another;[47] 'the most
unpleasing situation I ever was in', according to James Grant.[48] All
thought of an early end to the war had to be abandoned. Another
campaign was needed.

*

The British government was displeased by Howe's failure to crush the rebellion and, according to one report, privately blamed him for too inhibited a conduct of the war: 'By what ministers said, it seemd as if they had wish'd that Fort Washington had been storm'd, & some of the garrison put to the sword'.[49] Those of his subordinates inclined to conspiracy theories claimed that Howe deliberately prolonged the war so that members of the army's supply services could increase their profits.[50] A more plausible explanation for his caution was the difficulty of maintaining an army at such a distance from home. Howe seems to have been very aware of the need to avoid heavy casualties, which could not easily be replaced. This real-ization, as much as any desire to mix diplomacy with military operations, probably accounts for his seeming timidity. But however displeased British ministers might have been, little changed. Howe kept his command, and British plans for the 1777 campaign in many ways repeated what had been attempted in 1776. Given the disaster at Charleston, we should not be surprised that no southern dimen-sion was included, but the idea of an army advancing south from Canada and coordinating its operations with the main army in lower New York remained a central feature.

John Burgoyne, who had acted as Carleton's subordinate in 1776, returned to London that winter to lobby for command of the troops in Canada. He argued that the northern army should capture Ticon-deroga and could then choose between two alternatives: marching south to the Hudson or south east into New England, where it could cooperate with British troops advancing from Newport. After Trenton and Princeton, Howe reduced the strength of the British forces in Rhode Island in order to reinforce New Jersey, which made a co-ordinated New England campaign more difficult to envisage. But Germain supported Burgoyne's proposal to march into the Hudson Valley, by which means New England, the heartland of the rebel-lion, might be cut off from the other provinces, causing American resistance to crumble. In March 1777, Germain instructed Carleton to organize two detachments from his Canadian command; the principal one, under Burgoyne, would advance southwards to junc-tion with Howe, while a smaller force, led by Lieutenant Colonel Barry St Leger, would provide a diversion to facilitate Burgoyne's progress by marching eastward along the Mohawk Valley from Lake Ontario. But coordination with Howe, vital if the intended junction were to take place, was never properly pinned down.

At the end of November 1776, Howe had suggested that he would send 10,000 men up the Hudson to Albany, leaving 8,000 to cover New York and New Jersey and compel Washington to tie up the main Continental forces protecting Philadelphia. But the success of British operations in New Jersey caused Howe to scale back his commitment to supporting Burgoyne's advance. Howe now believed that the priority was attacking Washington and taking Philadelphia. In a letter to Germain written on 20 December, Howe allocated not 10,000 but 3,000 troops from his command to assist 'in some degree the approach of the army from Canada'.[51] Trenton and Princeton, far from discouraging Howe from focusing to the southwest, seemed to increase his determination to concentrate on Washington and Philadelphia. On 2 April 1777 he told Germain that Burgoyne should not expect much help from his army as he would be busy campaigning in Pennsylvania. Howe added that he intended to attack Philadelphia by sea, rather than try to advance across New Jersey. On 20 April he suggested that it was quite possible that he would not be in a position to complete operations in Pennsylvania in time to offer any assistance to the northern army.[52]

Germain, we might say, should have ensured greater coopera-tion; after all, it was his responsibility to provide strategic oversight. He appears to have done little to persuade Howe of the need to offer proper support for Burgoyne. On 18 May, Germain, knowing that Howe intended to campaign in Pennsylvania, wrote of his hopes that 'whatever you may meditate will be executed in time for you to co-operate with the army to proceed from Canada'. But he seems not to have pressed the general further. Claims that he had prepared a much fuller set of instructions but failed to send them surfaced later in the writings of one his political opponents. Such claims seem very unlikely; William Knox, one of Germain's under-secretaries of state, explained that Christopher D'Oyly, the other under-secretary, sent Howe a copy of Burgoyne's instructions.[53] Even so, Germain seems personally to have done little to ensure proper coordination. From a modern perspective, his unwillingness to impose himself seems difficult to fathom. In part, his diffidence perhaps arose from his political insecurity; he had come into high office less than two years earlier, and had still not recovered from the charges of cowardice levelled at him while he was a senior officer in Germany during the Seven Years War.[54] But Germain's reluctance to push Howe probably owed more to his recognition of the difficulties of transatlantic communication. He took the view that it was not for him to dictate the precise course of a campaign at such a distance; he believed that a considerable element of latitude had to be given to local commanders.

Howe's determination to bring Washington to battle led him to advance into New Jersey in June 1777, only to withdraw when it became clear that Washington would not oblige. On 23 July, a great British fleet of warships and transports left New York harbour to approach Philadelphia by sea. Progress was slow, and made slower still by Howe's decision not to sail up the Delaware, where he believed that Washington would be waiting for him, but go the longer route into Chesapeake Bay. British troops eventually landed at Head of Elk, Maryland, on 25 August. Washington marched rapidly south, through Philadelphia, to contest the British advance. He prepared to stop Howe's army at Brandywine Creek, Pennsylvania, a naturally strong defensive position. On 11 September 1777, Howe repeated the tactics that had proved so successful at Long Island the year before. German auxiliary troops kept the Americans focused on the centre of their line, while Howe and Cornwallis led the bulk of their forces in a long march around Washington's right flank. However, the Americans were not taken by surprise as they had been at Long Island, and they had time to respond when Howe's column arrived. The British emerged as victors, but the Continental troops retreated in good order. Howe had not been able to deliver a knockout blow.

Ten days later, British troops achieved a more decisive, if smaller scale, victory. After much manoeuvring by the main armies, but no further battle, light infantry led by General Charles Grey launched a night-time attack of considerable ferocity on American troops at Paoli, west of Philadelphia. The sleeping Americans offered little resistance, but Grey's men wreaked a terrible toll with their bayonets, killing or injuring more than 300 men: only 100 were taken prisoner. Decorous and even staid as Howe's formal operations appeared, Paoli was a reminder of the less restrained side of the Revolutionary War, and perhaps a sign of the increasing frustration of the British at their inability to extinguish the rebellion. Just before Howe's army sailed for Philadelphia, Richard Fitzpatrick, a Guards officer, had written that his fellow officers were 'discontented & exasperated to the most violent degree and seem to consider laying the whole Country Waste & extirpating the inhabitants as the only means of putting an End to the war'.[55] Fitzpatrick, it should be said, was uncomfortable about the war in America and might have been inclined to exaggerate to make a point. Even so, his testimony chimes with the increasing commitment to a hardline approach evident in other officers' accounts.[56] On 26 September, shortly after the bloody action at Paoli, Howe achieved his secondary objective of occupying Philadelphia, but it brought him little advantage. His primary target, the overwhelming defeat of Washington's Continental army, continued to elude him.

Indeed, Washington soon showed that his troops were still capable of striking back. As if he were trying to repeat his triumph at Trenton, on 4 October the American general attacked the British troops encamped at Germantown, just north of Philadelphia. Thick fog added to the confusion of the battle, and the Americans' early success was halted by the staunch British defence of Chew House. At length, Howe's forces rallied and repelled Washington's troops. But again, Howe gained little from his victory. His army was now confined to Philadelphia and cut off from supplies from the surrounding countryside. The sea route to the city was still closed, as the Americans remained in control of the river defences downstream. In order to open up the Delaware to supply ships from New York, on 11 October the British tried to shell Fort Mifflin on Mud Island into submission, but its garrison refused to surrender. Fort Mercer, on the eastern Delaware shore, was attacked by Hessian troops led by Count von Donop on 22 October. The Germans won American plaudits for their 'great bravery & firmness',[57] but their assault produced nothing but a long casualty list. Nearly 400 of the Hessians were killed or injured. Donop himself died of his wounds. Only in November did the Americans evacuate their defences, by

A 1777 mezzotint of General Sir William Howe.

which time British relief was overshadowed by bad news from the north.

Burgoyne began his operations in June, while Howe was still probing Washington's defences in New Jersey. The northern army comprised about 8,500 officers and men, most of them British and German regular troops, with 650 loyalists and Canadians and around 400 Indian auxiliaries. St Leger's diversionary force of regulars, provincials and Indians was 1,600 men strong. At first, all went well for Burgoyne. His troops took Ticonderoga in early July, after its garrison, under the command of Arthur St Clair, abandoned the fortress. The British then chased St Clair's troops south, catching his rear guard at Hubbardton on 7 July. A brisk action ensued, and only the arrival of German reinforcements tipped the balance in favour of the British. But pursuing St Clair had taken the British forces away from their planned route south, and Burgoyne was now obliged to march through difficult territory – with no proper road – to reach Fort Edward and the Hudson. Progress was so slow that Burgoyne's supplies began to run short. From Fort Edward, where his troops encamped on 31 July, Burgoyne felt obliged to send a detachment of men into the Connecticut Valley to gather food and secure horses for his dismounted Brunswick dragoon regiment. That detachment, made up of 600 Germans, loyalists and Indians, suffered a crushing defeat at the hands of a much larger body of New Hampshire militiamen at Bennington, on 16 August. A few days later, St Leger's little army, intended to draw the American troops away from Burgoyne's advance, began to retreat. St Leger, who had landed at Fort Oswego, on the shores of Lake Ontario, a month before, was held up by the need to capture Fort Stanwix, in the Mohawk Valley. As an American relief force approached the fort, the Indians accompanying St Leger decided to leave. With his numbers severely reduced, St Leger concluded that he had to abandon the siege and begin the return journey to Canada. Burgoyne was now unsupported, either by St Leger or, more seriously, by Howe.

The American position, by contrast, was steadily strengthening. On 19 August, Horatio Gates, yet another former British army officer in congressional service, took over command of the army assembled at Saratoga to block Burgoyne's progress. He replaced Philip Schuyler, a wealthy but unpopular New Yorker, who, like Gage on the British side, was suspected by some of his subordinates of sympathizing with the enemy, and was certainly prone to pessimism.[58] Gates inherited a growing army; his Continental troops were now reinforced by considerable numbers of New England militiamen galvanized by Burgoyne's use of Indian auxiliaries. Burgoyne's army remained in good spirits; as one of his junior officers noted later, the ease with which they had captured Ticonderoga had misled them into thinking that they were 'irresistible'.[59] On 13–14 September, the British forces crossed to the west bank of the Hudson and a few days later began to approach the American defensive works on Bemis Heights. Benedict Arnold, one of Gates's senior officers, took a strong body of troops from the American defences to stop the British advance. The two sides met on 19 September at a woodland clearing around Freeman's Farm. The battle was fought with great determination by both the Americans and the British. Even though Arnold's forces at length disengaged, leaving the British masters of the battlefield, to call this a British victory would surely be most inappropriate: Burgoyne's army was now too weak to make further progress. As a British officer noted, 'Notwithstanding the glory of the day remains on our side . . . the real advantages . . . will rest on that of the Americans'.[60]

Burgoyne was still convinced that help was at hand. Clinton, left at New York by Howe, was indeed making every effort to rescue the beleaguered northern army. Burgoyne learned, on 21 September, that Clinton had promised a push at the American defences upriver from New York City. Burgoyne no doubt believed that such a diversion would draw some of the increasing numbers of Americans away from Gates's army, and so take the pressure off his tired and hungry soldiers; he may even have thought that the original plan of a junction at Albany was still possible. Clinton was true to his word. On 3 October he set out with 3,000 men – half the garrison of New York City and its environs – up the Hudson. Two days later he took Verplanck's Point and, on 6 October, Forts Montgomery and Clinton, north of Peekskill. The next day Clinton reached Fort Constitution. He sent on 2,000 men under General John Vaughan to take supplies up to Albany for Burgoyne's army. But Vaughan was unable to proceed when, on 15 October, his river pilots refused to go any further. A frustrated Vaughan proceeded to burn Esopus, which he described with much exaggeration as 'a nursery for almost every Villain in the Country',[61] but there was no escaping the fact that the diversion designed to save Burgoyne had petered out.

By this stage Burgoyne was on the verge of surrender. He made one last attempt to attack the American defences on 7 October, only to be overwhelmed by the Americans' superior numbers. The Battle of Bemis Heights, as the action is now called, finally convinced Burgoyne that he needed to abandon the advance and turn back to Canada. But he had left his retreat too late. On 12 October, Gates

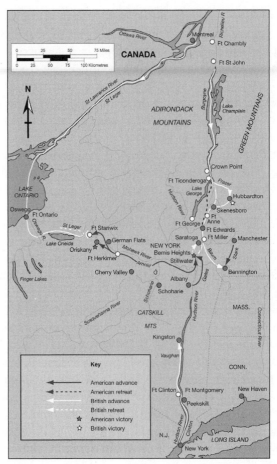

The Northern Campaigns, 1777, after Robert Middlekauff, *The Glorious Cause: The American Revolution, 1763–1789* (New York, 1982), p. 375.

cut off the British escape route and Burgoyne reluctantly opened negotiations. The Americans had nearly twice as many troops as the British, so Gates held all the best cards, but his nervousness about Clinton and Vaughan's advance up the Hudson led the Continental general to offer Burgoyne much more generous terms than the British position merited. The convention, signed by the two commanders, allowed Burgoyne's troops to march to Boston and from there to proceed to Europe, on condition that they took no further part in the war. Congress failed to honour Gates's terms, no doubt recognizing that much of Burgoyne's army would be redeployed to garrison duties at home, freeing up a like number of British troops to come across the Atlantic to reinforce Howe's army. Burgoyne's soldiers – now known in official correspondence on both sides as the Convention army – became prisoners, confined first at Cambridge, Massachusetts, and then in Virginia.

For the British, Burgoyne's fate was a disaster of the greatest magnitude. The catastrophe owed something, without doubt, to Burgoyne's overconfidence and impetuosity. He greatly underestimated the Americans and should have recognized that the odds were stacked against him after the defeat of a detachment of his army at Bennington. He also placed too much faith in Clinton's push up the Hudson. A more prudent general would have realized that he was in great danger much sooner; Burgoyne attempted to turn back only when it was too late.

Howe perhaps deserves a larger share of the blame. He knew that the British strategy for the 1777 campaign required him to cooperate with Burgoyne; his friend D'Oyly, as we have seen, had sent Howe a copy of Burgoyne's instructions. Nor can we excuse him by saying that Howe received no local advice on the need to coordinate his activities with Burgoyne's forces advancing south from Canada. Clinton, who had learned of the government's strategy while he was on leave in England early in 1777, impressed upon Howe the need to support the northern army. Yet Howe allowed himself to be distracted by Washington and Philadelphia. What was originally intended as a single campaign to end the rebellion therefore ended up as two completely separate campaigns carried out with only fitful reference to each other.

For this lack of coherence, Germain was principally responsible. His reluctance to micromanage commanders on the spot seems reasonable, given the slowness of transatlantic communications, but he surely should have made greater efforts to make Howe adhere to the agreed strategy. As it was, Germain left Howe largely to his own devices. Remarkably, Germain's friend and confident Sir John Irwine, commander-in-chief of the army in Ireland, was still completely in the dark about Howe's intentions in the autumn; from London he wrote on 29 September: 'Not a word from S^r: W^m: Howe ... Various opinions whether he is gone to the northward, or to Philadelphia; ... no man on this side of the Atlantic knows'.[62] Still more remarkably, a month later, on 28 October, before news of Saratoga reached England, Lord North was still 'in hourly expectation of good news' from Sir William Howe in Pennsylvania, and seemed to have forgotten all about Burgoyne.[63]

Rumours of Burgoyne's defeat reached Howe's army on 20 October. Howe, surely by now conscious of his share of culpability, offered his resignation two days later. The mood in British-occupied Philadelphia was understandably sombre. Ambrose Serle, Admiral Howe's secretary, noted in his diary the 'Disposition ... among some principal officers to throw the Blame on others'; 'every thing', Serle wrote gloomily, 'wears a melancholy aspect'.[64] A little later, a British military surgeon serving with the army in Philadelphia questioned the whole rationale of the campaign; why had the government in London ('The Cabinet Generals', as he contemptuously called the ministers) imagined that it was a good idea to bring Burgoyne and Howe to a junction in the Hudson Valley, and for what purpose? Surely, he argued, the troops sent across the Atlantic to form Burgoyne's army would have been better deployed in New York as reinforcements for Howe's forces?[65]

If the British were downcast, the Americans were correspondingly elated by their triumph. A professional field army had been compelled to surrender to rebel forces that British officers and men alike had regularly dismissed as untrained, inexperienced and amateurish. As a result, the British regulars lost some of their ability to inspire awe in the rebels: a significant psychological barrier had been overcome. 'It was a glorious sight', wrote an American soldier who witnessed Burgoyne's humiliation, 'to see the haughty Brittons march out & Surrender their arms to an Army which but a little before, they despis'd & called paltroons'.[66]

The impact on the French government was also important. Saratoga was not the cause of French intervention; Louis XVI's ministers had already decided on that course but wanted to complete their own war preparations before they formally became belligerents. Saratoga speeded up the process. Once the news of Burgoyne's surrender arrived at Paris, in December 1777, the French government made a commitment to the American commissioners to recognize the United States. Crucially, Louis' ministers also promised to enter into an alliance with the Americans. Lord North and his colleagues, as soon as they learned of the disaster that had befallen Burgoyne, did all they could to prevent a Franco–American junction, approaching the Americans in Paris to see whether they would agree terms, and even putting out feelers to the French to see whether they might be persuaded to respond to an appeal to European imperial solidarity.[67] But the Americans would not renounce their independence – George III's precondition for talks – and the French government, not without some reservations on Louis XVI's part, had decided that the opportunity to reduce British power outweighed the risks involved in supporting colonial rebels. The treaties between the French and the Americans were finally signed in February 1778. As North and his ministers fully appreciated, the American rebellion was about to turn into a much wider and more demanding conflict.

3

THE WORLD WAR

Long before they knew of the signing of the Franco–American alliance, British ministers were preparing for a war against both France and Spain. Such a war would be much bigger in scale than the conflict with the rebel colonies. Every area of imperial competition between the British and the Bourbons – in America, Africa and Asia – had the potential to become an arena of conflict. Britain's Mediterranean outposts of Gibraltar and Minorca might be attacked and the home islands themselves would be exposed to invasion. In these circumstances, the British government even considered a complete withdrawal from the rebel colonies and concentration of resources on the impending clash with the Bourbon powers. Such a course might well have created national unity at home. The parliamentary opposition and their supporters in the country had been unhappy about the American war from the beginning, and ending the struggle in the rebel colonies would have reduced the domestic pressure on the government. But the conflict in America was not abandoned. Lord North and his colleagues felt a continuing obligation to the loyalists. British ministers habitually exaggerated the strength and willingness of American 'friends to government' to assist British arms, but their hopes for loyalist support were not unfounded. Loyalism received a boost in 1778, as a good many Americans found it difficult to stomach an association with their ideological opposites; Catholic and absolutist France made a strange ally for Protestant and republican America. Perhaps more importantly, ministers in London believed that the viability of the West Indian sugar economy

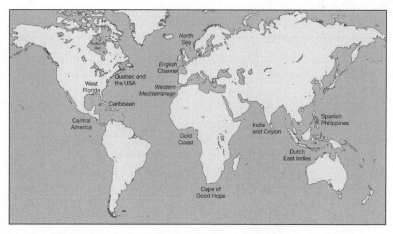

The World War: from 1778 the conflict became much more than a war for, and in, North America, but a struggle waged in all areas of competition between Britain and its European enemies.

would be undermined if the British could not keep at least the southern mainland to support the islands with foodstuffs and other vital supplies.[1] The war in America, however, was now to be part of a much wider and more complex struggle, and for Lord North's government it was by no means the most important theatre of the new global conflict.

In such a situation, British ministers naturally looked for new friends. In February, another approach was made to Catherine the Great of Russia. However, the only possible interest she could have in a British alliance was if North and his colleagues were willing to pledge military assistance in the event of a Russo–Turkish war. Ministers in London understandably baulked at the prospect of being drawn into another conflict,[2] and so turned to Prussia, Britain's main ally in the Seven Years War. A renewed Prusso–British axis seemed distinctly possible in April 1778, as Prussia and Austria were heading for a war over the disputed succession to Bavaria. Frederick the Great recognized that a conflict with Austria could easily escalate into another war against France, Austria's ally since 1756. If France and Austria were pitted against Prussia, would Frederick seek to revive his old British connection? The British press, perhaps longing for a return to

A contemporary miniature of Sir Henry Clinton, who took over command of the British army in North America when General Howe returned home.

the simplicities of the last war, devoted much attention to Frederick, as if to rekindle the public's enthusiasm for the king of Prussia.[3] But for Frederick himself, the attractions of a British alliance waned once it became clear that the French would not be drawn into a central European war in support of the Austrians. The British government was therefore obliged to prepare for a much broader conflict unaided by European allies who might have compelled the French to commit resources to defending their position on the Continent.

If America were not to be abandoned, British ministers realized that they could not continue the struggle there on the same basis as before. In early March 1778, Germain ordered Clinton, who had succeeded Howe as the commander-in-chief, to conduct a predominantly naval war from the British posts at New York and in Nova Scotia. Clinton was also urged to withdraw his troops from Philadelphia and assemble forces for a southern campaign.[4] On 21 March, once the reality of a Franco–American alliance had been confirmed, Germain issued new instructions, emphasizing the need to strike against the French in the West Indies and reinforce the garrison in the Floridas, which might soon come under Spanish attack.[5] The logic of the Caribbean expedition, though not spelled out, was almost certainly the same as in the Seven Years War. British governments assumed that the sugar of the French West Indies provided the public revenues that supported France's war machine; if the flow of sugar from the French islands could be reduced, or even stopped, then French war finances would be undermined and the French government would be forced to come to terms. Germain was explicit about what Clinton should do with the rest of his army; Philadelphia was to be abandoned and British forces were to be concentrated in New York. In a bid to separate the new allies, the Earl of Carlisle would lead a peace commission that would seek to negotiate an end to the American aspect of the war.

At the same time as it appointed the peace commissioners, Parliament agreed to surrender up its right to tax the colonies – the original cause of the dispute. North and his colleagues still hoped to salvage parliamentary trade regulation, which they continued to see as vital to British interests.[6] Carlisle, however, was soon to find that negotiations with Congress were not possible. His terms, which may have satisfied the Americans in 1775, would not do so in the very different circumstances of 1778. The continuing fund of goodwill towards Britain felt by many congressmen before the fighting started had largely disappeared after three years of war. Too much blood had been spilled and too much property destroyed. As a Virginia gentleman put it, 'The Die is Cast – the Rubicon is passed – and a Reconciliation with Great Britain, upon the Terms of returning to her Government is impossible'.[7] And with their new French alliance to sustain them, the Americans had no need to compromise. They would now settle for nothing short of complete withdrawal of the British army from the territory of the United States and a full acknowledgement of independence. Since the British commissioners were not empowered to offer anything of the kind, Carlisle was not even given the courtesy of a meeting. Congress let it be known via newspapers that it would not receive the commissioners.[8]

Clinton, meanwhile, had decided to delay sending detachments from his army to the Caribbean and Florida until he had successfully evacuated Philadelphia and brought his forces to the safety of New York. In June 1778, the British began to depart from Philadelphia, accompanied by nearly 3,000 loyalists who were unwilling to remain in the city. Given the number of loyalists who wanted to follow the British forces, Clinton judged that travelling by sea was not possible. To move such a large number of troops, refugees and baggage by land was a painfully slow business; to reach Allentown, 35 miles from Philadelphia, took six days. Washington's army, which had wintered at Valley Forge, Pennsylvania, shadowed Clinton's column as it crossed New Jersey. Charles Lee, recently exchanged and so back with the Continental army, was reluctant to harass Clinton's retreating troops, but Washington sensed an opportunity to attack an exposed enemy. On 28 June, in searing heat, Lee, leading the advance guard of the American army, began to engage with the British rearguard under Cornwallis near Monmouth Court House. Lee, concerned that the main British army would turn to assist Cornwallis, failed to press on and decided to pull back. Washington, advancing with the rest of the American troops, then took charge, and prepared his army for the British counterattack. He succeeded in repulsing several British assaults before the two armies disengaged. Both sides claimed success; the Americans because they had held off the British counterstroke, and the British because Washington had failed to inflict serious damage on their army when it was vulnerable to attack. On 29 June, Clinton's column resumed its slow progress, reaching Sandy Hook on 1 July and crossing over to New York City five days later.

Though Clinton would not have known it, he had arrived not a moment too soon. On 11 July, the importance of French intervention was underscored when Admiral Comte d'Estaing arrived off New York with 16 French ships of the line. His objective was to deliver a knockout blow to the British forces and bring the war to a speedy end.[9] The French had hoped to persuade the Spanish to join the struggle as their allies; after all, the Spanish, like the French, had good reason to want to recover territory and prestige lost in the Seven Years War. The Spanish fleet, when added to the French, would have given the Bourbon powers more ships of the line than the British. But the Spanish government, perhaps inhibited about assisting a rebellion that might set an example to its own American colonies, refused to enter the war at this point. Ministers in Madrid preferred to wait and see which side offered them the most attractive terms. Unable to bring the Spanish into the conflict in the spring of 1778, the French might reasonably have decided to hold back themselves. Without the Spanish their chances of success were much more limited, as France possessed only 52 capital ships to Britain's 66. But the French government opted instead for boldness.

D'Estaing had brought the French Mediterranean fleet out of Toulon in April. The Earl of Sandwich, the British first lord of the admiralty, believed that d'Estaing's intention was to join the French Brest fleet and sail into the English Channel. Sandwich, who had a keen sense of the Royal Navy's primary responsibility to protect the country from invasion, was reluctant to allow reinforcements to be sent to Admiral Howe until he was sure that d'Estaing was heading across the Atlantic rather than for a rendezvous with the Brest fleet.[10] Even then, Sandwich rightly recognized that British naval strength had to be husbanded in home waters rather than distributed throughout the globe. French troops were massing in Brittany and Normandy, as if to invade. On 13 July 1778, two days after d'Estaing's arrival in North America, the Brest fleet under Admiral d'Orvilliers appeared off the Isle of Wight. The French then sailed down the Channel to engage with the British western squadron under Admiral Keppel. The two fleets met off Ushant on 27 July. The action was inconclusive, but the French performed strongly enough to shake British confidence in their naval superiority. According to a British marine officer, 'It is agreed by every body that no fleet could go thro' the different motions better than the French did'.[11]

The very appearance of d'Estaing off New York demonstrated how much the war had changed. Up until that point, the British army operating in North America had no real need to worry about the Atlantic Ocean behind it. Despite occasional successes by American privateers, the extended supply line back to Britain and Ireland was reasonably secure. The Royal Navy ruled the waves and could move British troops to wherever they wanted to go. French intervention changed all this. The transatlantic supply line became much more vulnerable; Clinton was to complain in November 1778 that since he had taken charge, his army had been 'within 3 weeks of Starving' on no fewer than four occasions.[12] Fears that he might not have enough provisions no doubt inhibited Clinton from launching offensive operations. More serious still, isolated British coastal outposts were now exposed to coordinated attack from American soldiers by land and the French navy by sea. D'Estaing had failed to pull off such a coup at New York in mid-July, but at the end of that month his fleet sailed into Narragansett Bay to threaten the British garrison at Newport, Rhode Island.

At New York, Washington had been in no position to support d'Estaing, but at Rhode Island the situation was different. At the beginning of August American troops under General John Sullivan landed near Newport. Sullivan soon had some 10,000 Continentals and militiamen at his command. As the allies prepared to launch a coordinated attack, Admiral Howe, reinforced by ships newly arrived from Britain, unexpectedly arrived off Rhode Island. D'Estaing set off to engage with the British fleet, but Sullivan, rather than wait for the French ships to return, resolved to press ahead without French naval support. An American attack on the British defences was repulsed and the militia, discouraged by the setback, began to melt away. D'Estaing, with several of his ships damaged in the engagement with Howe's fleet, was not willing to stay off Rhode Island and sailed for Boston. As the Americans began to withdraw, the British garrison sallied forth to attack, only to pull back in the face of determined resistance. But Sullivan had little reason to celebrate. The aim of trapping the British at Newport and forcing them to surrender had not been realized. The Americans, many of whom were instinctively uncomfortable working with their former enemies, wasted little time in blaming their new allies: 'Mr Frenchman Left us ... in the Lurch' was one New Englander's bitter verdict on d'Estaing's departure for Boston.[13]

As soon as he had learned of the predicament of the Newport garrison, Clinton had assembled a rescue mission. The 4,000 troops he had brought with him from New York arrived off Rhode Island on 1 September. Too late to catch Sullivan, Clinton decided to raid the New England coast and even planned to attack the French fleet at Boston. Conscious that he was soon to lose a substantial portion of his command to the West Indies and Florida, Clinton wanted to make the most of the few weeks campaigning left to him. Admiral Howe vetoed the Boston enterprise, leaving Clinton to focus on drawing Washington's army into a decisive battle. But a British advance into New Jersey failed to persuade the American commander to engage. Attacks on the frontier of the rebel colonies, involving mixed forces of Indians and loyalists, caused much misery in Pennsylvania and New York, but it was not until the next year that Washington was willing to detach part of his army to counter these incursions. Clinton was unable to achieve much, other than antagonize the Americans further with some very destructive coastal raids before he was obliged finally, in November, to release many of his troops for service in the Caribbean and Florida. Though he claimed that his army had been effectively dismembered and that the loss of so many troops was 'fatal to the hopes of any future vigour',[14] he still responded to Germain's earlier request to shift the focus of the war to the south. Clinton decided to send 3,000 soldiers under Lieutenant Colonel Archibald Campbell to take Georgia. Campbell arrived off Tybee Island, some 15 miles from Savannah, in late December 1778. The American forces in the area, after offering token resistance, abandoned Savannah, leaving the British troops to occupy the town in the last days of the year.

By this time, the first clashes between the British and French had occurred in the Caribbean. The French had taken the initiative, attacking Dominica in September 1778. The island, which had been French until the end of the Seven Years War, was weakly defended and rapidly fell. The British forces detached from Clinton's command arrived in the West Indies in December and immediately proceeded to land troops on St Lucia, the objective identified by Germain in the spring. D'Estaing, now at the naval base at Fort Royal, Martinique, conveyed a strong body of French soldiers to St Lucia a few days later. On 18 December the French troops attempted to dislodge the British invaders. The subsequent battle demonstrated how much the British army had learned from the war in America. British light infantrymen subjected the advancing French to a constant fire. The attackers, according to one British participant, were thrown into 'consternation'.[15] The French soldiers tried to take the British defensive positions three times, but were driven back with heavy casualties. In all, they lost 1,500 dead and injured, or 30 per cent of their force. The French defeat that day, as a leading historian of the war describes it, was 'the Bunker Hill of the Caribbean'.[16] On 29 December, the French re-embarked and, on the thirtieth, the island's governor formally surrendered to the British commander, General James Grant.

If the British and French each had their successes in the war in the West Indies in 1778, the British clearly won the first round of the struggle that spread to India that year. The British East India Company, a military and territorial power as well as a trading entity, was already engaged in a war with the Maratha confederacy of Indian princes, which involved the company's Bombay forces and eventually much of its main Bengal army too. That conflict was to continue until May 1782. But, despite this major commitment, the company seems to have welcomed the opportunity presented by a new war with France. Company forces moved quickly to occupy French trading posts, many of which were only lightly defended. The most powerful, Pondicherry, had to be laid under siege. It held out, much to the admiration of the commander of the surrounding army, for 77 days.[17] But by the end of October 1778, only one French post remained in India, at Mahé, on the Malibar coast.

If the first stage of the wider war had gone better for the British than might have been predicted, 1779 was to prove an altogether tougher year. Spain signed a new treaty of amity with France in April and, two months later, entered the war. Continuing Spanish qualms about supporting the American rebels meant that there was to be no alliance with the United States, but Spanish intervention made the prospect of British victory in North America even more remote than it had been since the French entered the war. Perhaps unwisely, the British government had refused to buy Spanish neutrality by offering up either Gibraltar or Minorca. The French, who needed the support of the Spanish fleet, were more willing to bend. Vergennes, while complaining that 'the views and pretensions of Spain are gigantic', acceded to Spanish demands for French help in securing Gibraltar, Minorca and their lost American territories.[18]

In North America, Lieutenant Colonel Campbell's forces consolidated their hold on Georgia in January 1779. 'I have taken a Stripe and Star from the Rebel flag of America' was Campbell's understandable boast.[19] In March, civil government was restored in the province and Brigadier General Augustine Prevost, who had joined Campbell from East Florida, now took charge of the little British army in Georgia. He was convinced that the new royal government would never be secure unless dissident elements were denied support from neighbouring South Carolina. In Prevost's view, an attack on that state was therefore imperative. He had already sent a detachment of British troops to Beaufort, but on 3 February it had been obliged to withdraw. In March, Prevost advanced into South Carolina and defeated American troops at Briar Creek. Benjamin Lincoln, the local American commander, undeterred by Prevost's success, decided that the best means of defence was attack. Accordingly, he advanced into Georgia in late April while Prevost, rather than pull back, pressed on. Each side, it seems, was trying to persuade the other to abandon its offensive and return to defend its territory. Prevost reached Charleston, where John Rutledge, the revolutionary governor of South Carolina, was prepared to surrender so long as his state could be declared neutral for the rest of the war: Prevost insisted on unconditional surrender. In the end, the British general overplayed his hand; news that Lincoln was marching north to Charleston's aid forced Prevost to lift his siege on 12 May.

In the same month, Clinton sent an expedition to Virginia to support Prevost's operations. The British troops destroyed all the stores and shipping they could reach, hoping to prevent Virginian supplies from sustaining Lincoln's southern army. They probably also expected to occupy local military forces, stopping them marching south to oppose Prevost. But local resistance was very limited, so much so that some British participants concluded the population was well disposed to the British presence.[20] Sir George Collier, in charge of the naval forces supporting the troops, even contemplated staying to establish a naval base. But Major General Edward Mathew, the army commander, insisted on sticking to Clinton's instructions and leaving as soon as the work of destruction was completed. On 24 May, the British expedition returned to New York. This episode demonstrated that, even after French intervention, the Royal Navy was still able to give the British army great mobility. But the changed nature of the war was soon to be underlined afresh when the French navy sailed up from the West Indies to assist the Americans in Georgia.

Prevost had managed to extricate himself from the environs of Charleston, and in June his troops held off an attack by Lincoln's forces at Stono Ferry. To prevent the British from launching a further attack on South Carolina, the Americans summoned French help. D'Estaing arrived off the coast of Georgia on 1 September. He landed 5,000 French troops to assist Lincoln in capturing Savannah, but bad weather slowed down the allied siege preparations and gave the British garrison the chance to improve its defences. Prevost refused to surrender and d'Estaing's siege artillery proceeded to pound the town for three days. French engineers had concluded that the strength of the British works made a long siege the only option, but d'Estaing, mindful of a growing sick list in his fleet and the damage being done to his vessels by the bad weather, convinced himself that the town would have to be stormed. His officers warned him that an assault would be very costly, but d'Estaing would not listen. Some 900 French and Americans were killed or injured in an unsuccessful attack, while Prevost's troops suffered only 54 casualties. On 18 October, the allies raised the siege.[21]

At Newport, in August 1778, the French and Americans had failed to realize the potential of their alliance. Now at Savannah, a little over a year later, they again were unable to deliver a devastating blow to an exposed British garrison. After Newport, Admiral James Gambier had written of the 'reciprocal enmity and contempt' of the French and Americans for each other.[22] But after Savannah Clinton, only too aware that the French and Americans might sooner or later coordinate their efforts more effectively, saw no cause for gloating. He remained very much alive to the danger of the French navy's cooperating with American land forces. Savannah's survival was a cause for celebration but also for reflection; shortly afterwards, Clinton ordered Newport's garrison to be brought back to New York.

The war in the north did not go according to plan for Clinton in 1779. He repeatedly tried to bring Washington to a set-piece engagement and repeatedly failed. Washington detached part of his Continental forces to attack the native peoples who had ravaged the frontier in 1778. Sullivan, who led the American troops, proceeded to wreak an awful revenge in August and September, first pushing the Amerindians back to the British post at Niagara and then devastating their lands in the Mohawk Valley. But Washington would not oblige Clinton by moving his main forces from his New Jersey defences towards the principal British army. A British expedition sent from Halifax, Nova Scotia, captured Penobscot, in modern-day Maine, in June, at least partly in the hope of drawing off some of the main Continental army. But Penobscot was too remote to cause Washington any alarm. It was left to forces from Massachusetts to try (and fail) to dislodge the British in July.

Washington even refused to be drawn by British advances much nearer his base. In June, just as Penobscot fell to the British, Clinton attempted to lure the American general from New Jersey by advancing up the Hudson to threaten his communications with New England. But Clinton could not entice his opponent into leaving his defensive positions. He then sent an expedition to raid the Connecticut coast, in the hopes that this might provoke a response from Washington. New Haven, Fairfield and Norwalk were all burned. However, the American general, rather than advance towards New England as Clinton hoped, launched his own attack on the Hudson River forts that Clinton had recently taken. When Clinton recalled his troops from Connecticut to push north and challenge Washington, the rebel forces withdrew. The American mouse continued to elude the British cat.[23]

Clinton, growing more and more frustrated by his inability to compel Washington to fight a set-piece battle, asked permission to return home in August. The government refused to accept his resignation, perhaps wrongly. Clinton's sullen resentment at having to manage with fewer troops than his predecessor, together with his anxieties about his army's exposure to defeat by the French and Americans working together, made him a less than ideal commander-in-chief.[24] His mood could hardly have lifted when he learned that the British defences in Florida, which he had been ordered to strengthen at the expense of his main army in 1778, had proved too weak to withstand Spanish attack. Recovery of Florida was a priority for the Spanish government and, once news arrived of Spain's entry into the war, Bernardo de Gálvez, the governor of Louisiana, reinforced by Spanish troops from Cuba, moved rapidly against the British bases in West Florida. In September, Gálvez took the British garrisons at Manchac, Baton Rouge, and Natchez by surprise.[25]

In the Caribbean, the French had already been making significant headway before the Spanish became belligerents. Grant, still holding on to St Lucia, was reluctant to split his forces, which meant that most of the thinly defended British islands were open to attack. St Vincent fell to the French in June; Grenada in July. For the British, Spanish intervention made matters appreciably worse. Jamaica, their largest and most important island, became more exposed; in August a descent was 'daily expected'.[26] John Dalling, the governor, was not content to wait for the Bourbons to attack; he decided to go on the offensive. As early as the end of May, he was urging Germain to permit an attack on Hispaniola, with a view to the annexation of the island.[27] In September, he sent an expedition to support the British settlers in Belize and seize the Spanish base at Bacalar. But before the Jamaica forces arrived, the Spanish captured the British base at St George's Cay on 15 September. The troops from Jamaica therefore moved to attack the Spanish fortress of Omoa, in modern-day Honduras. Omoa was duly taken on 20 October, with the help of British settlers and the native population, only for the new British garrison to be obliged to abandon the post and return to Jamaica a few weeks later when sickness made it untenable to remain.

Spanish Central America was not the only new theatre of operations. Hostilities even spread to West Africa, where the European powers had established fortified posts from which they could buy slaves to work on the Caribbean and American plantations. In January 1779, a French expeditionary force captured St Louis in Senegal. The next month, the British base on James Island was also compelled to surrender. Further south, a French ship attacked and severely damaged the British post at Secondi, on the Gold Coast, in May. Later in the year, the British occupied an abandoned French fort at

Gorée, near the mouth of the River Gambia, but this gain offered scant compensation for the loss and damage inflicted on the British slave traders. The British marines who took Gorée had been landed from a squadron sailing for India. On the subcontinent, the sole remaining French post, at Mahé, fell in March 1779. The British might have been wiser to leave it in French hands, for Haidar Ali of Mysore regarded Mahé as being under his protection. Over the next few years, he and his son Tipu were to prove formidable adversaries of the British and strong allies of the French.

Europe also became a scene of much military and naval activity. As soon as the Spanish entered the conflict, they began a blockade of Gibraltar. The British post was difficult to attack and strongly defended, but by the end of August the governor, George Augustus Eliott, reported that provisions were running low.[28] Not until January of the next year did a relief convoy arrive. The most important development, however, from a British point of view, was the junction of the French and Spanish navies and a serious threat posed to England itself. In 1778, the French had pretended that they intended to land troops in order to prevent British ships following d'Estaing across the Atlantic; in 1779, the French and Spanish were not engaged in a feint. As a condition of entering the war, the Spanish insisted on a joint attack to bring the British government to terms. By 16 August the combined fleet – with some 66 ships of the line – was off Plymouth. Admiral Hardy, in command of the British fleet in the Channel, had only 39 battle ships at his disposal and was far to the west, deployed to prevent an anticipated landing in Ireland.

British fears for Ireland were understandable. The leaders of its Catholic majority professed their allegiance to the Crown, but many of their Protestant neighbours worried that any French and Spanish descent on Ireland would spark off a general revolt of the Catholic peasantry. To Lord North's beleaguered government, the Irish Protestants themselves must have seemed doubtful, particularly the Presbyterians in Ulster. The Protestants had begun to form volunteer companies the previous year, when France entered the war. The ostensible purpose of these paramilitary volunteer bodies was to overawe the Catholic population and help defend the country from invasion. But the volunteers soon acquired a political dimension, and worked with the Patriot opposition in the Dublin Parliament to press for concessions, first on trade and then on the constitutional relationship between Britain and Ireland.[29] As the lord lieutenant wrote of the volunteers, 'the lyon walks abroad without his chain, and tho' he wags his tail, his fangs may prove dangerous'.[30] Small wonder Hardy was stationed off Ireland to contest any attempted landing of troops by the Franco–Spanish fleet.

Once he realized that the enemy were not heading for Ireland, but had moved into the Channel, strong winds stopped Hardy from sailing to engage the French and Spanish, who were able to remain off Plymouth. On shore, feverish preparations were underway to resist an invasion. The governor of Plymouth organized the strengthening of its fortifications, and a local naval officer even contemplated giving weapons to the tin miners, despite his concern that they were 'such an unruly and ungovernable a set of men that the greatest disorders may be apprehended from them, should arms be put in their hands'.[31] All along the coast of Devon and Cornwall, local volunteer units sprung up; according to a militia officer, almost every village raised a company.[32] Hardy's inability to defend the country was roundly criticized ('English shyness is a revolution in the maritime System of Europe', complained an opposition MP),[33] but if a battle had occurred, British victory must surely have been doubtful. As it was, the allies started to fall out and sickness undermined their strength. In late September, the great Armada sailed away. For a crucial few weeks, however, the Royal Navy had effectively lost control of the Channel and invasion seemed a real possibility.[34]

At the end of 1779, Lord North's ministry faced a major domestic crisis, thanks in part to the exposure of England to an enemy landing during the summer. At its height, the crisis threatened to topple not just North and his colleagues, but the very system of political management on which all eighteenth-century British governments relied. Lack of success in the war, high taxes (apparently yielding no positive ends), concerns about the misuse of public funds, and a credit crisis brought on partly by government borrowing at high rates of interest all combined to create a mood of great discontent. In December, landowners in Yorkshire formed an association to press for a reduction in public spending and a more independent House of Commons better able to check and control government. Over the next few months, Yorkshire's lead was followed across the English counties, and many boroughs started to agitate for their own preferred reforms to the political system.[35]

Across the Atlantic, Clinton, despairing of bringing Washington to decisive battle in the north, finally decided to concentrate resources on the southern theatre. On 26 December 1779, he sailed from New York with 7,600 troops for South Carolina. His aim was to return to Charleston, the city that had defied the British in the summer of 1776 but looked distinctly vulnerable when Prevost had approached it earlier in 1779. By January 1780, British transports reached Tybee Island, near Savannah, where the ships were repaired and the troops rested after a gruelling voyage in severe winter storms. On 10 February, the British forces sailed north towards Charleston, arriving at North Edisto Inlet, about 30 miles from the city, the next day. The American defenders, commanded by Lincoln, sat tight and awaited reinforcements from the north. Clinton methodically approached the city, occupying ground across the harbour to the south in early March. At the beginning of the next month, British troops started digging siege trenches on Charleston Neck to the north. When a British detachment seized Monck's Corner a few days later, Lincoln's garrison was effectively cut off. On 21 April, recognizing that his situation was hopeless, Lincoln offered to surrender, but only if his garrison were allowed to leave without becoming prisoners of war. Clinton refused. For another three weeks the siege continued, with the city experiencing heavy bombardment, before Lincoln finally capitulated on 12 May.

When news of the fall of Charleston reached London, the pressure on Lord North's beleaguered government noticeably slackened. Over the preceding months calls for reform had been mounting, and North himself had, in March, been obliged to concede a royal commission to examine the public accounts. The appetite for change had already been declining before Clinton's success became known in England, largely as a result of the anti-Catholic Gordon Riots that rocked London in June 1780; many gentlemen in the counties lost their enthusiasm for reform when confronted with major disorder in the capital. But news of Charleston's capture further boosted the government's standing as exaggerated tales of the consequences circulated; according to John Gibbons, a London clergyman, the fall of the southern city had caused '*All North America*' to submit to British rule.[36] By the end of the year, Sir George Savile, a leading opposition politician, judged that the public had lost interest in any kind of parliamentary reform.[37]

If North was relieved by the British victory in South Carolina, Clinton was little short of euphoric. Not even news of the fall of Mobile, in West Florida, to the Spanish dimmed his joy. Clinton's response to the British commander at Mobile wasted little space on commiserations and took the form of an extended description of his own triumph at Charleston. The British commander-in-chief had cause to be pleased. His army had captured the principal city in the south, and with it 2,500 Continental troops. In the days following, local people flocked in to take the oath of allegiance. On 29 May, a British force led by Lieutenant Colonel Banastre Tarleton defeated a body of Continentals at the Waxhaws, reinforcing the impression that the whole province would soon be back in British hands. But even at this moment of optimism, Clinton's anxieties about the French continued to be influential. On 8 June, he sailed back to New York with 4,000 troops to counter what he believed was a threat to New York City's weakened garrison.

Clinton's concerns were justified; a French expeditionary force, led by the Comte de Rochambeau, was on its way to North America. In July the French landed at Newport, Rhode Island.[38] Clinton feared that the French would join Washington, and their combined forces would be in a position to attack New York. The American commander-in-chief was indeed keen to launch operations in conjunction with Rochambeau, but the French were unwilling. Rochambeau saw his role as supporting the French fleet, not reinforcing Washington's Continental army. The French troops therefore remained inactive at Rhode Island. Clinton, still buoyed up by his success at Charleston, momentarily threw aside his customary caution and considered an attack on the new French post. But any thought of a British strike evaporated when Washington threatened the outer defences of New York. In September, the arrival of naval reinforcements from the

Caribbean under the energetic Admiral Rodney offered a further opportunity, but this time Clinton decided that the defences of Newport were too strong to risk an attack. Instead, he hoped to capture the key American forts on the Hudson, which controlled communications between New Jersey and New England. Benedict Arnold, the commandant of West Point, had opened negotiations with the British to hand over the fort. Arnold's motives were mixed. He was heavily indebted, which no doubt made the British offer of a substantial sum of money particularly attractive. But he was also hostile to the French alliance and married into a family with loyalist inclinations. Whatever his reasons, his treachery was discovered when the Americans fortuitously captured John André, a British officer who was carrying incriminating documents. Arnold escaped to the British lines, but the Americans hanged the unfortunate André as a spy.[39]

When Clinton sailed back to New York in early June, Cornwallis was left in command in the south. Despite the reduction in the British forces in the region, his subordinates remained confident. As one officer wrote from Camden on 10 June, 'This Country is intirely conquered'.[40] But British optimism was soon to be eroded by a revival of resistance in the South Carolina back country. British troops advancing inland behaved almost as badly as they had done in New Jersey in late 1776; their brutality and licentiousness, in the view of at least one historian, provoked the population into an armed response.[41] Perhaps even more culpable were the newly formed loyalist militias, which contained many men who were keen to settle old scores. But even if the British and their loyalist allies had conducted themselves impeccably, problems were almost bound to arise, as the army was moving into an area denuded of foodstuffs over the preceding months by the need to supply the American garrison at Charleston; the local people understandably resisted attempts by the British troops to gather provisions. Rumours also abounded that South Carolinians were about to be pressed into Hessian service.[42] Nor did Clinton's attempt to force Americans into choosing sides help pacification. Shortly before he sailed north, he ordered the revocation of the paroles given to rebel militiamen who had surrendered; from 20 June they were obliged to take an oath of allegiance to the

Crown or be treated as open enemies: passive acquiescence was not enough. The result, according to a British officer writing from Camden on 7 July, was that 'nine out of ten of them are now embodied on the part of the Rebels'.[43] Most importantly, resistance in the back country was sustained by support from North Carolina. As another British officer noted as early as 16 June, American forces based in the neighbouring state 'over awes a great part of the Country and keeps the Candle of Rebellion still Burning'.[44]

News of the approach of an American army, led by Horatio Gates, the victor of Saratoga, no doubt encouraged further resistance in South Carolina. But even when an outnumbered Cornwallis crushingly defeated Gates at Camden on 16 August, the British could not pacify the province. Cornwallis complained that large parts of the back country never knew of his victory; 'any person daring to speak of it being threatened with instant death'.[45] It seems more likely that resistance continued because reports circulated that more American troops were on their way. Cornwallis concluded that the only answer was to advance into North Carolina. Until South Carolina was denied physical and moral support from its neighbour, Cornwallis reasoned, it could never be properly brought to order. He was also attracted by the prospect of many loyalists in North Carolina, whose support might prove more resolute than that of the South Carolina 'friends to government'.

Cornwallis began to advance into North Carolina in September. His progress was halted the next month when a detached part of his army, made up of loyalist provincials and militiamen, was destroyed at King's Mountain on 7 October. The savagery of the war in the southern theatre was underlined after the battle, when, according to one of the loyalist officers, the rebels conducted a 'mock tryal' and then executed several of their captives.[46] Clinton sent a force to Virginia under Major General Alexander Leslie to assist Cornwallis's operations by destroying supplies and drawing off American soldiers who might have reinforced North Carolina; after King's Mountain, Leslie's troops were ordered south to join Cornwallis. The invasion of North Carolina was abandoned, at least for the time being, and Cornwallis's little army withdrew to Winnsboro, South Carolina, where it went into winter quarters. The

British troops soon found themselves exposed to the same sort of harassment that had been their fate in New Jersey in the winter of 1776–7. The war in the back country seemed to be degenerating into extreme violence and destruction. Nathanael Greene, the new commander of the American forces in the south, wrote at the end of December of 'the relentless Fury' of the local rebels and loyalists, noting that 'a great Part of this Country is already laid waste & in the utmost Danger of becoming a Desert'.[47] Small wonder Cornwallis wanted to renew his advance into North Carolina as soon as possible.

1780 was also a year of mixed fortunes for British arms beyond North America. Germain regarded Spain as the weak link in the enemy coalition. He hatched ambitious plans for a coordinated attack on the Spanish empire in the Pacific, approaching it both from the west, via India, and the east through Central America. The capture of Manila in 1762 had effectively knocked Spain out of the Seven Years War; Germain seems to have thought a similar blow now would have the same effect. Reinforcements were allocated to Jamaica to carry out the Central American part of the plan, but even before they arrived, Dalling, perhaps overly anxious to acquire Spanish booty, sent another expedition to the mainland. The objective was the San Juan River and control of a route to the Pacific. Once on the west coast, a fortification could be established from which predatory raids could be launched along the length of the Pacific littoral and further afield. British troops, led by Lieutenant Colonel Stephen Kemble, captured San Juan Castle, near the shore of Lake Nicaragua, on 29 April. But, as at Omoa in 1779, the tropical environment proved the most potent Spanish weapon. Sickness debilitated Kemble's forces, making it impossible for them to press on. When they retreated back to the Caribbean coast, the Spanish had little difficulty in taking back San Juan Castle from the small garrison Kemble had left to defend it.[48]

In the Caribbean itself, Admiral Rodney engaged with the French fleet in April and again in May, but in June he failed to intercept a Spanish fleet bringing 10,000 troops to Havana. Illness on board the Spanish ships meant that the Spanish reinforcements were in no condition to attack Jamaica or any of the other British islands. Sickness also ensured that British troops remained largely inactive. General John Vaughan, Grant's successor as local British commander, had wanted to recapture St Vincent and Grenada in March, but his army became so weakened that he had to abandon the enterprise. 'The unhealthiness of this Island has almost destroyed the few troops that came from America', an officer wrote from St Lucia in July, 'and the recruits of new Corps are fast following them'.[49] On St Lucia alone, 568 British troops died in the three summer months. In September, Vaughan reported that the 'great mortality' caused by sickness 'must effectively check all hopes of active operations'. He even doubted whether his forces were strong enough to defend what they held.[50]

The British position in India was hardly less parlous. In July 1780, Haidar Ali of Mysore began his long-planned attack in response to the British seizure of the French post at Mahé. Haidar's great army launched itself into the Carnatic, laying siege to Arcot. British forces marched to counter Haidar, but in September a detachment of nearly 4,000 troops under Lieutenant Colonel William Baillie suffered a complete and catastrophic defeat at Pollilur; 'the severest blow the English ever sustained in India', according to one East India Company officer.[51] The main British army retreated in some haste to Madras. If the French had been willing to intervene at this point, Madras itself might have fallen. The French governor of Isle de France had already begun talks with Haidar, and French ships and troops were available to help, as the Paris government had dispatched reinforcements to Isle de France and Isle de Bourbon in December 1778. Yet, unaccountably, the local French commanders did not commit themselves at this vital juncture and so the opportunity to inflict a crushing blow on the British in southern India was missed.

By the close of 1780, then, the British government must have recognized that the war was not going well. In North America, the hopes kindled by the fall of Charleston were largely extinguished when South Carolina descended into anarchy. In the north, Clinton continued to be unable to bring Washington to a decisive action, and now the arrival of a French expeditionary army increased the risk of an attack on New York. The early success in Central America was again followed by defeat at the hands of the unhealthy environment, and in the Caribbean sickness also inhibited offensive operations. After a flurry of activity in 1779, all was quiet in West Africa, but in southern India the British position appeared precarious. Ministers had missed the opportunity to detach the Spanish from their alliance with France at the beginning of the year; secret talks with Spanish representatives broke down when it became clear that the British government would not give up Gibraltar. Yet, amazingly, in December, British ministers chose to add to their list of enemies by declaring war on the Dutch Republic.

North's government resented the way in which the Dutch traded with the Americans, especially through their Caribbean island of St Eustatius. The Dutch, for their part, were angry that the Royal Navy assumed the right to stop and search Dutch merchant vessels, in contravention of the treaty of 1674 which allowed for the carriage on neutral ships of all goods (apart from carefully defined contraband) owned by or destined for a belligerent. British anxieties increased when the French entered the conflict. The French war effort, ministers in London believed, was sustained by Baltic naval

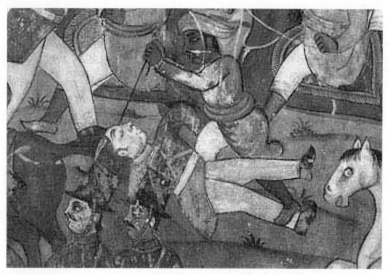

A contemporary Indian depiction of Haidar Ali's defeat of Lieutenant Colonel William Baillie at Pollilur.

supplies, brought to French ports in Dutch ships. The Royal Navy's seizure of Dutch vessels offended other neutral powers, particularly the Russians. In February 1780, Catherine the Great decided to form a League of Armed Neutrality, which would support the rights of all neutral shippers, by force if necessary.[52] If the Dutch joined the League, they would be able to deliver still larger quantities of naval stores to the Bourbon powers under Russian protection. One British minister even feared that the Dutch would take over the carriage of all French and Spanish seaborne goods, allowing the Bourbon governments to recruit nearly all of their trained mariners for naval service.

So, in December 1780, under the pretext of having discovered evidence of an imminent commercial treaty between the Dutch and the Americans, the British government declared war. In so far as North and his colleagues wanted to prevent the Dutch securing Russian protection, their plan worked. The empress would not come to the assistance of the Dutch once they became belligerents. But, in another sense, the British ministers seriously miscalculated. They allowed themselves to be convinced by Joseph Yorke, the long-serving British ambassador at The Hague, that a successful war against the Dutch would strengthen the hand of the pro-British House of Orange and weaken the position of its Francophile opponents in the Patriot party. The reverse happened; the Orangist regime was fatally undermined and the Dutch were driven into the arms of the French.[53]

1781, which would prove to be the decisive year of the war in North America, began badly for Washington. In January, mutinies amongst his Pennsylvanian and New Jersey troops suggested that the Continental army was in no condition to undertake offensive operations. The French even considered withdrawing their expeditionary force from Newport, so unpromising did prospects appear. At this time, congressional delegates worried that Russia and Austria might impose a compromise peace, which would have left the British in possession of what they held in North America.[54] The delegates would have been even more concerned had they known that Vergennes was willing, if the worst came to the worst, to contemplate such a settlement.[55] But the Americans were not the only ones to be fearful about the future in the early months of 1781. Clinton remained worried about a Franco–American threat to his headquarters at New York: news that French naval reinforcements were crossing the Atlantic increased his anxieties. Through the spring and summer he asked Cornwallis to send him troops from the south to make the British better able to fend off an attack in the north. Far to the south, in West Florida, Gálvez continued to make progress against the British outposts, taking Pensacola, the remaining British stronghold, in May.[56]

But it was in the Carolinas and Virginia that the American aspect of the war would be decided. At the beginning of January, Cornwallis left Winsboro for North Carolina. He had only a small army but expected soon to be reinforced by Leslie's troops. At the same time, a British detachment sailed from Charleston to establish a base at Wilmington on the Cape Fear River, from where supplies could be gathered for Cornwallis. The British soon experienced a significant setback. On 17 January, a force led by Tarleton was shattered by Daniel Morgan's Continentals and militia at Hannah's Cowpens. Tarleton impetuously attacked, but was bettered by Morgan's skilful battlefield tactics.[57] The British defeat was at least as much of as a blow as King's Mountain had been the previous autumn, yet, this time, Cornwallis refused to retreat back into South Carolina. Instead, he determined to press on and pursue the Americans. Morgan's detachment and then Greene's main army successfully eluded him, and the Americans crossed the Dan River into Virginia on 13 February. After rapid forced marches, Cornwallis's army was too exhausted to follow any further. The British general ordered his men back to Hillsborough and called on the North Carolina loyalists to come forth and support him. Any inclination local 'friends to government' might have had to put their lives at risk were dampened when a body of loyalists setting off for Hillsborough under Colonel John Pyle were cut to pieces by American cavalry.

Once he learned that Greene had recrossed the Dan into North Carolina, Cornwallis left Hillsborough to confront the American army. Greene eventually offered battle at Guilford Court House on 15 March.[58] Cornwallis was outnumbered more than two to one, but still decided to attack. The Americans were able to defend in depth and then counterattack. In the end Greene withdrew from the battlefield, but if this was a British victory it would be difficult to imagine a more Pyrrhic one. Cornwallis, whose army was already small, had lost twice as many men as Greene. As one British officer put it with much understatement, they may have won, but 'without any very brilliant advantages arising from it'.[59] When his commander appealed again for local loyalist help, none was forthcoming. Few of the loyally disposed were willing to join such a palpably weak force of British troops. Cornwallis had little choice but to limp to the protection of the outpost established at Wilmington.

Greene, meanwhile, decided to march into South Carolina, which was only lightly defended by British and loyalist troops left there under the command of Lord Rawdon. Greene's logic was simple: Cornwallis would have to give up the British posts in South Carolina 'or return to support them'.[60] Either way, Greene concluded his army would be able to undo all that the British had achieved. Cornwallis waited to see what happened further south. His preference was to march from Wilmington into Virginia. As in 1779 and 1780, Clinton had sent a British expedition to the Chesapeake to support the progress of the southern army; Cornwallis, despairing of rallying the North Carolina loyalists, wanted to join the British forces in Virginia and make it the main scene of operations. But if he learned that Rawdon was struggling to hold off Greene, Cornwallis was prepared to abandon any advance into Virginia and return to South Carolina.

Rawdon, although heavily outnumbered, defeated Greene at Hobkirk's hill, near Camden, on 25 April. But, as a North Carolina militia officer involved in the battle later claimed, the British victory was strategically worthless; it did not afford 'the least advantage to Lord Rawdon'.[61] The American forces soon gained the upper hand. The British evacuated Camden on 10 May, and a string of outposts in South Carolina and Georgia fell to the Americans over the next few weeks. Rawdon became ill and was replaced by Lieutenant Colonel Alexander Stewart, who showed no inclination to do more than hold on to the remaining British posts. Stewart fended off Greene's attack at Eutaw Springs in September 1781, but then pulled back to Charleston. Despite his failure to win a battle, Greene had recovered most of South Carolina and Georgia for Congress.

By this stage, Cornwallis was running into trouble further north. He had left Wilmington even before learning of Rawdon's victory at Hobkirk's Hill, but once he received news of his subordinate's triumph he decided that South Carolina was safe and pressed on to join the British troops already in Virginia, giving him command of some 7,000 soldiers. Cornwallis was opposed by a small American force led by the Marquis de Lafayette, a French volunteer serving in the Continental army. Lafayette's advanced guard narrowly escaped destruction at Green Spring in early July. But Cornwallis's objective was not just to defeat the American troops deployed against him; he also wanted to establish a naval anchorage. Clinton, though he had initially thought of Virginia as a diversion from his plans for the war in the north, was equally committed to Cornwallis's establishing 'a station in Chesapeake for ships of the line, as well as frigates'.[62] After some deliberation, Cornwallis chose Yorktown, which could accommodate large battleships. In early August, his troops started to construct defensive works. In retrospect, we can see this was a fateful decision. On the move, burning and destroying stores and chasing the American forces, Cornwallis was a formidable enemy: once he dug in at Yorktown he became a sitting target.

In June, Rochambeau's troops had already left Newport to rendezvous with Washington's army at Phillipsburg, New York. Clinton was convinced that the long-feared attack on the British headquarters at New York City was in the offing. But on 19 August, the French and American forces began to march south. A few days later, French ships carrying heavy siege guns sailed from Newport for the Chesapeake, where they were to meet another French fleet coming up from the Caribbean with 3,000 more troops. To keep Clinton fearful for New York, Washington and Rochambeau proceeded as if to attack the city from Staten Island or Sandy Hook. Not until 31 August, when he had been reinforced by British ships from the West Indies, did Admiral Thomas Graves sail to protect Cornwallis from the French navy. On 5 September, Graves fought a two-hour battle with Admiral de Grasse off the entrance to Chesapeake Bay. No ships were lost on either side, but the damage to the British fleet encouraged Graves to return to New York to refit.

Cornwallis was now trapped unless the Royal Navy could return and defeat the French fleet. Even before Washington and Rochambeau arrived, his army was outnumbered by the American forces already in Virginia, reinforced by the French troops that de Grasse had landed. Belatedly realizing that Cornwallis was in danger, Clinton launched an attack on the Connecticut coast. But not even the storming of Fort Griswold near Groton, and the burning of most of New London, persuaded Washington to turn back. Clinton now took the desperate step of assembling as many troops as he could spare for a rescue mission. The slowness of the naval repair work delayed his departure, with 7,000 soldiers, until 19 October, by which time he was too late to do anything for Cornwallis.

The allied army, now 16,000 strong, began a close investment of the Yorktown defences on 28–9 September. Heavy artillery bombarded the British positions relentlessly from 6 October, and when the French and Americans took two British redoubts on 14 October, the chances of Cornwallis's army holding on all but disappeared. An attempted break out across the river at Gloucester was stymied by bad weather, and so, on 17 October – the very day when Burgoyne had surrendered at Saratoga four years earlier – Cornwallis recognized the inevitable and began negotiations. Two days later, the British troops laid down their arms.[63]

To lose one field army might be counted as unfortunate; to lose two smacks of carelessness. At any rate, it was too much for the British political nation, which decided that the war in North America was no longer worth pursuing. 'A general despondency was the first effect of Lord Cornwallis's surrender', wrote Lord Loughborough, a government supporter.[64] In the words of an opposition MP, 'every Body seems really sick of carrying on ye American War'.[65] The American aspect of the conflict ground to a halt. The British went onto the defensive, concentrating on holding what they had, while Washington found it impossible to persuade the French to join him in an attack on either Charleston or New York. The French, for their part, wished to follow up Yorktown, not by another campaign in North America, but by building on their earlier triumphs in the Caribbean. They had taken Tobago in June and in November recaptured the Dutch island of St Eustatius, which had been occupied by the British

John Trumbull's 1797 painting of Yorktown depicts the surrender ceremony. Cornwallis, claiming illness, delegated the act of capitulation to his second-in-command, Charles O'Hara, who tried at first to give his sword to the French commander. When Rochambeau declined, on the grounds that the French were merely the Americans' auxiliaries, Washington insisted that his second-in-command, Benjamin Lincoln, accept O'Hara's submission.

since the beginning of March. De Grasse returned to the Caribbean in December hoping to seize Barbados.

Elsewhere, the British experienced further setbacks in 1781. Once the Dutch war began, ministers in London abandoned their ambitions plans for a campaign against the Spanish in the Pacific and turned their attention to the even more exposed Dutch overseas possessions. A tempting target was the Cape of Good Hope, at the southern tip of Africa, where a Dutch base commanded the sea route to India. A squadron of British ships, carrying 3,000 troops, set sail from England in March under orders to capture the Cape. But Baillie de Suffren, a highly enterprising French Admiral, not only attacked the British ships while they were taking in water and undergoing repairs in the Cape Verde Islands, but also reached the Cape first, on 23 June, landing two French regiments to reinforce the Dutch garrison. When the British arrived, they realized that the Cape was too well-defended. Most of the British ships returned home, but some of the squadron's vessels conveyed the troops on board to India.

In India itself, the British were more successful. The failure of the French to intervene allowed Sir Eyre Coote, the new British commander-in-chief, supported by reinforcements from the East India Company's main Bengal army, to recover the psychological advantage lost to Haidar Ali in 1780. In July, Coote defeated the Mysore forces at Porto Novo. Retrospectively, one of his officers considered the British victory the turning point, 'the most critical battle that had been fought for a long time in India'.[66] Coote followed this up with a further triumph at Pollilur in August, and another at Sholinghur in September. The British also went onto the offensive against the Dutch, easily seizing all their factories in India apart from Negapatam, which was taken in November after a brief siege. In August,

Copley's much-reproduced Death of Major Peirson, a striking example of a military hero dying under the flag (see also Trumbull's images of the Death of General Montgomery p. 61 and the Battle of Bunker Hill on p. 58).

British East India Company troops even captured the Dutch base at Padang and all the forts and factories on the west coast of Sumatra.[67]

Even in Europe, the British managed to hold off their enemies in 1781. The exposed British garrison on Jersey repulsed a French attack in January. The gallant defence, led by a young officer in a newly raised regiment, inspired one of the war's most memorable images, John Singleton Copley's *Death of Major Peirson* (1783). Gibraltar, still under siege, received fresh supplies when a convoy of nearly 100 provision ships arrived under Admiral Darby's protection in April. In August, the Royal Navy's engagement with the Dutch fleet off Dogger Bank in the North Sea, while hardly a decisive victory, obliged the Dutch ships to return to the safety of the Texel. But elsewhere, August saw less welcome developments for the British government. A combined French and Spanish army landed on Minorca and began to besiege St Philip's Castle at Port Mahon. Shortly afterwards, the allied fleet that had landed the troops on Minorca sailed out into the Atlantic and northwards to the Channel approaches, causing renewed alarm in southwest England and Ireland about a possible invasion. As in 1779, sickness on board the allied armada may have spared the British Isles from attack, but on this occasion the excessive caution of the elderly Spanish admiral, Don Luis de Córdoba, was perhaps just as important.

Though the war in America effectively ground to a halt after Yorktown (apart from an unexpected French attack on the forts of the British Hudson's Bay Company as late as August 1782), the wider war not only continued, but in many ways became more intense. North's government lost parliamentary support, and in April a new administration was formed, headed by the Marquess of Rockingham. The new government sought to negotiate with the Americans, while pressing on with the conflict against Britain's other enemies. The Dutch, as in 1781, appeared to ministers in London as a soft target. In West Africa, British forces attacked the Dutch fortified slave trading stations. After an unsuccessful assault on Elmina in February 1782, in March the British were able to take Mouri, Kormantin, Apam and Beraku without opposition and Accra after a brief siege. In May, the Dutch post at Kommenda also surrendered. Meanwhile, in India, the British captured the Dutch base at Trincomalee in Ceylon (Sri Lanka) in January 1782.

However, the British also experienced setbacks and defeat in the early months of 1782, which suggested that they might lose far more than the rebel colonies in North America before the war could be brought to an end. In February, Admiral de Suffren landed French troops to support Haidar Ali of Mysore, and challenged the Royal Navy in the waters off eastern India, while Haidar's son Tipu compelled the surrender of a British detachment in Tanjore. February also saw the British and Hanoverian garrison at St Philip's Castle on Minorca, weakened by scurvy, surrender after a six-month siege. The fall of Minorca inevitably increased the pressure on the other British Mediterranean foothold at Gibraltar. In the same month, the French took the West Indian island of St Kitts, after a month-long siege of the British post on Brimstone Hill and an unsuccessful attempt to relieve the garrison. Montserrat was captured by the French shortly afterwards and, in March, the Spanish seized the British base on the Rio Negro in modern-day Honduras. The Bourbons began preparations for a combined attack on Jamaica, the island that many contemporaries – including George III – regarded as the British Crown's most valuable overseas possession.[68]

Admiral Rodney's great victory over de Grasse's French fleet at the Battle of the Saintes on 12 April 1782 both saved Jamaica and boosted British morale.[69] The Saintes was one of the few decisive naval engagements of the eighteenth century. Rather than persist with the conventional tactics of line-abreast firing, Rodney's ships boldly forced their way through the enemy line, broke it again, and then subjected the French centre to a concerted attack. De Grasse and his flagship, the *Ville de Paris*, were obliged to surrender; four other French ships, together with all the heavy artillery intended to be used against Jamaica, fell into British hands. Rear Admiral Sir Samuel Hood, Rodney's subordinate, complained that an opportunity had been missed to inflict even more extensive damage on the French fleet.[70] A Swedish officer on one of de Grasse's ships shared this view; had Rodney pursued the French through the night, he wrote, 'the victory of the English would have been still greater'.[71]

But there can be no doubt that the British admiral had done enough to secure Jamaica. Rodney sailed into Port Royal on 28 April to a hero's welcome. Spanish forces assembled on Hispaniola redirected their attention to the north, taking the weakly defended Bahamas as a consolation prize in May.

The Battle of the Saintes probably saved more than just Jamaica. It helped the British in their negotiations with the French, who began to fear a revival of British naval strength and so became more amenable to a peace settlement. But the Saintes was not the only reason that the war ended on a better note for the British than looked likely in the first months of 1782. The successful defence of Gibraltar also boosted British confidence and deflated the Bourbon powers. The French and Spanish laboriously constructed floating batteries from which to bombard the British defences, and then began a bombardment from both land and sea. On 13 September, the heavily armoured floating batteries, like 'so many invincible Aligators', in the evocative words of one of the British defenders, deployed in a semicircle below the King's Bastion, the central point in the British works.[72] Both sides fired away at the other furiously. A contemporary British calculation suggests that, on that day alone, 'not less than Twenty Thousand Shot & Shells were fired by the Enemy, and perhaps half that number by the Garrison'; the same source claims that some 3,000 rounds were expended per hour between ten in the morning and six in the evening.[73] For a while, it seemed as if the floating batteries would 'bid defiance to the powers of the heaviest ordnance';[74] but at length red-hot shot set the vessels alight. Though the French and Spanish maintained their siege until news arrived of the signing of the peace preliminaries, they attempted no further major attack.[75] Against considerable odds, the British and Hanoverian garrison had held on.

In India, however, the British position looked much more precarious in the final stages of the war. The French expeditionary force took Cuddalore on 8 April 1782. Although Coote defeated Haidar's forces at Arni on 2 June, and Admiral Edward Hughes prevented the French recovering Negapatam a month later, French troops – with Dutch support – recaptured Trincomalee at the end of August. Haidar Ali's death at the end of 1782 meant that the British were opposed by an even more formidable enemy in the form of his son Tipu, who successfully fended off a threat to his western flank posed by East India Company troops from Bombay led by Brigadier General Richard Matthews. The British hold on the Coromandel Coast meanwhile remained tenuous; French reinforcements under de Bussy landed at Porto Novo in March 1783. Major General James Stuart, who commanded the royal and company forces in the area, tried to dislodge the French before Tipu could join them. In June, the British began to besiege Cuddalore. However, when they attacked the French lines, the British and Hanoverian troops were thrown back easily; 'never was there a greater panic than now prevail'd amongst the runaways', wrote a disgusted British officer.[76] The French admiral de Suffren added to British discomfort by compelling Hughes's squadron off Cuddalore to withdraw to Madras. The French troops in the town, their morale boosted by de Suffren's success, proceeded to launch an attack on the besiegers on 25 June, but the French sally was repulsed by Stuart's forces. Neither side, it seemed, could establish dominance over the other. Even so, when news arrived from Europe that a peace had been signed, Stuart readily agreed to suspend hostilities; abandoned by Hughes, he recognized that his position was far from secure. Tipu continued his own struggle into 1784, capturing Managalore from Matthews's forces at the end of January, and only coming to terms with Lord Macartney, the British governor of Madras, in March.

4

CIVILIANS

To capture the impact of the War of Independence on those not engaged in the fighting is no easy matter. The very term 'civilians' is problematic. It was not in use at the time, at least partly because distinctions between combatants and non-combatants were still not firmly established. The almost universal male obligation to defend one's community by serving in the militia meant that many men that we might regard as civilians received military training and carried arms. This was particularly true in North America, but also occurred in other imperial theatres and even in the European countries. In the British case, the existence of volunteer units, formed on an associational basis when invasion threatened, and often distrusted by the authorities, further complicates the situation. So, too, do the Irish volunteers, whose functions were at least as much political as military; their aim was not simply to protect their country from Bourbon attack, but also to exert pressure on the British administration in London and Dublin to win commercial and constitutional concessions for Ireland.[1]

A similar blurring of the boundaries occurred at sea. The navies of the belligerents were supplemented by officially sanctioned privateers; private sailing vessels authorized to seize any ships. These privateers sometimes served alongside the navy, but more often they continued their peacetime role as merchant carriers, only becoming fighting ships when they saw the opportunity to attack and capture an enemy merchant vessel. But whether we refer to them as civilians, or non-combatants (another anachronism), or 'inhabitants' (the label used by contemporary soldiers), the people we are considering are those who were not primarily involved in the war as active military or naval participants.

To understand the civilian experience, we have to be aware of the variables that affected it. The country in which civilians lived made a difference. The war had a more immediate and intense impact on American non-combatants than on Europeans, because the rebel colonies were the scene of extensive military operations, whereas most of Europe was untouched by the ravages of war. For the same reason, the peoples of the other imperial theatres – in the West Indies, Central America, West Africa and South Asia – experienced war more directly than most Europeans who remained at home. The conflict's shadow also fell in different ways on various types of civilians. Women were often presented with opportunities and challenges distinct from those faced by men. Similarly, blacks often experienced the war in different ways to whites: slaves in the rebel colonies who received their freedom saw their status transformed much more than indentured servants and apprentices who took advantage of the war to escape from their masters; the latter were freed from temporary servitude, the former from permanent enslavement. Blacks were also disproportionately affected by the turmoil and dislocations of the war; while reliable figures are not available to us, it seems very likely that a higher percentage of blacks than of whites had their lives transformed by flight and relocation in North America, or ended prematurely by food shortages in the West Indies.[2] And, as one would expect, the impact of the war varied according to the social status of the civilian. Those common merchant seamen who escaped impressment no doubt welcomed wage rises caused by a wartime shortage of skilled maritime labour, whereas ship owners cursed an increase in their costs. Wealthy investors in the public debts of the belligerents became richer thanks to higher interest rates, while the regressive tax systems that paid their interest took money disproportionately from the less well off.

Rather than try, in very limited space, to present a picture of the full range of different ways in which civilians were affected in each of the countries involved, it seems better to be selective. We will focus on three categories of place, determined not by political boundaries but by the intensity of their wartime experience. The first comprises the war zones, where civilians came into direct contact with fighting soldiers or sailors and saw the struggle in its most dreadful guise. The second looks at areas exposed to attack, or near enough the fighting to become war zones, but which avoided such a fate. The third considers the locations remote from the fighting and in no real danger of attack; the bulk of the territories of the European belligerents. We should not consider these categories as completely distinct; civilians in more than one category – or even in all three – may have experienced certain features of the war in much the same way. Increased taxation, to give an obvious example, was common to the war zones, the areas under threat of attack, and the locations far away from any hostilities. In addition, a particular place could move, as it were, from one category to another. No part of the United States was so nearly continuously on the front line as New Jersey, described by one historian as 'the cockpit of the Revolution'.[3] As a result of its proximity to British-held New York City, it experienced military operations in most years of the conflict from 1776 onwards. More usual was a period as a war zone followed by a period of less intense engagement with the conflict, or vice versa. Long Island in New York was, during late August 1776, the scene of full-scale combat, and thereafter an area of settled military occupation; it was not far from the fighting and exposed to possible attack, but spared any further contact with the active military operations, and the quality of its inhabitants' experience of the war changed accordingly. Britain and Ireland – and southern England in particular – moved in the opposite direction. For the first years of the war, this area was remote from all military and naval operations and not exposed to attack. However, from 1778 it was threatened with invasion by the French and was the scene of extensive military activity.

We start with those civilians living in the war zones. Their experience was not always negative. For many of the enslaved in North America the arrival of the British army was something to be welcomed as an opportunity for liberation, even if disappointment often followed. From the moment in 1775 when Lord Dunmore, the last royal governor of Virginia, offered freedom to slaves who would join him in trying to put down the rebellion, blacks saw the British armed forces in a positive light. Robert Honyman, a doctor in Virginia, noted in 1781 that British troops acted like a magnet as they snaked across the state: 'these poor creatures', Honyman wrote of the slaves, 'flocked to the Enemy from all quarters, even from very remote parts'.[4] More prosaically, some white settlers appear to have regarded the appearance of soldiers in their neighbourhood as a matter for curiosity, a diversion from their humdrum lives. Charles O'Hara, a senior British officer in Cornwallis's army, noted that in North Carolina 'The novelty of a Camp in the back Woods of America … brought several People to stare at us'.[5] Others recognized the chance to make money from trade with the military. American farmers seem to have brought their goods to British and French camps in the hope of earning some hard currency, and the Continental army also purchased readily available local produce, at least until the value of the paper money it had to offer diminished almost to nothing. When British troops landed on Staten Island in July 1776, the local people seemed pleased to see them, not least because the soldiers bought their foodstuffs 'at reasonable rates'.[6]

But for most inhabitants of the war zones, life could be decidedly grim. For non-combatants unfortunate enough to be trapped on Gibraltar when the Spanish began their siege, food shortages soon became an acute problem. In early January 1780, the governor reported that many civilians were 'near starving'.[7] The arrival of a relief convoy only a few days later transformed the situation, but over the long siege the inhabitants were to face further difficult times. Residents and refugees in Boston, effectively besieged for nearly a year at the beginning of the war, complained of shortages of food and fuel. Richard Reeve, a customs officer, noted that 'Fresh Provisions' had become 'extremely scarce' by the end of July 1775; in November he wrote that 'scarcely any thing can be procured by the inhabitants for Money. The Army and Navy engross every thing'.[8] A local loyalist was equally aggrieved: 'There are a few of the Army who monopolize, & distress us', Peter Oliver claimed. 'A load of Sea Coal is just bought by them at 10 Dollars P Chaldron & we are forced to pay £3.5/Sterling for it.'[9]

For civilians everywhere in the war zones, anxieties about security were never far away. John Miller of Germantown, Pennsylvania, who encountered the British army for the first time in September 1777, confessed in the privacy of his journal that he was 'in great fear, especially of the foreign Mercenaries'.[10] Many farmers, rather than engaging in consensual trading with the army, were given no choice but to part with their crops and livestock, which were taken from them by forcible requisition. If they were lucky, they received receipts for the goods taken, but even then their chances of securing any payment were distinctly limited. Dr Alexander Garden, a South Carolina loyalist, had cattle, horses, sheep, pigs, 'together with Corn Rice, pease, long Forage &c&c', taken from his plantation by various parties of British troops during the siege of Charleston in the spring of 1780. Receipts were given for some of these items, but long after the war was over he had still not received the money he was owed.[11] Simply by camping on their land, armies inflicted losses on civilians. Crops were trampled and left unfit for harvest; trees were cut down to provide makeshift shelters; fences and even outbuildings dismantled for fuel. Losses of this kind were often regarded by those who caused them as regrettable but unavoidable. 'Such must ever be the wretched situation of a Country the seat of war', a British officer noted during the advance of Burgoyne's army in the summer of 1777.[12]

Destruction could, however, be more malicious. In India, Haidar Ali's forces devastated the Carnatic when they invaded in 1780; his cavalry, in particular, were responsible for the burning 'and pillaging the whole Country', according to a British account, 'even to the Gates of Madras'.[13] Native Americans, sponsored by the British forces in Canada, and often accompanied by regular troops and American loyalists, similarly laid waste parts of the frontier of the rebel colonies. Raiders destroyed crops and buildings, and carried off or killed livestock. In retaliation, Washington sent American troops to the frontier in the summer of 1779 to ravage the lands of the native peoples who had been attacking settler communities. The express aim of the expedition was to cause as much distress as possible; 'the total destruction and devastation of their settlements', in Washington's words.[14] General Sullivan's soldiers appear to have carried out their instructions with relish, laying waste to large tracts of Indian country, burning crops and villages as they proceeded.[15] Despite the extensive destruction wrought by Sullivan's troops, the Native Americans were not cowed. In 1780, New York frontier communities suffered devastating raids from Canada, and in October, Ballstown and Schoharie, near Albany, were both put to the torch.

British raids on coastal communities were similarly intended to maximize damage. Falmouth, in modern-day Maine, attacked in the autumn of 1775, was one of the first places to receive this treatment. Many other towns were raided before the war ended; New London, on the Connecticut coast, was the target as late as September 1781. Everywhere, buildings and shipping were burned; in Virginia, where attacks penetrated along the riverine network, tobacco stocks were treated in the same way, and even orchards were set alight. Inland communities were not necessarily safe from soldiers advancing from the coast. From the Cheraw district of South Carolina a British officer reported in September 1780 that his troops had 'burnt & laid waste about 50 Houses & Plantations'.[16] The aim behind such destructive attacks varied. Some were intended to destroy supplies useful to the American war effort, or incapacitate privateers; Germain recommended raids on New England in March 1778 specifically to prevent the Americans from 'Continuing their Depredations upon the Trade of the Kingdom'.[17] Other British attacks were designed to tie down rebel troops, still others to induce the elusive Washington to offer battle. We can also discern a desire to punish and intimidate the population at large. William Tryon regretted the loss of two churches in Fairfield, Connecticut, during the raids that he led in July 1779, but shed no tears for the incineration of the rest of the town, which he regarded as justified by the need to inspire 'a general Terror and despondency'.[18]

Soldiers acting on their own account, rather than under orders, could be equally vindictive. When they were compelled to retreat, their frustration and anger – and perhaps a sense that they would not return – meant that they could engage in an orgy of destruction. In the days before British troops left Boston in March 1776, they vented their spleen. John Rowe, a merchant, recorded in his diary that officers in one house 'broke a looking glass over the chimney which cost twenty guineas'.[19] When the British army evacuated Philadelphia in the summer of 1778, several accounts suggest that all manner of rubbish, including large quantities of excrement, were left in the streets.[20] As Prevost's little army withdrew from the vicinity of Charleston in the early summer of 1779, some of his soldiers appear to have wreaked a more thoroughgoing revenge on Ashley Hall, the estate of the absent William Bull, the last royally appointed lieutenant governor of South Carolina. The damage was comprehensive, and seemingly without purpose. It went as far as the cutting open 'every bed & Mattress', the smashing of all the 'china glass & other crockray', the breaking a fish dam, and even the scattering of Bull's private papers 'over the pasture & garden'. Prevost denied that his troops were responsible, trying to put the blame on Pulaski's Legion of the American army, or even the 'Myriads of Negroes' running wild in the confusion. But whoever inflicted the damage, it was obviously a consequence of the estate's unfortunate location in an area through which the competing armies passed.[21]

Soldiers in the war zones also took the opportunity to steal civilian property. At the point of first contact with an area, soldiers were particularly prone to plunder, because the dangers they faced either removed their inhibitions or increased their sense of entitlement. Continental troops even stole from their own people, and their French allies, although kept away from the population at Newport, took advantage of their march south to Yorktown in 1781 to take what they wanted from unfortunate inhabitants. Once in Virginia, French troops were criticized for their thefts of local property. But it was the British army that acquired the worst reputation. In New Jersey, in November and December 1776, victorious British and German soldiers in pursuit of Washington's disintegrating army pillaged extensively. According to one contemporary observer, 'To give a Particular Account of Every Robery and outrage committed by the Hessians and Regulars In and within five miles of Princetown ... would fill a Vollum'.[22] Daniel Coxe, a loyalist living in Trenton, later claimed that his 'Rooms, closets Stores and Cellars were all broke open ransacked & pillaged'.[23] As they advanced into Chester County, Pennsylvania, in September 1777, General Howe's troops even broke into the Baptist meeting house at Tredyffrin, taking the sacramental dishes, a table cloth, a bible, miscellaneous items of clothing and assorted burial tools.[24] When British troops landed on St Lucia in December 1778, they appear to have been no less prone to pillaging. An inventory of the plunder of a British soldier, executed shortly after General Grant's forces landed on the island, contains assorted forms of male clothing – breeches, coats, waistcoats, shirts, stockings – but also women's caps.[25] In Gibraltar, Spanish shelling exposed cellars full of wine, which members of the garrison proceeded to consume before engaging in widespread looting: 'Robbery, Moroding, Housebreaking and shoplifting by the Soldiery', in the words of an appalled British officer.[26]

Civilians were not just robbed; they were also physically maltreated. On the frontier, Native Americans killed women and children, as well as men, in the towns that they attacked; British and loyalist officers accompanying the Indians claimed that it was impossible to control the blood lust of their allies ('I could not prevent some of them falling unhappy Victims to the Fury of the Savages').[27] Native women and children experienced equally brutal treatment at the hands of American troops. In the longer-settled areas, the civilians' ordeal was scarcely less awful. Men were assaulted, usually when they tried to resist the predatory attentions of the soldiers, and a few were even killed – sometimes by accident, but on other occasions deliberately. Many reports suggest that large numbers of women were raped. The British advance through New Jersey in November and December 1776 appears to have been particularly notorious in this respect. Congress naturally made the most of the propaganda opportunity, but we should not assume that all rebel accounts deliberately exaggerated the incidence of such offences. The private correspondence of revolutionary soldiers suggests that they were genuinely outraged: 'The Devils', an American officer wrote, 'have waged War against Decency'.[28] Nathanael Greene was more explicit, emotionally reciting to the governor of Rhode Island his horror at British troops' activities: 'little Girls not ten Years old ravish, Mothers and Daughters ravish in presence of the Husband and Sons who were obliged to be spectators'.[29] We also know from the testimony of women themselves that particular individuals were attacked. Mary Johnston, raped when British troops landed on Long Island in August 1776, appears in the army's own court martial records;

in a remarkable act of forgiveness, she tried to secure a pardon for her attackers when they were sentenced to death.[30] In May 1781, Jean Blair, from North Carolina, wrote to her sister of the victims of the rapes committed by British soldiers, 'amongst them, my Brother says, was H. Montfort's Wife and John Rights. Langfords wife was served in the same manner'.[31]

The inhabitants of places in North America fortunate enough to be some distance from the fighting could hardly have forgotten about the war; they felt its impact in many aspects of their lives. They might not themselves be at immediate risk of death at the hands of the enemy, but some succumbed to diseases generated in the war zones and transmitted to their locality by disbanded soldiers. The smallpox that swept through New England in 1775–6, and then spread much further afield, can be linked to the siege of Boston, which seems to have been the epicentre of the outbreak.[32] Nor did distance from the battlefields offer any protection from the loss of a husband, brother or son who had joined the Continentals. Even if civilians were spared such a family tragedy, they might find the absence of so many men caused difficulties. Many communities gave up a staggeringly high proportion of their male population for military service, either in the Continental army or the embodied militia. More than two-thirds of the men aged 16 to 50 in Chatham, New Jersey, enrolled in a military unit during the course of the war.[33] Peterborough, New Hampshire, had a population of 549 in 1775. About 170 of its men performed some form of military service during the war, which means that almost every male of the appropriate age must have carried a musket at one time or another.[34] Women filled the gap to some extent, taking on new roles – as a Connecticut farmer's wife wrote, in the absence of her soldier-husband, 'What was done, was done myself'.[35] But military mobilization was not the only cause of labour shortage; the flight of many slaves and indentured servants made matters much worse. Employers of labour complained at the lack of hands, and in some areas crops lay unharvested: in March 1779, Sarah Thomas of Marshfield, Massachusetts, bemoaned 'the want of bread', which she attributed to so many men 'imployed in destroying one another' rather than 'Cultivating the ground that there poor unhappy Famalys may have bread to eat'.[36] For civilians in all the newly independent states, increased taxation was an extra burden, especially in the second half of the war. Inhabitants of the territories under rebel control also experienced severe dislocations caused by hyperinflation, brought on primarily by Congress and the states issuing large quantities of paper money; between 1775 and 1778, currency issue accounted for a staggering 86.47 per cent of congressional revenue.[37] In Pennsylvania, prices rose sevenfold in the course of 1779; in Maryland, the cost of foodstuffs such as beef, butter, corn, wheat and salt went up by between 1,900 and 5,043 per cent between 1777 and 1780.[38] Consumers protested bitterly, especially in the urban centres. But the deflationary policies adopted by Congress in the last years of the war dismayed many producers, who saw their profits evaporate. Nor was loss of property confined to the areas where the fighting took place. In all the states, Americans identified as loyalists had their homes, lands and goods confiscated by the revolutionary authorities and sold to help pay for the war effort.

Even so, those who lived away from the fighting were in a better position than those who found themselves face to face with military men in the combat zones. Opportunities to profit from the war were much greater for those at some distance from its sharp end. The enforced sale of loyalist estates benefited many wealthy Americans with money to buy up new land, and even enabled some tenants in states like New York, Virginia and Maryland to become freeholders of the land that they farmed.[39] The needs of the Continental army stimulated American production of firearms, gunpowder, footwear and clothing. Farmers, who before the war had concentrated on providing for their families and immediate localities, were drawn into more distant and more commercial exchanges as commissaries made large-scale purchases of foodstuffs for the army.[40] The promise of hard specie lured Americans into bringing their produce to British bases. From New York, a Hessian officer wrote of the inhabitants who drove cattle 20 miles to sell them to the garrison.[41]'Wagons with tobacco', James Simpson wrote from newly captured Charleston, 'have come upwards of two hundred and thirty miles'.[42] A French officer passing through Philadelphia in September

1781 wrote that he had met several merchants in the city 'who assured me that peace would only hurt their trade, for business reasons, they did not want it'.[43]

The people in the territories under British control were also better off than inhabitants of the war zones, though they may not always have appreciated their comparative good fortune. Martial law operated in all the British enclaves in the rebel colonies, which meant that civilians suspected of committing offences were tried before military courts. Punishments were often the same as those meted out to soldiers; severe floggings were not unknown. As William Rawle of Philadelphia reflected many years later, 'There is something in the air of a military government extremely disagreeable to those who have experienced another'.[44] Civilians were often obliged to accommodate military personnel in their own homes, and often complained at the disruption and damage caused. In New York, Joshua Pell complained that the 27 soldiers quartered on his property had 'behaved in a very unruly manner by breaking open an Appartment and taking away his Poultry, making use of his Hay and burning his Fire Wood in a very lavish manner, as also being very Noisy & troublesome to himself and Family'.[45] Overcrowding, caused by the presence of large numbers of refugees as well as the military, meant that the British-occupied towns became perfect breeding grounds for disease; 'In the city it has been sickly this month', a German pastor in New York wrote at the end of August 1777, 'many people, especially children, died.'[46] The inhabitants' houses were not usually deliberately burned by British troops, but they might lose outbuildings dismantled to provide fuel for the garrison, or see their property levelled to create clear fields of fire from defensive positions. Farmers living on the western end of Long Island were subjected to more and more onerous requisitions of timber and horses and wagons; either through disaffection or inability, they showed an increasing disposition not to comply.[47] Inhabitants of the British enclaves also had to endure the predatory attentions of soldiers. In October 1779, James Edgar of Flushing, Long Island, found three British light dragoons attempting to rob his sister's house. Fearing for his life, Edgar shot one of the intruders dead.[48] Long Island experienced a very different scourge in the form of the so-called Hessian fly, a small insect responsible for the destruction of wheat in the late-1780s, which some Americans claimed (or at least implied) was brought into their country by the German auxiliaries.[49]

Nonetheless, the experience of American non-combatants in the areas under British control was, in many ways, better than for those who lived in the war zones. In a few cases, civilians living in a British enclave were lucky enough to have a sympathetic local commander, who tried to ensure that the inhabitants were as little inconvenienced as possible. Earl Percy, in charge of the Newport garrison in the first months of 1777, refused to provide more forage for Howe's main army than he thought the local people could spare; 'it is absolutely necessary', Percy wrote on 9 February, 'to leave at least 800 Ton for the Stock of the Inhabitants, without which, they must be reduced to the greatest State of Misery'. Small wonder Newport residents thanked Percy fulsomely when they learned that he was about to return to England.[50] Brigadier General Francis McLean, in command at Penobscot in 1779, was no less solicitous for the local inhabitants, and worked hard to ensure that his troops refrained from plunder and generally behaved well. In August, McLean proudly informed Clinton that 'not an Article [has] been taken by the Navy or Army since our arrival, without payment'.[51]

But while leadership made a difference, civilians in British-controlled territory had a less awful experience than those in the war zones even when they lived in areas not blessed with a local protector like Percy or McLean. Army officers found it easier to control their men in garrison than in the open country, or on a raid. More importantly, civilians were much more likely to secure redress when they complained about mistreatment. Joshua Pell's protests about the bad behaviour of the troops quartered on his property led the British commander in New York City to order an inquiry 'into the Grounds of these Complaints that the Persons may be punished who have been guilty of such Irregularities, and Mr Pell's grievances be immediately redress'd'.[52] Women in the British enclaves might be attacked by soldiers, much as they were outside, but we know from various sources that far from negligible numbers of women in the British garrisons married into the army. In Philadelphia, one Hessian chaplain reckoned that he had married as many as a hundred local women to German soldiers.[53] Most of all, the opportunities for the inhabitants to profit, as in the territory firmly in rebel hands, were much greater than in the combat zones. The British army had money to spend, and local manufacturers and merchants wasted little time in offering goods and services to the troops. New York City, under British occupation from September 1776 until the end of the conflict, had experienced nothing like it since the golden days of the Seven Years War. William Faulkner sold large quantities of beer to individual British regiments and to the commissary general,[54] and the account-books of the city's merchants and shopkeepers suggest buoyant business. In Charleston, the number of retail outlets increased dramatically, while in Philadelphia one merchant observed that 'the Army of itself takes off large Quantities of Goods & by giving Employ to many of the Inhabitants enables them to become Purchasers also, by which means there has been Considerable Sales.'[55]

Similar observations can be made about areas under risk of attack – but not the scene of combat – outside North America. On Jamaica, the threat of invasion frequently led to the calling out of the militia, regarded by one correspondent as 'that worst of enemies', because it badly affected the productivity of the sugar plantations and imposed cost burdens on local property owners. The island was also cut off from its main supply source of the mainland colonies, resulting, as one estate attorney reported, in a severe 'scarcity of Provisions amongst ye negroes'.[56] On the whole, however, civilians in the areas not subject to actual fighting suffered less and benefited more than the people in the combat zones. British planters on Dominica, taken by the French in September 1778, were compelled by the occupying forces to provide a quota of cattle per week for the supply of the military hospitals, but at least they received some recompense. They were also able to continue their commercial activities, despite the French takeover of the island.[57]

In Britain and Ireland, the Europeanization of the American war brought difficulties but also created opportunities. Access to European markets was impeded, and French successes in the Caribbean campaigns further reduced exports. British overseas trade contracted sharply; officially measured exports for 1778–81 were, on average, worth 24 per cent less than in 1774.[58] But, considering the economy as a whole, losses for exporters were roughly counterbalanced by the large increase in government spending associated with the intensification of the war effort once the French became belligerents. True, increased state borrowing had its downside. It drew savings away from land improvement – the number of enclosure acts diminished during the second half of the war – and starved infrastructure projects, like canal construction, of the funds they needed. Wartime taxation, especially in the later years of the conflict, when it started to fall on items of popular consumption, may have reduced demand for certain products; it certainly contributed – along with wartime failures and the threat of invasion – to the extra-parliamentary movement for tighter control of public expenditure, which unsettled Lord North's government from the end of 1779.[59] Furthermore, the faster pace of military preparation caused labour shortages in some areas, particularly the Highlands of Scotland, which were subject to heavy recruiting. Yet for all these drawbacks, increased government spending on war-related activities undoubtedly provided a stimulus to industry and agriculture. Clothiers like William Wilson, who produced tartans for the Highland regiments, did well out of the war.[60] So, too, did manufacturers of other uniforms; producers of cannons, small arms and gunpowder; private shipbuilders, who received many more contracts for war vessels; and farmers and merchants providing foodstuffs for the expanded armed forces. In August 1779, Joseph Jacob, a Waterford provision merchant, looked forward to 'a handsome Share' in new naval contracts; in November he wrote that he had already salted almost 5,000 barrels of beef and pork. His good fortune was shared, of course, with the farmers of Waterford's hinterland, who supplied him with the meat.[61]

However, not everyone welcomed the presence of the military in their communities. Prices rose in places like Plymouth, where large numbers of soldiers, militiamen and sailors assembled. In the summer of 1780, the mayor of Norwich noted that the price of hay had been pushed up by the large number of dragoon horses stabled in the city.[62] Publicans protested at having to accommodate military personnel at lower rates than they would charge civilian customers, and the War Office received a flood of complaints about misbehaving soldiers. William Joliffe, MP for Petersfield in Hampshire, harrumphed in April 1779 that the troops quartered in his neighbourhood had 'stolen more than twenty Sheep and Lambs a great number of Hogs, and poultry without number'.[63] The next year, Sir Francis Buller, a Devonshire baronet, was even more vocal about the problems caused by soldiers based in his area: 'hardly a Night passes that some Felony is not committed by them, they have broken open several Houses, committed Highway Robberies, stolen four sheep from one man & three from another, stripped a third of all his poultry, & robbed Orchards & Gardens without End'.[64]

But, outraged as some local worthies undoubtedly were, nowhere in Britain or Ireland suffered the fate of New Jersey, or Virginia, or South Carolina. The camps formed to assemble and train troops probably produced more benefits than drawbacks. Owners of the land were paid for its use, and compensated for damages to their property. Small-scale thefts caused loss to local people, and outbreaks of sickness caused an increase in death rates amongst the surrounding civilian population, but the opportunities to supply the camps – and the large number of visitors they attracted – were seized with relish. Local inns profited from increased trade; a coach service was even established to carry London sightseers to one of the larger camps in Essex. Newspapers cashed in on public interest by carrying regular items of 'Camp Intelligence'; printmakers produced salacious images depicting the supposed delights of the tented military town at the appropriately named Coxheath in Kent; and the playwright Richard Brinsley Sheridan brought out a musical comedy, *The Camp*, in 1778.[65]

Finally, we turn to those places remote from the war, and in little or no danger of enemy attack. The continental European belligerents – France, Spain and the Dutch Republic – would have to be included in this category, both before and after they became formal enemies of the British. So, too, would Britain and Ireland between the beginning of the war and the end of 1777; in other words, before French intervention intensified the experience of the war and invasion seemed a real possibility. We also need to consider civilians in some of the neutral powers, who felt the ripple effects of a faraway conflict.

Distance from the war could encourage a sense of detachment and lack of interest. Jabez Maud Fisher, an American Quaker visiting Britain at the beginning of the conflict, recorded in his journal that the Welsh paid scant attention to the struggle across the Atlantic; 'they know as little as they care'.[66] Most evidence, however, points to a higher level of engagement elsewhere. In the first months of the conflict, borough corporations, and even county meetings the length and breadth of England and Scotland, sent in loyal addresses supporting the war, or petitions calling for reconciliation with the Americans.[67] No doubt this partisanship was based, in many instances, on long-standing local antagonisms, but the American war gave them a new salience. The corporation of London called for the healing of the rift with the colonists on the basis that the war was bound to lead to more taxes, a higher debt, and 'we fear, the Loss of the most valuable Branch of our Commerce'.[68] In Lichfield, Staffordshire, church bells rang out to celebrate the capture of New York and the fall of Fort Washington; in Nottingham, a scuffle ensued in the Exchange Hall when one merchant proposed a toast to the American commander-in-chief.[69] English Protestant Dissenters tended to be well-disposed to the Americans, at least in this early part of the war, while members of the Church of England were more clearly split; Anglican clergymen overwhelmingly supported the government, but a significant part of the laity did not.[70] Parliament was no less divided, with a vocal minority of opposition MPs hostile to the war and fearful of the government's authoritarian intentions. As the Marquess of Rockingham, leader of the principal opposition group, wrote in June 1775, 'If an arbitrary Military Force is to govern one part of this large Empire, ... it will not be long before the whole ... will be brought under a similar Thraldom'.[71]

Ireland's Anglican landowning elite, keen to rule the country with minimum interference from London, readily drew parallels between their situation and that of the Americans, who, at least at the beginning of the war, seemed to be seeking only to assert their British rights. Presbyterians in Ulster were generally enthusiastic supporters of the rebels; for many of them political and religious sympathy was bolstered by familial links, as large numbers of 'Scotch–Irish' Presbyterians had migrated to North America in the course of the eighteenth century.[72] Many Irish Catholics were no doubt ambivalent about a war between Protestants, and welcomed British difficulties. But some of their leaders sensed an opportunity to parade their loyalty as a means of securing relief from legislative restrictions on their participation in public life; Charles O'Conor, a Catholic spokesman, emphasized the contrast between Catholics' quiet obedience and the rebelliousness of the Protestant Dissenters in the colonies.[73]

Controversy over the war encouraged great interest amongst the reading public. William Robertson, the Scottish historian, apparently brought out the first two volumes of his *History of America* in 1777 in the hopes of capitalizing on public fascination with all things American.[74] Poets, seizing on the sentimental possibilities of an internecine conflict, published accounts of the miseries of a civil war, such as Thomas Day's *Desolation of America* (1777). Verses on war-related topics, like the death of a British officer at Bunker Hill or the Battle of Long Island, similarly appeared in the *Gentleman's Magazine*, one of the leading periodicals of the day.[75] London, English provincial, Scottish and Irish newspapers carried extensive coverage of the struggle in America between 1775 and 1777. Official dispatches and casualty lists, as well as reports from American sources, filled column inches; from a business point of view, editors must have regarded the conflict as a godsend. Most importantly, it increased circulation figures; the number of readers grew as the public sought out every scrap of information available.

France had a more restricted press than Britain or Ireland, but its officially sanctioned newspapers experienced a similar boost. The *Gazette de France* had sold well in the Seven Years War, but in the peace that followed circulation dropped back appreciably. The same pattern was discernible in the War of Independence. By 1781, the *Gazette de France* was selling as many copies as at the height of the previous conflict. After the war, circulation again contracted.[76] Other evidence suggests substantial French interest in the American conflict. Young male members of elite British and Irish families travelled on the Continent to complete their education, or simply for leisure.

Many of them who went to France in the first years of the War of Independence reported home on the great sympathy for the American cause. In September 1775, Lord Lewisham, the son of the Earl of Dartmouth, wrote that 'our American dispute' was one of the chief items of his conversation with the French, whom Lewisham believed were 'universally favourable to the Americans'.[77]

Physical remoteness from the fighting did not mean that civilians in Europe were unaffected by the war. Soldiers and sailors sent overseas were rarely accompanied by their families. Separation itself could cause distress and anxiety. Captain William Congreve, serving in North America with the Royal Artillery, learned that his wife was much 'affected by yr leaving her';[78] while Lady Louisa Conolly reported that General Howe's wife was 'in such a miserable state of anxiety that I tremble for her continually'.[79] For poorer women, the absence of a husband could lead to more than just worry. In November 1775, Wiltshire magistrates categorized Martha Hudd, the wife of an absent marine, as a rogue and vagabond and packed her off to her husband's native parish.[80] Separation, furthermore, could be permanent. By no means all soldiers and sailors returned home. Some deserted while abroad and established a new life for themselves. Others died, either in battle or more often of disease; the West Indies, West Africa and India were particularly unhealthy postings for Europeans unaccustomed to the local environment; ships, where crews and passengers were cooped up for months at a time, were breeding grounds for all manner of illnesses. When news arrived of the death of a loved one the impact would surely have been the same whether the relative lived in Barcelona, Bergen-op-Zoom, Besançon, Birmingham or Boston, Massachusetts.

Troop movements, although not as extensive as in the war zones or the areas seriously threatened by attack, caused disruption and pressure in the European belligerent countries. Even before the British government declared war on the Dutch Republic in December 1780, ministers in London ruled out a rapid strike at the Dutch fleet in harbour, after having been warned by Sir Joseph Yorke, the British ambassador at The Hague, of the difficulties involved. Unsurprisingly, however, the States General took no chances, and immediately hostilities commenced, Dutch coastal defences were strengthened by moving army units into the seaboard provinces and constructing shore batteries.[81] France was not threatened by invasion, but was still the scene of considerable military activity. Even in 1775, Lord Lewisham reported that 'The town of Tours is continually full of soldiers in their way to Nantes', from where they were to sail to the French West Indies, either to strengthen the garrisons there in case of British attack, or, Lewisham implied, to be in a better position to intervene in the American war.[82] Soldiers marching for embarkation points, and then gathering in the ports, created both opportunities and problems for the local population. Accommodation became limited and prices rose, but local shopkeepers and merchants usually profited. Governments often dispersed money into the local economy by hiring merchant shipping to act as troop transports. The benefit could even flow in the direction of neutrals; in 1776 the British government hired Dutch vessels to carry their German auxiliaries from the mouth of the Rhine. Likewise, the expeditionary force of Spanish and French troops sent to capture Minorca in the late summer of 1781 (originally only 8,000-strong, but by the end of the siege in February 1782 consisting of more than 14,500 officers and men) drew on food supplies from across the western Mediterranean – not just from Spain itself and southern France, but also from Italy.[83] Encampments had a similar impact on the areas in which they were established. When, in the spring of 1778, more than 30,000 French soldiers were assembled in Normandy to persuade the British government not to send further ships across the Atlantic, it seems very likely that local people experienced some of the disadvantages of a military presence, particularly thefts and price rises, but also the pluses, especially the opportunity to supply the troops with local produce.

The most widespread consequences for non-combatants in Europe surely came in the economic sphere. Many people found themselves paying more taxes. The experience, it should be said, was not universal. In Britain, Lord North managed to limit tax rises before 1778 to an increase in the land tax, which fell only on the propertied, and various duties on luxuries – such as a tax on employers of servants – which he reckoned would not affect the poor. But in France and Spain it was often the privileged classes that escaped the burdens, which were felt disproportionately by the less well-off. In France, the war was paid for largely by borrowing, although indirect taxes, many of which fell on popular items of consumption, were subject to a 10 per cent increase in August 1781 in response to the need to raise more money for large interest payments on the debt.[84] The chief beneficiaries, attracted by interest of up to 10 per cent on life annuities, were the big investors, many of whom came from the Dutch Republic (where interest rates were much lower) or Switzerland (where the Genevan Jacques Necker, the French finance minister, had good contacts). The chief losers were the payers of taxes on items of mass consumption, such as salt.[85] The Spanish state had no tradition of deficit financing; its access to Central and South American bullion enabled it to pay for extraordinary expenses out of accumulated specie. However, from 1779, the Madrid government felt obliged to abandon its balanced-budget approach and borrow substantial sums. The interest rates offered were lower than on the French debt, but still required an increase in domestic taxation. State-controlled sales of tobacco produced reliable revenue for the government; from 1780 the money raised from tobacco was earmarked for debt servicing. Tobacco taxes went up, too, from 1779, although the rise appears to have diminished rather than increased government income, as consumers cut back on purchases, or turned to illegal alternatives.[86]

Particular sectors of the economies of the distant belligerents did well out of the war. Shipbuilding was stimulated by the demand for larger naval forces, and even before the Dutch Republic joined the war, its different provinces debated whether it was best to expand the army or the navy. The landward provinces, not surprisingly, preferred army augmentation; they feared a war on the Continent. The seaward ones, heavily dependent on overseas trade and antagonistic towards Britain as a commercial and imperial rival, argued for an increase in the size of the navy. Holland, the richest and most important province, which paid a high proportion of the total taxes, was committed to naval expansion and so this was eventually the path pursued. The Dutch navy grew significantly during the period of Anglo–Dutch hostilities. Between 1781 and 1785 the States General allocated more than 73.6 million guilders to the building, equipping and manning of warships, compared with only 20.7 million between 1771 and 1780: in October 1782, 16 vessels of between 40 and 76 guns were under construction.[87] The Spanish government also devoted considerable resources to developing its naval strength. Expenditure of 55.4 million reales a year between 1770 and 1779 was increased between 1780 and 1783 to an annual average of 92.7 million reales.[88] In 1776, the Spanish navy had 57 ships of the line; an undated 'Estado de los Navios', probably drawn up when Spain entered the war in 1779, suggests that by then the number had increased to 64.[89] Losses to the enemy during the conflict meant that the Spanish fleet had only 48 ships of the line in service in 1780, but over the next two years the number went up to 54.[90] In France, naval expansion was pursued more vigorously. Determined to avoid another land war in Europe, the French government felt free to pour resources into the navy rather than the army. Some 35 million livres (about £1.5 million) went to the navy in 1776 but by 1782 this had increased to 200 million livres (nearly £9 million), and so the number of French ships of the line went up accordingly: from 52 in 1778 to 73 in 1782.[91] The building of warships not only provided work in dockyards, perhaps the greatest industrial enterprises of the time, but also had a beneficial effect on a whole host of subsidiary traders, from rope makers and sailcloth manufacturers to iron founders.

In all of the belligerents, arms manufacturing was boosted by the war. The French, Spanish and Dutch armies may have remained at their peacetime establishment strength, and so created no call for new weapons above the normal replacement rate, but more warships meant a greater demand for cannons. A ship of the line might carry between 60 and 120 guns; 20 new capital ships could therefore generate a demand for at least 1,200 new pieces of ordnance. The beneficiaries were not always subjects of the states that were spending the money. Spanish cannon requirements were met in the years before 1779 partly by a contract with the Scottish Carron Company, and by purchases from France.[92] In all the belligerents, small-arms sales increased thanks to the need to arm the crews of naval vessels and privateers. Gunpowder production, a Dutch speciality, was also stimulated by the war. Nor should we forget that French, Dutch and Spanish munitions found their way to the American rebels. According to evidence gathered by British agents, in the winter of 1776–7 the Continental army received some 200 field pieces and 30,000 muskets from French royal magazines, with another 12,000 French army muskets following in the summer of 1777. American uniform requirements were also partly met by supplies from their European friends; Spanish 'Cloathing for Soldiers to a great Amount' was sent to New Orleans, for collection by American agents in April 1777, and the following September Congress purchased French-made uniforms in blue and brown. Manufacturers based in powers that remained neutral throughout the war gained, too: Prussian cloth was sent down the Elbe to Hamburg, and from there to Amsterdam for shipment to North America.[93]

Food producers and retailers also benefited from increased demand. A fleet about to set out on voyage required vast quantities of foodstuffs to sustain its crews over a prolonged period at sea, and if the ships carried troops on board then the demand for victuals was even greater. Naval forces were like towns; they produced almost no food of their own (apart from some fish caught on voyage) but consumed voraciously. Cork, surrounded by a rich agricultural hinterland, was a major provisioning centre for the Royal Navy, and for the army sent to America in 1776. To preserve stocks and control prices, the government imposed embargos on Irish provision exports, much to the irritation of local merchants and their political supporters, who claimed that foreign markets would be lost forever to their European competitors. Perhaps German and Danish meat producers did indeed take advantage of the new opportunities presented to them, but imposing an embargo was not the same as enforcing it: scattered evidence suggests that Irish merchants continued to trade with many of their old partners, and even catered for the demands of the French fleet, which purchased large quantities of Irish beef in preference to meat from French farms.[94]

The stimulus provided by increased military activity, and naval activity in particular, needs to be set against the damage done to overseas trade. In Britain, manufacturers and merchants suffered in the first stage of the war from the almost complete cessation of formal trade with the rebel colonies. As early as July 1775, the metalworking industry of the English Midlands was feeling the pinch, with one businessman complaining of the 'baleful effects in the iron manufacture particularly nails'.[95] Textile manufacturers were even more badly hit; woollens had made up some 30 per cent of Britain's exports to the mainland colonies in 1772, and now the American market was largely closed. In Glasgow, tobacco weighing 46 million pounds was imported in 1775; the next year the figure plummeted to a mere £7 million; and in 1777, to a paltry £210,000.[96] More generally, war increased the cost of transporting goods by sea for all of the belligerents, partly because insurance rates rose to reflect the increased risk of loss, but also due to sailors' wage rates going up as navies recruited heavily from the available pool of mariners. Even before the French entered the war, American privateers captured large quantities of British merchant vessels, mainly in the Atlantic and Caribbean, and then, when they were able to operate from European ports, in waters closer to Britain. Once their countries joined the war, French, Spanish and Dutch merchant ships were also exposed to attack. The Dutch sustained considerable losses, both to privateers and the Royal Navy, in the first months of their participation in the conflict, but the French merchant marine suffered more sustained blows: between 1778 and 1783 nearly 1,500 French vessels were taken as prizes.[97]

But if the American conflict was bad for the merchants and shipowners of the European belligerents, it opened up new opportunities for neutrals. The Dutch, before they were dragged into the war, profited greatly from carrying much of the overseas trade of the United States. St Eustatius had acted as a great *entrepôt*; a storehouse for American exports to Europe, and European (including British) exports to America. Admiral Rodney, who captured the Dutch island in February 1781, considered the trade it had handled 'more detrimental to England than all the forces of her enemies'.[98] Dutch merchant ships, furthermore, had carried naval stores – mainly timber, tar and hemp – from the Baltic to the French and Spanish ports. At least one British minister, as we have seen, feared that the whole of the overseas trade of the Bourbon powers might soon be carried in Dutch vessels, enabling the French and Spanish navies to maximize the number of trained mariners they took from their countries' merchant ships.[99] When the Dutch were forced to enter the war at the end of 1780, the opportunities for profit evaporated immediately, but others were ready to fill the gap. In 1782, Weymouth's overseas trade, according to what a visitor could gather, continued almost entirely in 'neutral bottoms', probably German and Scandinavian vessels.[100] Direct British trade with the Dutch Republic all but ceased once the two became formal enemies, but it seems that many British exports to the Dutch, and Dutch exports to the British, were merely re-routed through the neutral Austrian Netherlands (roughly the equivalent of modern-day Belgium). Small wonder a British visitor to Ostend reported, in 1782, that local merchants were concerned that peace would bring an end to their prosperity, as they had benefited from the diversion of British trade with the neighbouring Dutch Republic and feared that the prewar pattern would soon be re-established.[101]

5

ENDINGS AND EXPLANATIONS

How did the war end? And why did the British lose the Thirteen Colonies, yet cling on to most of the other parts of their extended empire? Some answers have been provided in the preceding chapters, but we now turn to consider these questions more systematically. The first section looks at the peacemaking, both between the British and the Americans and the British and their European enemies.[1] The second considers the wider issue of why the war ended as it did; why the British lost the war in America but held on, or even gained the upper hand, in the last stages of the wider war.

In the spring of 1782, the Marquess of Rockingham's new government was committed to ending the war with America, but its ministers disagreed about how this should be done. Charles James Fox, who had consistently opposed the American aspect of the war since 1775, became the foreign secretary, a new post created by the new government. Fox wanted to come to terms with Congress as speedily as possible, in order to concentrate British resources on the continuing war with the Bourbons and the Dutch.[2] To this end, he was willing to acknowledge the United States and accept its independence. But his colleague Lord Shelburne, who filled the new post of secretary of state for home and colonial affairs, argued that negotiations with the Americans came within his remit; as the United States had not been recognized by the British government the Americans remained rebel subjects who came under his jurisdiction.

Behind this rather arcane piece of power play lay an important difference, not just of approach but of objective. Shelburne, in contrast to Fox, had no wish to acknowledge American independence until a comprehensive settlement had been reached with Britain's European enemies. He may even have hoped that it would not be necessary to recognize the independence of the United States, or at least that some form of political connection between Britain and America could be salvaged from the wreckage of the British Atlantic empire; the idea of a federal union certainly seems to have been discussed in the peace negotiations, even if no one on the American side seems to have taken it seriously.[3] But Shelburne was also more interested than Fox in Britain's European position. He hoped that a comprehensive settlement with the French might pave the way to a Franco–British understanding and cooperation against the rising eastern powers of Russia, Prussia and Austria, which he identified as posing the greatest threat to the European balance of power.

The struggle between Fox and Shelburne led each to appoint their own representatives to negotiate in Paris. Shelburne had been in contact with Benjamin Franklin even before Lord North's government fell; as soon as the new administration was formed, Shelburne sent Richard Oswald, a wealthy Scottish merchant, across the Channel to act as his envoy. Fox, determined not to surrender his position, responded by dispatching Thomas Grenville, a government-supporting MP, to speak on his behalf. Franklin knew Oswald and so willingly talked with him; 'the Doctor showed me a good deal of civility', Oswald reported to Shelburne, while Franklin himself told Shelburne that he found Oswald to be 'a wise and honest man' with whom he could do business.[4] Grenville, on the other hand, made little progress, either with Franklin (who wanted to deal only with Oswald) or with Vergennes. The French foreign minister was distinctly unimpressed by Grenville's suggestion that the Franco–British discussions should be based on the peace of 1763, which the French government, hardly surprisingly, interpreted as an insulting failure on Fox's part to recognize how much Britain's position had been weakened.[5] Fox was in a minority in the cabinet and the king was far from well-disposed to him. Even so, he held his ground until Rockingham's unexpected death in July 1782 put Shelburne in charge of the government. Fox resigned and Grenville returned from Paris, leaving Shelburne free to pursue his own course.

Shelburne was predisposed to believe that generosity to the former colonies would weaken American ties with the French. Like most British politicians, he continued to think that the Americans were instinctively hostile to the Catholic and absolutist Bourbons and much more inclined, despite the experience of the war, to amicable relations with the British. Franklin, for his part, encouraged Oswald to believe that generosity to the United States would pay dividends to Britain, as the French and Spanish would come to terms if they thought the Americans and British were about to reach agreement. Franklin pushed too far in suggesting that Canada might be ceded to the United States, but Shelburne was willing to give a good deal. Progress stalled, however, when Franklin fell ill. John Jay, his replacement as chief American negotiator, was far less well disposed to Oswald, who found him truculent and disinclined to offer anything to the British. Jay even caused difficulty over Oswald's credentials. Only with Franklin's return did the prospect of an early settlement between the British and Americans revive. The issue of the loyalists proved contentious, however; Franklin urged Oswald to drop any reference to compensation, on the grounds that 'They have done infinite mischief to our Properties by wantonly burning and destroying Farmhouses, Villages and Towns'.[6] If the British government insisted on trying to secure compensation for the loyalists, Franklin continued, then Congress would present counterclaims for the property seized or destroyed by the British and loyalist forces during the war. As late as November 1782, a fortnight before the preliminary peace terms were agreed, Oswald tried to persuade the American commissioners to give proper consideration to the loyalists, but they again refused. They responded, as before, by referring to British depredations, citing the way in which the British forces that had evacuated Savannah in July had taken away large numbers of slaves who had fled from their American owners.[7] The British and American negotiators finally reached agreement on 30 November. The preliminary terms, as they were called, would remain provisional until the conclusion of a general peace: but they did not change. The British government conceded the independence of the United States and accepted that it would withdraw its forces from Charleston and New York. The United States was given much more generous boundaries than Congress could reasonably have expected; Shelburne, still hoping for a postwar rapprochement, and seeking to drive a wedge between the Americans and the French, gave up the territory between the Great Lakes and the Ohio. The Americans were even granted fishing rights off Newfoundland. The best that the British negotiators could secure in return was an agreement that the Americans would honour their debts and a promise that Congress would recommend to the states a restoration of British and loyalist property; Oswald must have known that the chances of the states responding positively to such a recommendation were very limited indeed.

While the British and Americans negotiated, talks proceeded between the British and the French. Vergennes wanted to reverse as much of the 1763 settlement as he could, hence his horror when Fox, via Grenville, suggested that the peace agreed at the end of the Seven Years War should form the basis for negotiations. In June 1782, Vergennes told Montmorin, the French ambassador at Madrid, of his desire to 'forget all that had gone before' and reach a new settlement 'based on justice and mutual convenience'.[8] De Grasse, captured at the Saintes and detained in England, conversed with Shelburne in August 1782 about the shape of a future peace; his report to Vergennes encouraged the French foreign minister to believe that the British would be prepared to move at least some way towards the French objective. Gérard de Rayneval, Vergennes's under-secretary, crossed the Channel to speak directly with Shelburne, but at a meeting on 13 September, Shelburne appeared less willing to compromise than de Grasse had suggested; on India, he explained to Rayneval that 'things must remain there as they were established in 1763', as 'it was not to be expected that the King could cede two continents'.[9] More positively, Shelburne hinted that if Britain and France settled their differences, they might together act as the arbiters of Europe.

While he could not have welcomed Shelburne's obdurate resistance to concessions in India, Vergennes would have been more receptive to Shelburne's suggestion of Anglo–French cooperation in Europe. Vergennes already believed that the Russians posed a threat to the European balance of power: the Austro–Russian alliance of June 1781 convinced him that Catherine the Great would soon engage in another war with the Ottoman Empire, France's long-standing friend. In late September 1782, just as he learned of the outcome of Rayneval's meeting with Shelburne, Vergennes discovered that the Russians were indeed preparing for war. Other developments encouraged him to be more willing to move towards the British position. Rodney's victory at the Saintes was an uncomfortable reminder that the Royal Navy was still a formidable force. French public debts were also a consideration. The war was proving very expensive; for two years Necker, the finance minister, had been arguing that France could not afford to prolong the conflict.

But if Vergennes was now more willing to compromise, Spain proved reluctant to end the war without the tangible gain of Gibraltar. The Spanish government continued to want the Rock back even after the defeat of the besiegers in September 1782. The Conde de Aranda, the Spanish minister in Paris, went so far as to suggest a complicated land swap to overcome the problem. Under Aranda's scheme, the French could be given Santo Domingo (and therefore acquire the whole of Hispaniola) so long as one of their overseas territories was offered to the British so they could give Gibraltar to Spain. Shelburne briefly considered relinquishing Gibraltar in return for Spanish and perhaps even French concessions. But such a trade-off was ultimately unnecessary as, in December 1782, with the Anglo–American preliminaries signed, the Spanish reckoned that their chances of regaining Gibraltar had gone and dropped it from the list of their demands.

The Dutch remained obdurate for longer, but in the end even their resistance was worn down. Gerard Brantsen, the Republic's emissary at Paris, was under instructions to make no concessions. The demands he tabled were totally unrealistic, given the disastrous showing of the Dutch in the war. The States General wanted the return of all territory and trading bases captured by the British, recognition of the rights of neutral shippers and compensation for Dutch losses at sea. Vergennes took it upon himself to negotiate on behalf of the Dutch, and secured the restoration of Trincomalee, but he could not persuade the British to part with Negapatam. The

Dutch agreed to an armistice only on 20 January 1783, just days before the other powers accepted preliminary terms. No Dutch signature was appended to the final settlement until 20 May 1784. The reluctance of the Dutch representative to put his name to the treaty was understandable; the British not only kept Negapatam but won the right to trade in the Dutch East Indies.

The definitive peace, signed by the Americans, French, Spanish and British on 3 September 1783, confirmed everything that had been agreed in the preliminaries. The United States secured a British recognition of its independence, with boundaries far more extensive than any American could have expected in July 1776, or even in the aftermath of Yorktown. The French did not make the gains they had hoped for in India, but their prewar trading stations on the subcontinent were restored, they regained St Lucia and retained Tobago, recovered Senegal, won better fishing rights off Newfoundland and the right (denied them in 1763) to fortify Dunkirk. For Spain, there was no Gibraltar, but Florida and Minorca represented acceptable consolation prizes. The British, who entered the war to keep control of the old mainland American colonies, saw those colonies become independent states. But George III's empire was not completely dismembered; the British held on to most of their Caribbean possessions and resisted French pressure for concessions in India, where they strengthened their position by retaining the Dutch base at Negapatam.

On any objective reckoning of the strength of the two sides fighting in America in the first years of the war, the British should have put down the colonial rebellion. Why did they fail to do so? Traditional explanations tend to highlight the revolutionary fervour of the Americans, their superior tactical skills, the leadership of Washington and the incompetence and unsuitability of the British army. Not only is each of these explanations unsatisfactory in itself, even taken together they do not account for why the Americans were able to hold off the British and sustain their independence.

American enthusiasm was palpable at the beginning of the conflict. The militiamen besieging Gage's army in Boston were truly motivated by a desire to defend their communities from the British army.

At this stage, a genuine *rage militaire* seems to have gripped the colonists, who were drilling and preparing to fight further south, as well as in New England.[10] But we should not make the mistake of assuming that enthusiasm is a guarantee of success. The Declaration of Independence, when read to the Continentals at New York, inspired cheers, but the American performance in the subsequent fighting on Long Island hardly suggests that fervour was an adequate substitute for professionalism. Indeed, when he learned of Howe's victory, Charles James Fox reflected ruefully on the 'melancholy consideration ... that no people animated by what principle soever can make a successful resistance to military discipline'.[11] We should also note that by the closing stages of the conflict in America, war-weariness seems to have been more conspicuous than passionate support for independence. In Virginia, one of the cradles of the Revolution, British forces met with remarkably little local resistance in 1779, 1780 and even 1781. On that last occasion, Benjamin Gilbert, a Massachusetts soldier serving in Virginia, was dismayed by what he saw: 'it is as hard a matter to find a sincere friend to his Country in this part of the State', he wrote, 'as to find a Tory in the State of Massachts Bay'.[12] John Bannister, a Virginian officer, was unsurprisingly more forgiving ('the People are tired of the War & come to the Field most reluctantly')[13] but his judgement throws equal doubt on the importance of American revolutionary fervour as a general explanation for British failure.

Nor should we exaggerate the significance of the Americans' use of what would later be termed guerrilla warfare. Militiamen did take pot shots at British troops at various moments in the war; most familiarly, perhaps, during the opening engagement when the redcoats retreated from Concord, but also during the winter of 1776–7 in New Jersey and in the South Carolina backcountry in 1780. The testimony of British officers themselves reveals that this irregular fighting caused the British army some distress and dented its morale, but we should not assume that it constituted the main part of the rebels' military effort, and certainly not imagine that it won the war in America. Washington appreciated that 'partisan' tactics had a part to play, but he was keen, as we have seen, to keep control over the conduct of the war.[14] Temperamentally and socially conservative, he saw his Continentals as a military force that should fight a conventional war, in much the same manner as his British opponents. As the war dragged on, his dream of creating a European-style military came nearer to reality; the New England militia army that Washington inherited in the summer of 1775 (and much disliked) had, by the end of 1779, become a more recognizably professional force, with new uniforms and European drill inculcated by the Prussian instructor General von Steuben. Many of its soldiers, furthermore, became much like the rank-and-file of European armies as the war progressed: they were drawn disproportionately from the bottom of the pile. An indication of the poor background of many of the Continentals is the significant number of black recruits, especially in the northern part of the army. A German officer in the French army, viewing Continental troops at White Plains, New York, in 1781, noted that 'A quarter of them were negroes.'[15] From a military point of view, one of the great virtues of such men was that their poverty encouraged them repeatedly to re-enlist, which meant that the American rank-and-file became increasingly experienced and less of an annual levy.

To deny Washington a role in the survival of the United States would be churlish in the extreme. His bold counterattack at Trenton, in December 1776, may even have saved the Revolution from collapse. He was admired, even revered, far beyond the boundaries

A contemporary depiction of American troops;
note the black soldier on the left.

of the new United States; he gave the Revolution a respectable face to many Europeans, including many Britons.[16] Even General Howe, while not recognizing him as an equal, addressed him as though he were almost a fellow-professional. But the quality of Washington's generalship can easily be overstated. He was comprehensively defeated in the New York campaign of 1776, losing heavily on Long Island, and was beaten again at Brandywine Creek in Pennsylvania the following year. Most of the battles he fought he lost, or at least failed to win. In 1778, some congressional delegates seriously considered replacing him with Gates, the victor of Saratoga. Washington's real achievement was to keep his troops in the contest. He embodied American determination to carry on, despite setbacks and defeats, and his army became the symbol of American resistance, or what his colleague, the Rhode Islander Nathanael Greene, called the 'Stamina of American liberty'.[17] So long as the Continental army survived to fight another day, the American cause survived with it. Washington's personal preference was to attack and finish the war quickly, but he ended up pursuing a strategy of avoiding battle wherever possible, denying his opponents the opportunity to deliver the knockout blow they needed to end the conflict. His unwillingness to oblige Clinton by joining battle in 1779 drove the British commander-in-chief to distraction.[18]

The British army was far from hopelessly unsuited to winning the war in America. Many historians suggest that it was as much a reflection of all the ills of an aristocratic order as the American armed forces were the embodiment of the liberty-loving society from which they sprang. But if many of the British army's senior officers were indeed aristocrats, they were by no means all foppish incompetents. A good number took their military duties very seriously and worked hard to acquire professional skills. William Howe, though the brother of a viscount, won his appointment to American command at least partly because he had served in America in the Seven Years War and had experience of light infantry tactics.[19] Cornwallis, an earl, was a daring commander who pushed himself, as well as his men, to the limit. Clinton, grandson of an earl, although much criticized for his seeming inactivity, showed occasional flashes of boldness and a keen strategic appreciation of the realities of the war in America. The soldiers they led, while punished severely at times, were not simply terrorized into doing their duty by violence or its threat; generals like Howe, Clinton and Cornwallis appealed to their men's better natures, and even their appreciation of the political dimensions of the war. The few scraps of testimony we have that illuminate the attitudes of the common redcoats suggest that at least some of them were motivated not just by fear or money, but by a sense of loyalty to their king and their country. If historians have overstated the fervour of the rebels, they may have underrated the ideological commitment of their opponents.

The British army, furthermore, adapted remarkably quickly to American conditions, just as it had done in the Seven Years War. Not only were its uniforms modified, but its tactics changed, too. Already, in the spring of 1775, its light infantry companies were used to firing and reloading while lying flat on the ground.[20] During the early years of the war, the rest of the army acquired experience in similar methods. The British troops, whose skirmishing techniques caused such devastating damage to the tightly packed French soldiers on St Lucia in December 1778, had been serving in North America for more than two years, during which time they learned to deploy in looser formations and use light infantry tactics. In July 1781, during one of the last battles in the war in America, at Green Spring, Virginia, the British troops even turned the tables on their Continental army opponents, who had adopted European close-order formation and were exposed to a withering fire from their hidden British enemy.[21]

So, if the British failure to win the war in America is not attributable to superior American morale, or leadership, or tactics, what is the explanation? Before the war started, as we saw, ministers in London had believed New England to be the epicentre of resistance; by concentrating the army in Massachusetts, they intended to overawe both it and its New England neighbours. But the experience of the first months of fighting, when the army had been confined to Boston, discouraged ministers and senior commanders from thoughts of further campaigning in New England, and led them instead to consider ways of cutting the region off from the rest of the rebel provinces.

Perhaps if the British government had sought to exploit more effectively the very real divisions between New England – with its Puritan and democratic traditions – and the more religiously hierarchical and socially stratified provinces in the south, the rebellion might have been broken, or at least contained. But no concerted effort was made to deepen this sectional division; Germain was too fixated on the more recent (and arguably more superficial) division between rebels and loyalists, which proved difficult to turn to British advantage.[22]

In truth, despite New England's prominent role in prewar opposition to imperial initiatives, in 1775 the revolt was general and had no readily identifiable geographical centre. The rebel colonies had no capital city in a European sense. As they had come together only to resist British authority, and had no tradition of unity, no American city could possibly fulfil that role. Philadelphia, though the home of the Continental Congress and the largest urban centre, could not be compared with a European capital, which meant that its capture by Howe's forces in 1777 had only a limited impact on American morale. The British occupation of other major towns – particularly New York City and Charleston – similarly failed to produce the psychological blow that could have been expected if a European city like Vienna or Berlin had been taken by an enemy. The rebel colonies were predominantly rural; the vast majority of the people were scattered across a large expanse of territory.

Much of that territory was difficult for armies to access. Areas like the Delaware Valley posed few challenges, as they were flat, possessed an established road network and had long been under cultivation. Virginia was also open to attack, thanks to the extensive and navigable riverine system that allowed British raiders to move far inland. Interior New England was altogether more difficult for military campaigning; 'covered with wood & hilly', in the words of one British officer, it was far from easy to penetrate.[23] Even more of a barrier was the forested wilderness of upper New York, through which Burgoyne's army attempted to proceed in the summer of 1777. Roads existed, but whenever the British and German troops departed from the established routes, they were obliged to cut down trees and construct new roads: small wonder that Burgoyne's expedition made such slow progress.

The very size of the North American theatre of operations was itself a problem for the British forces. It was much bigger than the army's traditional areas of European deployment in the Low Countries and even western Germany. The British troops that fought in the Austrian Netherlands in the 1740s, during the War of the Austrian Succession, would have thought of a theatre of operations stretching between the French and the Dutch borders, a distance of less than 80 miles. The British army's campaigns of 1758–62 in north-western Germany were conducted over a larger area; from Bremen in the north to near Frankfurt in the south is about 200 miles. But in 1779, Sir Henry Clinton commanded troops as far apart as Penobscot, in modern-day Maine, and Savannah, in Georgia. The distance between these two posts, as the crow flies, is about 1,200 miles. To coordinate the campaigns of British troops separated by large tracts of territory in rebel hands was no easy matter, as the fate of Burgoyne's expedition from Canada in 1777 emphatically demonstrated.

If distances within North America posed difficulties for the British army, the distance between the imperial centre and the colonies presented even greater challenges. Communication across the Atlantic was often very slow; it took a sailing ship approximately five to seven weeks to reach Boston from England, and four to five weeks to make the return journey. A voyage from England to the Chesapeake lasted nine weeks; to sail from the Chesapeake to England, about six.[24] To micromanage the war from London, as Germain appreciated, would have been a hopeless undertaking. But even setting the general strategy was hampered by the great distance of ministers from the American campaigning grounds. Germain's failure to coordinate the plans for 1777, when Howe effectively left Burgoyne to fend for himself, owed much to the problems of poor communication – some of it perhaps down to Germain's reluctance to impose his will, but at least as much to the time it took for instructions to reach the commanders on the spot. Howe replied to Germain's request that he complete the Pennsylvania campaign in time to help Burgoyne only at the end of August; it would be have been many weeks later that Germain learned that Howe was unlikely to be a position to oblige, by which time it was too late to do anything to remedy the situation.[25]

Transatlantic distances presented other difficulties for the British. When they had campaigned in North America in the Seven Years War, British troops had been able to draw on local sources of supply. In the War of Independence, by contrast, the British army was reliant on food and other essentials shipped more than 3,000 miles from Britain and Ireland. In 1776, Howe was pleased with the logistical support his troops received; at the end of that year's campaign, he announced that the army had never been in want of food.[26] But to sustain an army so far from home with supplies sent across the Atlantic was no easy undertaking, and every year it required a great effort to assemble and ship the provisions required. For brief periods the army controlled enough territory in America to reduce this dependence on an extended Atlantic supply line, but no British commander-in-chief could be confident of local sources. The Atlantic crossing was always hazardous: in wartime much more so. American privateers captured British supply vessels, and once the French entered the war the army's umbilical cord was frequently endangered. Anxiety about supplies, as we have seen, inhibited Clinton from launching offensive operations.[27]

The British army in North America was also a long way from its chief source of reinforcements. Again, the contrast with the Seven Years War is marked. In that earlier conflict the British army was able to call on local manpower to augment its strength. In the War of Independence, native peoples and parts of the settler population were certainly recruited to help the British war effort, but the bulk of the royal forces came from Europe. At the height of the Seven Years War, locally raised provincials comprised about half the total forces deployed against the French; in the War of Independence they never amounted to more than one third of the royal army. Every casualty amongst the regular troops took time to make good; much longer than for the rebels, who were fighting on home ground. As a German officer in the French army noted, 'The Americans lose 600 men in a day, and 8 days later, 1,200 others rejoin the army; whereas to replace 10 men in the English army is quite an undertaking'.[28] The need to protect the British army from heavy casualties may well have inhibited its senior officers even more than the exposed transatlantic supply line. It might also help to explain why General Howe regularly seemed to hold back from delivering a knockout blow. Perhaps he was influenced by a desire to avoid undue American bloodshed, which might have made pacification more difficult.[29] But if political considerations encouraged him not to press his advantage, it seems very likely that the need to preserve manpower strength was at least as important a cause of his inhibition.

The British army, as we have seen, did not expand dramatically in the first years of the war. The king, rather than agree to the raising of new regiments that would have facilitated rapid growth in the army's size, preferred to hire German auxiliaries who would be ready for immediate service in the 1776 campaign. Even when Washington's counterattack at Trenton and Princeton made a further British campaign inevitable, the government decided to hire yet more Germans rather than create new regiments at home. Reliance on the Germans made sense in military terms; the Hessians, at least the first contingent sent to America in 1776, were experienced professionals who acquitted themselves well in their first battles. American hopes that the Germans, as 'mercenaries', lacked commitment to the British cause and could be persuaded to desert, proved over-optimistic; not a single Hessian soldier deserted for months after their arrival in North America, and German desertion became a serious problem only once the war was effectively over.[30] But politically, the hiring of the Germans was perhaps a mistake. In late 1775, some Americans, on learning that the auxiliaries would be coming across the Atlantic, regarded the Germans' involvement in the war as a sign that the king had thrown his colonial subjects out of the British family. American fears that the British government was set on establishing an authoritarian order in the colonies were probably reinforced by the origins of the auxiliaries; they came from states that Americans regarded as despotic. If the war was all about allegiances, in Clinton's words, a contest to see who could 'gain the hearts & subdue the minds of America',[31] then hiring German troops may not have helped the British to win.

Perhaps even more damagingly, the British army became associated with parts of the American population that members of the

A contemporary picture of German auxiliary troops; they were a vital
component of the British army in North America, but their presence
probably increased American determination to resist.

settler community feared or hated. Native warriors allied themselves
to the British and raided the frontier. Their usefulness to the British
cause was questionable, however. On the positive side of the equa-
tion, they caused economic damage to the rebel colonies; a British
report claimed that a single raid in 1778 destroyed 'about 1000
Dwelling Houses, [and] all their Mills', and that the Americans had
also lost 'about 1000 head of horned Cattle, and sheep and swine
in great numbers', which had been driven to the British bases.[32]
Native attacks on the frontier also eventually compelled Washington
to weaken his main Continental army by sending a powerful detachment to neutralize the Indian threat. However, the British were not
necessarily advantaged. Many members of the settler population,
especially those near the exposed frontier, felt a deep hostility to the
natives based on generations of conflict and the passing down of

horrific atrocity stories. Some British officers had imagined that American fear of the Indians could be turned to good account; native incursions would terrorize the rebels into submission.[33] At least a few Americans were no doubt terrorized, but others seem to have been inspired to determined resistance. It was surely no coincidence that very large numbers of New Englanders flocked to join Gates' army in opposing Burgoyne's forces, which included an important Indian component. It helped, no doubt, that the natives' reputation was soon confirmed; despite Burgoyne's entreaties, his native allies tended to treat the settler population indiscriminately. The murder and scalping of Jane McCrea, a loyalist, gave the Americans a propaganda gift that they wasted no time in exploiting. Gates told Burgoyne that his use of the Indians would appear 'in every Gazette' to 'convince Mankind' of the British general's base conduct in paying for scalps.[34] It was hardly surprising, then, when one of Burgoyne's Brunswick officers concluded that 'It would certainly have been better if we had not had any Indians with us'.[35]

Equally damaging, so far as British attempts to win over the settler population were concerned, was the royal forces' association with the enslaved population of the colonies. If settlers on the frontier lived in constant anxiety about Indian attack, whites throughout the colonies worried about the flight or even mutiny of their slaves. Desperate British officers, cooped up in Boston at the start of the war, contemplated mobilizing the enslaved to overawe the rebels, particularly in the southern colonies where the enslaved population was concentrated.[36] In Britain itself, a few politicians also suggested that this might be a good way of overcoming the army's numerical weakness.[37] The British government, so far as we can tell, never seriously considered such an option; the reliance of the British Caribbean plantations on slave labour would have made any encouragement to large-scale slave rebellion a high-risk strategy.[38] But Lord Dunmore, the last royal governor of Virginia, attempted to rally the enslaved to his standard in 1775, and Clinton in 1779 effectively repeated Dunmore's offer of freedom for any enslaved person who left his rebel master and came into the British lines. Clinton's intention, it seems, was not to arm the enslaved and use them as military auxiliaries, but to encourage them to leave their owners to undermine the revolutionary economy; he also sought to entice white indentured servants for the same reason. Some enslaved Americans who reached the British lines did go on to serve in a military capacity, but many more acted as craftsmen, drivers and labourers in the army's ancillary departments, or became servants to officers and even to rank-and-file soldiers.[39] The experience was probably not as liberating as many runaways had hoped; a good number merely swapped one form of servitude for another. Even so, from the enslaved perspective, the British must have appeared more committed to liberty than most white Americans. From the British perspective, however, the help of the slaves was, at best, a mixed blessing. The number attaching themselves to the British army eventually became a burden rather than a help, as they consumed provisions that could not be spared. More importantly, the association of the army with the flight and freedom of slaves reduced the chances of winning over wavering whites. Far from being cowed by the threat of a great slave insurrection, or even by the seemingly unstoppable haemorrhaging of their black labour force, white slave owners seem to have become more determined to resist British authority. Even loyally inclined Americans complained bitterly at the loss of their slaves.

The loyalists themselves – or at least loyalists-in-arms – might be counted as another group that made the British task of securing American hearts and minds more difficult. Lord George Germain, as we have seen, envisaged the loyalists as a vital element in the British war effort; he continued to believe that most Americans supported a restoration of royal rule right through to the end of the conflict. Senior British officers, while becoming more sceptical about the number of loyalists as the war proceeded, recognized that arming the 'good subjects', as James Robertson put it, to help subdue the bad, would to some extent make up for the limited number of regular troops available in the rebel colonies.[40] But setting Americans against Americans made the war even more of a fratricidal contest, and added greatly to the animosities engendered on both sides. Loyalist military units might contain a sprinkling of British officers and sergeants, and include in their rank-and-file some former rebels, but they were mainly made up of 'friends to government' who had lost their property and were disinclined to treat their opponents with lenience. The desire of such loyalists for revenge made it difficult for British commanders to prevent them from ruining the chances of reconciliation. One particularly notorious unit was the Associated Loyalists, comprising militant refugees who refused to join the provincial line. They soon acquired a reputation for depredation and cruelty, leading one rebel to condemn Clinton as nothing but 'the ringleader of a banditti of Robbers!'[41]

At times, the British army was little better. Although some Americans benefited from the economic opportunities offered by the presence of British troops, others had good cause to rue the day they encountered the redcoats. British ministers and generals might see their forces as liberating Americans from the 'tyranny' of Congress, but the troops arrived, in the minds of most of the settler population, not as friends but as invaders. As a result of the concentration of British forces in Boston in the months before the outbreak of the war, the rebels easily established their authority throughout the Thirteen Colonies. In the summer of 1776, the British were therefore obliged to reclaim lost territory, not defend posts they already held. The first contact of the British troops with American civilians was often when the troops arrived in a locality in pursuit of, or having beaten, Washington's Continentals. Flushed with triumph, British soldiers tended at this moment to treat the inhabitants as fair game. In New Jersey, during November and December 1776, numerous local people had their property taken and their persons attacked; many different sources report a large number of rapes. The experience was repeated in other areas into which the British advanced, even if the inhabitants of places under more settled British occupation tended to be treated less harshly. British officers often blamed the Hessians for excesses, and American accounts also identified the German auxiliaries as particularly licentious. But British order-books and court-martial records, as well as private letters and diaries, make it abundantly clear that it was not just the Hessians who maltreated the inhabitants. Though by no means all Americans who suffered took to arms against their oppressors – some accepted their fate with remarkable fatalism – British depredations created enemies when the British army needed more friends.

Even if the British and German troops had behaved well, treating American non-combatants with the greatest courtesy and mildness, the army's peripatetic progress through the colonies would surely have discouraged potential loyalists. The army's practice of arriving in an area, staying for a while then moving on elsewhere, made it less and less likely over time that the well-disposed would come forward. As one contemporary account put it, 'The Friends of Great Britain whenever the Army came have been tempted to Declare themselves and afterwards left to pay the forfeit of their temerity'.[42] Those who were emboldened by the British presence to announce themselves 'friends to government' might momentarily feel more confident; but if the troops then withdrew, as they did in New Jersey in 1777, in Pennsylvania in 1778 and in Virginia in 1779 and 1780, the newly identified loyalists were exposed to the enmity of their neighbours. Reports of the unfortunate experiences of those who did rally to the British cause, only to be deserted a short time after-wards, hardly encouraged loyalists in other areas to put their heads above the parapet. Fears of imminent desertion almost certainly inhibited the North Carolina 'friends to government' from joining Cornwallis in 1781.

At the same time, the British army's mobility may also have driven neutrally inclined Americans into the rebel camp. When a British force arrived in a locality – and over the course of a long war, most areas of the rebel colonies experienced a British raid at one time or another – the militia would be called out to combat the attack. Male Americans who, until that moment, had managed to steer clear of trouble and maintain a low profile were now faced with an uncom-fortable choice; join the American defenders or be regarded as a closet loyalist. Most men put in this unenviable position probably chose to turn out with the militia; however dangerous it was to take up arms, they probably calculated that it was more dangerous to be exposed to the wrath of your community when the British left. And after having served in the militia against the British army, it became more natural for these colonists to identify with the American cause. The experience of combat, and particularly of being shot at by British troops, must have made it very difficult to remain neutral or uncommitted.[43]

But if the British army could have done more to avoid large numbers of Americans gravitating towards the revolutionaries, its fundamental problem – the problem that made the war in America all but unwinnable for the British government – was the entry into the conflict of France, then Spain, and finally the Dutch Republic. Even before formal French intervention in the summer of 1778, foreign aid had underpinned American resistance. Money and munitions were the most important contributions; in 1777, the first large French loan and a substantial delivery of French muskets sustained the rebel war effort. Even European manpower, in the form of small numbers of trained officers who arrived as volunteers, helped the Americans to hold off the British forces. Foreign money and munitions continued to flood in after 1778 – the former may even have saved the American economy from total collapse in 1781 – but once the French government committed itself to joining the war as a fully-fledged belligerent, the nature of the conflict changed dramatically and the American debt to Britain's European enemies increased accordingly.

The British position might not have been so difficult if North's government had been able to secure European allies. Britain had never before in the eighteenth century fought France without the help of another major European power. The key to British success in the Seven Years War had been using subsidies to pay for German troops to tie down French resources on the Continent while British fleets and troops mopped up French overseas possessions. Without any European allies to play the same role, the British could not deflect the French from devoting most of their efforts to a naval war. The French government poured money into building ships before and during the conflict; its 52 ships of the line in 1778 had become 73 by 1783. For a brief moment in 1778 it seemed that the French government's strategy might unravel; Austria and Prussia clashed over the Bavarian succession, and their local dispute threatened to bring on a much wider European war. But French ministers avoided being drawn into the conflict alongside their Austrian ally, and kept their focus austerely on the struggle with Britain.

Naval historians reasonably argue that the French had not as great an advantage as it seemed; effective navies could not be created overnight, by transferring resources from the army to the fleet, but took years of steady investment to build up.[44] But if France lacked the naval infrastructure that Britain possessed, in the short but vital period between 1775 and 1782 it was able to do enough to challenge the dominance of the Royal Navy and help to end British hopes in America. If the British government had secured a major continental ally, perhaps the French would have been compelled to devote more spending to their army, and their navy would therefore have been much weaker. Britain's isolation was not, however, a chosen course, or at least not a chosen course from the mid-1760s. Many British politicians and diplomats, both before and during the War of Independence, sought to forge new links with one or more European powers to counterbalance France, only to find that none would join them. British victory in the Seven Years War had convinced most European states that France no longer posed a real threat to the balance of power; none of them any longer feared France enough to want to form alliances against it. Indeed, the general assumption across Europe was that Britain was now the overmighty one, whose power should be checked. The League of Armed Neutrality of 1780 was directed against British naval bullying; there was no Grand Alliance of the kind formed against Louis XIV at the beginning of the century, or against revolutionary France at its end.

The most obvious consequence of foreign intervention against Britain was the geographical expansion of the war to the Caribbean, Central America, West Africa, Europe and Asia. The British government now had to fight a multi-front conflict. Ministers in London agreed to continue the war in America, but with more limited ambitions. They no longer thought it likely that they would be able to reclaim all the rebel provinces; their primary aim was to peel off the southern mainland colonies, which could sustain the British West Indian islands with vital supplies. British military and naval resources were diverted to other theatres of operation, particularly the Caribbean and home defence. In February 1778, on the eve of French intervention, 65 per cent of British military manpower was based in North America; by September 1780, only 29 per cent.[45] In these circumstances, with other arenas of conflict competing for troops and ships, the British forces in the rebel colonies were never strong enough to achieve even the government's attenuated American aims.

Within North America itself, foreign intervention made a material difference. Early in 1778, in anticipation of a Spanish entry into the war, Germain ordered Clinton to send troops from his army to reinforce the garrison of West and East Florida. Once the Spanish eventually became belligerents – in the summer of 1779 – the government in Madrid instructed the governor of Louisiana to begin operations to reclaim Florida. Gálvez's campaign was outstandingly successful; he had taken all the British posts in West Florida by May 1781. But for Clinton, the war in Florida was never more than a sideshow; his real fear was French involvement in North America. The arrival of the French expeditionary force led by Rochambeau in 1780 made him fearful for his New York headquarters, but his nightmare was that the French navy would effectively cooperate with American troops to trap isolated detachments of his army. Franco–American coordination was lacking at New York in July 1778, and failed to materialize at Newport, Rhode Island, not long afterwards. It produced no positive results at Savannah in 1779. However, in the autumn of 1781, the French and Americans finally pulled it off in spectacular fashion, compelling Cornwallis to surrender at Yorktown after de Grasses' ships had secured control of the Chesapeake.[46]

To say this is not to belittle the rebel contribution to British defeat in the mainland colonies. Washington's counterattack at Trenton, as already noted, breathed new life into the dying embers of the American cause at the very end of 1776. Saratoga was an even bigger coup for American arms; a major British field army surrendered and the rebels became confident – perhaps for the first time – that they could hold off the highly professional British military. But, contrary to the commonly held view, the French did not become belligerents as a result of Burgoyne's defeat. Saratoga hastened rather than produced French intervention. Vergennes had already won the internal battle in the French government over whether to join the war. The Americans' ability to sustain their rebellion, simply to remain unvanquished, despite repeated battlefield setbacks, convinced ministers in Paris that they were worth supporting and that French intervention would materially harm British interests. Vergennes needed time, however, to build up the navy and to try to persuade the Spanish to enter the war alongside the French. Saratoga encouraged him to believe that the time was ripe for French involvement, with the Spanish, if possible, but without them if necessary. Americans had known from 1775 that their fortunes depended upon their ability to secure foreign help; their real achievement was to hold on until that help was forthcoming and then, after several false starts, to work effectively with their French allies to inflict a crushing defeat on the British army.

If the British lost the war in America, their successes elsewhere meant that they emerged more powerful than had seemed likely in the immediate aftermath of Yorktown. In essence, as we have already noted, Rodney's victory at the Saintes and the heroically protracted defiance of the Gibraltar garrison boosted British morale and undermined the confidence of the Bourbon powers.[47] Each of these British triumphs can be explained by local and personal circumstances – such as Rodney's boldness and the strong natural defences of Gibraltar – but they are both linked by one fundamental factor: British naval power. Rodney commanded a larger number of ships of the line at the Saintes than his opponent de Grasse; the British admiral's superior tactics may have been important, but he was undoubtedly helped by his possessing numerical superiority. Rodney had at his disposal the largest fleet that the Royal Navy had deployed outside European waters.[48] Similarly, Gibraltar could not have hung on without relief convoys arriving during the siege. By the end of August 1779, the governor of Gibraltar was reporting that 'very little fresh Provision is left',[49] and, in January 1780, not a moment too soon, a first relief convoy arrived. A second reached the Rock in June 1781, just in time to prevent the lack of food reducing the garrison to a dangerously weakened state. The safe arrival of another convoy of supply vessels in October 1782 finally led the besiegers to despair of their chances of taking the British outpost. Each of these convoys was supported by large numbers of British warships and would not have been possible without a powerful Royal Navy. The British fleet could not outgun all its enemies combined from 1779, when the Spanish joined the war; even so its expansion was spectacular, particularly in 1778–9, when the number of ships of the line increased from 66 to 90. The French navy also grew in the same period, but not as greatly; its 52 ships of the line in 1778 had risen to 63 the next year.[50]

The increase in the size of the Royal Navy was merely one aspect of a much more concerted British war effort from the time when Bourbon intervention looked inevitable. The mobilization of military manpower was also much greater from 1778 than it had been before, when the British armed forces faced only the colonial rebels. Twelve infantry regiments were added to the army's establishment in 1778, and another 14 the following year, plus four regiments of light dragoons. Between September 1777 and September 1778, 24,000 soldiers were added to the army, excluding the regiments based in Ireland, compared with less than one third of that number in the preceding 12 months.[51] Financial mobilization changed pace with French intervention, too. Lord North introduced new taxes in 1778, many of them falling more generally than the taxes levied earlier in the war. More and more taxes on popular items of consumption followed in the next few years. Government borrowing also increased dramatically; North had secured loans for a total of £7.5 million between 1776 and 1778; from 1778 to 1780 he raised £13 million; in 1780–82, a staggering £24 million.[52]

Why did the British state mobilize for the wider war so much more effectively than for the purely American war before 1778? To some extent, the answer is technical. The king's resistance to the raising of new regiments, as we saw earlier, was finally overcome when a French war seemed imminent. New regiments were the best way to recruit the army rapidly, which meant that the land forces were able to expand at a much faster rate from the end of 1777 than they had done in the years of war against the Americans alone. But the explanation cannot rest simply on method. We need also to consider the role of ideology. British politicians and the wider public recognized that fighting the Bourbons in a worldwide war was going to be no easy matter. However, at least the conflict against the French and the Spanish – Britain's traditional Catholic and absolutist foes – united the country, in contrast to the American war which bitterly divided it. Enthusiasm, as we saw in the case of the Americans, is not in itself a guarantee of success, but, if enthusiasm leads to more soldiers and more ships, it certainly helps. In the end, however, the new tempo of British mobilization might have a simple geographical explanation. For most British people, the American war was remote. It posed little direct threat to the home territories before 1778, even if some government supporters feared that rebellion, inspired by American example, might break out in Ireland, or even in London.[53] The Bourbon war, by contrast, was much more immediate. France, populous and powerful, was also proximate. Its great army was poised across the Channel – at its narrowest point only 21 miles wide. The threat of invasion, in 1778 and still more so in 1779, when a Franco–Spanish armada appeared off Plymouth, helped to galvanize the British people; public subscriptions were formed, which raised money to encourage recruitment into both the army and navy.

The commitment of many different people, unconnected with government, may have helped the British war effort, but that it was sustained right through to 1782–3 owed a great deal to a tried and tested system of state finance. In the 1690s, English taxation and public borrowing were revolutionized by the demands of a great war with Louis XIV and a new constitutional settlement; once the monarch started to work with Parliament, tax revenues became more reliable, enabling long-term debt to be secured. What John Brewer called the 'fiscal-military state' emerged in this critical period; it was to produce vast sums of money, by the standards of the time, to support Britain's eighteenth-century military and naval forces.[54] In the War of American Independence, Parliament agreed to the raising, on average, of £12 million a year in taxation. Much of this money serviced the interest in the long-term debt, which rose from £127 million in 1775 to £232 million in 1783. High levels of taxation caused much grumbling. Indeed, in the crisis years of 1779–80, when the war appeared to be going very badly, fears that the government's bloated revenues were being wasted led to a popular movement for retrenchment and parliamentary reform. In addition, as the war dragged on, the government found it necessary to offer higher rates of interest to secure loans; in 1779, Lord North lamented 'the very high terms that had been insisted upon by the monied people', and two years later was similarly regretful at having to borrow 'on such disadvantageous terms'.[55] Even so, the British state continued to be able to raise the large sums it needed to sustain the war effort, right through to 1782–3.

The contrast with France, Britain's principal European enemy, is instructive. The French economy was probably no less strong than the British, yet the British paid more per capita in taxation.[56] In part, the French state's inability to assemble sufficient money to support a long war was the result of the way vested interests had secured important tax exemptions. Certain provinces had won the privilege of not paying some taxes, while the nobility throughout France also enjoyed freedom from particular types of impost. The nobility, who dominated the benches of the Paris and provincial *parlements* that registered the king's edicts, stubbornly resisted reforming attempts by successive French finance ministers. Even so, the exempted were gradually compelled to contribute more by the introduction of wartime taxes that applied more generally.[57] Perhaps as important as noble and provincial privileges was France's demographic structure. It was less urbanized than Britain and its population more scattered, which meant that indirect taxes were often more difficult to assess and collect.[58] Nor should we forget that large numbers of French taxpayers were in financially difficult circumstances; if the French state had tried to raise taxes more aggressively it would probably have reduced consumption of taxed products and therefore have diminished the tax take. The problems involved in trying to increase tax revenues meant that borrowing appeared to be the only way to fund the French war effort. However, a limited tax base also meant that investors were reluctant to buy into France's public debt without the inducement of high rates of return. Necker raised the equivalent of about £21.7 million between 1777 and 1781, but mainly in the form of life annuities at 10 per cent interest – almost double the yield on British government consols in 1781 and 1782.[59] French public finances, already staggering under the burden of paying for the ruinously expensive Seven Years War, were creaking alarmingly by the last phase of the War of Independence, whereas the British government was still, despite all its troubles, able to provide a reliable funding stream to sustain its armed forces. In the final analysis, the deeper pockets of the British state meant that it was able to keep going for longer than its main European opponent. British successes in the last years of the war, and the shape of the final peace settlement, ultimately owed much to French fears of financial exhaustion. As George III had predicted in September 1780, 'this War like the last will prove one of Credit'.[60]

6

EPILOGUE

The loss of the American colonies was a profound blow to British pride. In the years immediately following the end of the war, many commentators – both at home and abroad –assumed that Britain, shorn of most of its mainland colonies, had descended into the ranks of the second- or even third-rate European powers. National confidence was sufficiently shaken for proposals for constitutional reform to be high on the agenda; established institutions appeared to have failed to prevent government mismanagement and military defeat. The reform campaigns that had emerged in the crisis years of the war – pressing for a cut in public expenditure, a reduction in government influence over the legislature and a redistribution of parliamentary seats – continued into the peace. In 1785, William Pitt the Younger, the king's chosen prime minister, who had served as Chancellor of the Exchequer in Shelburne's government, led the calls for parliamentary reform.

Many Britons harboured great resentment at what they saw as American treachery. When Shelburne and then Pitt attempted to persuade Parliament to give significant commercial concessions to the new United States, the proposal was roundly rejected. Parliamentarians – and probably large parts of the wider public too – favoured excluding the Americans from the closed trading system created by the Navigation Acts; Lord Sheffield's polemical work *Observations on the Commerce of the American States* (1783), which recommended treating the Americans as fully fledged foreigners, seems to have struck a chord. The public was broadly behind the alternative national strategy of forging stronger connections with continental Europe; the Anglo–French trade treaty of 1786 was one of the fruits of this strategy, and British trade with the Continent boomed in the decade after the end of the American conflict.[1] To a good number of Britons, political connections with the European powers appeared no less desirable. In the aftermath of the war, a reflective debate took place on Britain's diplomatic isolation, widely perceived to be a crucial cause of defeat across the Atlantic.[2] The country, a newspaper contribution argued, presented a lamentable image in Europe, 'without one ally in the world'.[3] The search for a new connection of substance, begun in the 1760s and intensified during the war itself, was given added urgency. Some historians have even identified a new caution in British imperial affairs. After having provoked the Americans with parliamentary assertions of the right to tax, no further attempt was made to raise money in the empire on the authority of the Westminster House of Commons.[4]

Yet Britain's defeat was not as catastrophic as it might have been, and national recovery came remarkably quickly. Politically, as Shelburne and Pitt discovered, it was not possible to resurrect the prewar Atlantic trading arrangements let alone some form of political connection, which is what Shelburne had wanted; at a governmental level, relations between Britain and the United States remained frosty for many years. But if we look in other areas, beyond formal political connections, we can see that essential facets of the old order were soon reconstructed.[5] Migration, one of the defining features of the British Atlantic World since the beginning of the seventeenth century, resumed as soon as the war ended. New directions of travel emerged; for the first time, significant numbers of Americans left home to establish themselves elsewhere in the Atlantic basin. But many of the old patterns revived. Ulster Protestants and Scottish Highlanders flocked across the Atlantic, much as they had done in the decades before the Revolution. Family correspondence that criss-crossed the ocean kept alive the idea of a transatlantic community.[6] So, too, did a largely shared culture – books and pamphlets published in London were reprinted in Philadelphia, and early American political prints were often the work of British-born engravers. Religious connections, especially between Protestant Dissenters in Britain and Ireland

and their denominational brothers and sisters in America, remained strong. Trade between Britain and the United States also picked up, and eventually eclipsed prewar levels. By the mid-1790s, with European markets closing as a result of the French Revolutionary Wars, British exports to mainland North America were stronger than ever. American loyalist refugees played a key part in consolidating and even expanding the remainder of the empire. The great loyalist migration to Canada gave it an Anglophone Protestant population that British governments had been trying to create since the conquest in 1760, while the British West Indies received other loyalist refugees. Some American exiles exerted an influence at still greater distances from their old home. Sierra Leone, in West Africa, was established as a haven for free blacks in 1787; five years later it became the new home for more than one thousand former slaves who had tried first to establish themselves in Nova Scotia and New Brunswick.[7] Loyalists even found their way to India.[8] More importantly, from the British state's point of view, an Asian empire emerged in the 1790s and early part of the nineteenth-century that compensated for the loss of America. If the War of Independence brought an end to the First British Empire, a second soon took its place.[9]

For the victorious allies, the future was less rosy. The once-mighty Dutch East India Company had lost territory and influence in Asia: already tottering before 1780, it was never to recover. The Republic itself was plunged into political chaos. The pro-British Orange regime, which Lord North's government had misguidedly imagined would be strengthened by the war, was fatally undermined. The chief beneficiaries were the pro-French Patriots, who took inspiration from British defeat in America to press for fundamental changes in the constitutional arrangements in the Republic. The political conflict soon degenerated into a civil war. In September 1786, troops loyal to the Prince of Orange clashed in Gelderland with paramilitary Free Corps associated with the radical wing of the Patriot movement, and the following spring Orangist soldiers were forced to flee by Free Corps near Utrecht. The humiliated prince was rescued only by Prussian military intervention, encouraged and supported by the British government. Britain benefited, at least in the short term, from the defeat of the pro-French Patriots, and, perhaps more importantly, by the acquisition of new allies in the form of the Dutch and the Prussians. But the Patriot movement was not eradicated, and the Prince of Orange's reliance on Prussian bayonets did not augur well for the future. When the French Revolution came, the old order in the Republic was again put under pressure. In January 1795, French troops overthrew the Orangist regime and placed their Patriot allies in charge of the new Batavian Republic.[10]

Spain's postwar experiences were less immediately painful. National finances recovered remarkably quickly, thanks largely to the resumption of bullion shipments from Central and South America.[11] The government had achieved many of the aims it set itself when it took Spain into the war in 1779. Frustratingly, Gibraltar was still in British hands, as was long-lost Jamaica; but Minorca had been recovered, and so had Florida. Spain, in other words, had succeeded in reversing its Seven Years War losses. But, in the longer term, Spanish support for the Americans may have been a mistake. In 1777, the Conde de Floridablanca, the Spanish secretary of state, worried that the independence of the United States 'would be the worst example to other colonies'[12] – a point British ministers had already been making to the Spanish and French governments ever since the American rebellion began. When Spain entered the war, its ministers were careful to do so as allies of France, not the United States. But such punctiliousness provided little protection from the contagion of insurrection. Spain's American empire looked to be going the same way as Britain's in the early 1780s, with revolts breaking out from New Grenada in the north to Chile in the south.[13] In 1781, a royal official in Venezuela was reporting on the 'vehement desire for independence' among Spanish Americans.[14] His solution, and the one pursued by the Spanish crown after the war, was federal restructuring of the empire. In 1787, King Carlos formally abolished the distinction between *crillos* (American Spaniards) and *peninsulares* (metropolitan Spaniards): both were now theoretically eligible for public office in the 'mother country'. The intention was clearly to forge a common identity across the empire. Various schemes of imperial federation were canvassed, but none was implemented. Spanish Americans were not for the most part so easily appeased. Comparisons were readily drawn between the Spanish American provinces and the 'English colonies' that had 'fought for their liberty'.[15] Incendiary language became more and more common amongst Spanish creoles.

To establish a link between the creation of the United States and Spanish American independence is by no means easy. Spanish government reforms provoked colonial rebellions in much the same way as British imperial changes did; there was an internal logic, in other words, to Spanish American rebellions, even if they took place at the same time as the British American uprising, and were inspired by similar causes. The Spanish colonies only broke away once the Bourbon monarchy collapsed in Spain itself in 1808; Argentina began the process two years later, and it was not until 1824 that the Peruvians finally overthrew Spanish authority. Even so, it seems reasonable to claim that the American Revolutionary War contributed to the process that finally destroyed Spanish dominion in Central and South America.[16]

Nor did intervention in the American war work out to French advantage in the longer term. Hopes of forging lasting commercial relations with the United States, of opening up Atlantic trade and destroying Britain's monopoly in the process, were not fulfilled. Even before the end of the war, the British were squeezing the French out; between 1781–3 and 1786–9, the value of French commerce with the United States fell by 72 per cent.[17] But if, in this sense, the French ministers secured less than they desired, in other respects they received far more than they had anticipated. Like Spain, France was an imperial power that aided and abetted colonial rebellion at some risk to itself. Vergennes had put aside such disturbing thoughts to concentrate on seizing the opportunity to humble the British and restore French power. In the immediate aftermath of Yorktown, his judgement appeared to be triumphantly vindicated. A few years later, the situation was less clear. The great revolt in Saint Domingue in 1791, when the slaves rose up and overthrew the white planters, can be seen as a consequence of the turmoil created throughout the Atlantic world by constitutional discussions of slavery and liberty, and the more practical manifestations of a new spirit in the wartime emancipation offered to North American slaves by first Dunmore and then Clinton.[18] The spark in Saint Domingue, one might reasonably counter, was provided not by the American rebellion but by events in metropolitan France, which was plunged into its own revolution from 1789. But the collapse of the old order in France can itself be seen as an outcome of the American Revolution.

This is not to endorse the judgement of an embittered American loyalist cleric who claimed in 1797 that the French Revolution was a 'gigantic offspring' of the American.[19] The old argument that French soldiers serving in America brought back revolutionary ideas of liberty has now been largely discredited. A good number of the officers who served in the rebel colonies were far from impressed by what they saw; some ended up as counter-revolutionaries in 1789.[20] Equally doubtful are the claims that common French soldiers were inspired to participate in the rural unrest that was an important part of the Revolution by contact with an American society where freehold ownership was the norm.[21] Many of the French veterans of the American war did indeed come from areas that were to experience serious peasant uprisings in 1789, but this correlation proves very little, as these were the poorest provinces of France, from which the French army disproportionately recruited its soldiers. In truth, the French rank-and-file was largely kept away from the civilian population in the United States; the chances of French soldiers gaining an appreciation of American land tenure systems were very limited indeed.[22]

France was not able to avoid the wind of change blowing across the Atlantic, but the case for a link between the American and French Revolutions rests more on financial crisis than on ideological transmission.[23] Recent scholarship questions the scale of France's wartime debt, and suggests that the real financial damage was done either earlier – in the Seven Years War – or later, during the 1780s, when French controller-generals tried to bolster dented confidence by extravagant new spending projects.[24] But if Necker's heavy borrowing during the War of Independence was certainly not the only cause of France's financial woes, it contributed mightily to the crisis that overwhelmed the French monarchy in the late 1780s. Turgot, who lost the debate over whether to support the Americans in 1776, had surely been right to point to the need for a prolonged period of peace for France to recover from the financial strains created by the

Seven Years War. The American conflict provided exactly the opposite. Money was poured into naval expansion, but, given the resistance of vested interests to large increases in domestic taxation, most of the funding had to come from borrowing. As the French state's creditworthiness was questionable, loans could be secured only by offering very high rates of interest. France was on the slippery slope to financial disaster by 1783: postwar spending merely accelerated the rate of descent.

The United States, on the face of it, emerged from the war having achieved its goals. Independence from the British crown had been secured, and without turning the American states into clients of France. But success came with a large price tag attached. The war in the South had been particularly destructive. To recapitalize a severely damaged economy – to rebuild shipyards and farms, to replace livestock and produce harvests on a desolated land – took a long time. In 1786, Washington optimistically claimed that it was 'wonderful to see how soon the ravages of war are repaired', but this was in a letter to a French correspondent and was probably designed to create a favourable impression.[25] Exports from the southern states were still only worth half their prewar value in the early 1790s. According to one modern estimate, per capita income across the new United States fell by 46 per cent between 1774 and 1790. If true, that would put the decline on a par with what occurred during the Great Depression of 1929–33.[26]

The Revolution, furthermore, had done some damage to America's credentials as a land of liberty. The loyalists had been subjected to draconian confiscations, which helped to sour relations between the United States and the British government for years to come. In the end, compensation for their losses was delivered not by the American governments, as was envisaged in the peace treaty, but by the British Parliament, which eventually paid out more than £3 million to nearly 2,300 claimants following a lengthy investigation by a commission of enquiry.[27] Worst still, so far as America's reputation was concerned, the awkward issue of slavery had been highlighted by revolutionary rhetoric; the distance between what the white settlers claimed as their rights, and the rights that most of them were willing to allow to their enslaved labourers, exposed the rebels to accusations of hypocrisy. Even during the war, British government supporters had wasted no time in pointing out American inconsistency. In the aftermath of the conflict, when the London government was keen to restore its own image and even more keen to do down the new republic, and the religiously committed were keen to regain God's favour, British commentators made much of the movement to abolish the slave trade that had begun in their country in 1783, and readily drew a contrast with the United States, where slavery not only remained a vital institution but became enshrined in the new constitution eventually agreed in 1787.[28]

That constitution emerged only after a period of considerable political turbulence that further weakened the United States. The Articles of Confederation, the first attempt to define the relationship between the states and the central government, tilted so heavily in favour of the states that Congress was unable to raise the money required to fight the war. Yet reaching agreement on a better constitutional arrangement proved very difficult. Those opposed to a beefed-up federal government argued, with some justice, that granting tax-raising powers to Congress would be a betrayal of the Revolution, the fundamental purpose of which had been to repel the attempts of another strong central body – the Westminster Parliament – to encroach on the autonomy of the different colonies. Americans had come together to defend local rights to self-government; now they were being asked to give up those rights to a strengthened central authority. Advocates of a federal government maintained, with equal justice, that the loose arrangements of the Articles of Confederation simply did not work; they had undermined the war effort and were now preventing the United States from cutting any figure on the world stage. Unable to fund a substantial peacetime army, the Americans could not even compel the British to evacuate their remaining posts in the western lands granted to the United States in 1783. A few overseas enthusiasts for the American Revolution, like Richard Price in Britain, held up the new republic as a model for the world.[29] However, most foreign observers were less impressed. European statesmen questioned whether the Americans could sustain their independence; some even predicted that they would be forced into some form of new subservience to the British state.

The adoption of the Federal Constitution in 1787 did not settle the vexed issue of central authority versus states' rights. Nor did it complete the process, begun at Independence, of building an American nation. Sectional and provincial loyalties remained very strong. Sometimes these local attachments could live happily side-by-side with a sense of wider American-ness. But often state and regional loyalties acted as a powerful alternative allegiance; revealingly, it was not until after the Civil War of 1861–5 that the term the United States came to be widely used as a singular rather than plural form. Nor did America rapidly become the major figure on the world stage that some of the new republic's founders had hoped to see. The United States became an international force only once it industrialized in the second half of the nineteenth century; arguably, it exerted a significant global influence only from the early twentieth century.

In the decades following the end of the War of Independence, America was in a very much weaker position. Indeed, though political independence had been secured, and Americans were free to devote their energies to expansion on their own continent, they remained, in many senses, in a dependent relationship with Britain. True, free from British commercial legislative restrictions, they were able to forge new trading connections with parts of the world hitherto closed to them, or at least difficult to access. American commerce with northern Europe and the non-British West Indies increased markedly in the 1780s; by 1790–2, these two regions between them accounted for 40 per cent of American exports. But in the same years, Britain and Ireland remained the biggest market for American products, taking 31 per cent of all goods dispatched abroad from the United States. In the 1790s, furthermore, traditional American exports such as tobacco, cereal crops, timber and fish were supplemented by a new staple – cotton – which sustained the textile mills of Lancashire and the Clyde Valley of south-western Scotland. British manufactured goods, particularly metal-ware and textiles, continued to dominate American markets. The domestic industries that had sprung up while British imports were prohibited struggled to survive the great tidal wave of cheap British manufactures that engulfed the postwar United States. In economic terms, in other words, America remained trapped in an essentially colonial relationship with the old mother country.

The War of American Independence, then, defies the neat stereotypes of losers and winners that are usually imposed upon armed conflicts. The nominal loser – Britain –looked in bad shape immediately the conflict closed, but large numbers of its people soon began to appreciate that they had retained many of the benefits of the old imperial relationship with the American colonies but were no longer burdened by the costs. Britain's wider empire, far from beginning a slow but inexorable decline, was within a few years to become larger than ever before. The supposed winners, by contrast, were to experience much less fortunate consequences over the following decades. Remarkably, the French and Dutch old regimes both imploded, at least partly due to the impact – financially in the first case, politically in the second – of their states' involvement in the war. The Spanish, for their part, regained territory in the short term, but then went on to lose most of their American empire, a longer-term outcome that owed at least something to the influence of the successful revolt of 13 of Britain's North American colonies. Even the United States cannot be seen as a clear and unambiguous victor. Political independence was not to be matched by economic and cultural independence for many years.

Notes

Introduction

1 Robert J. Allison, *The American Revolution: A Concise History* (New York, 2011).

2 Stephen Conway, *The War of American Independence, 1775–1783* (London, 1995) and *The British Isles and the War of American Independence* (Oxford, 2000).

3 See, for example, Eliga Gould, 'American Independence and Britain's Counter-Revolution', *Past & Present*, no. 154 (1997), pp. 107–41; Hannah Smith, 'The Idea of a Protestant Monarchy in Britain, 1714–1760', *Past & Present*, no. 185 (2004), pp. 91–118; Jeremy Black, *The Continental Commitment: Britain, Hanover, and Interventionism, 1714–1793* (London, 2005); Andrew C. Thompson, *Britain, Hanover, and the Protestant Interest, 1688–1756* (Woodbridge, 2006); Nick Harding, *Hanover and the British Empire, 1700–1837* (Woodbridge, 2007); Brendan Simms, *Three Victories and a Defeat: The Rise and Fall of the First British Empire, 1714–1783* (London, 2007); Brendan Simms and Torsten Riotte (eds), *The Hanoverian Dimension in British History, 1714–1837* (Cambridge, 2007); Tony Claydon, *Europe and the Making of England, 1660–1760* (Cambridge, 2007); Marie Peters, 'Early Hanoverian Consciousness: Empire or Europe?', *English Historical Review*, cxxii (2007), pp. 632–68. My own contribution to this Europeanization of British history appeared as *Britain, Ireland, and Continental Europe in the Eighteenth Century: Similarities, Connections, Identities* (Oxford, 2011).

4 For the theoretical aspects of the 'spatial turn', see, for example, Barney Warf and Santa Arias (eds), *The Spatial Turn: Interdisciplinary Perspectives* (London, 2008).

5 The Contractor State Group, as it is now known, has published four volumes of essays so far: H.V. Bowen and A. González Enciso (eds) *Mobilising Resources for War: Britain and Spain at Work during the Early Modern Period* (Pamplona, 2006); Rafael Torres Sánchez (ed.),

War, State, and Development: Fiscal-Military States in the Eighteenth Century (Pamplona, 2007); Rafael Torres Sánchez and Stephen Conway (eds), *The Spending of States: Military Expenditure during the Long Eighteenth Century: Patterns, Organization, and Consequences, 1650–1815* (Saarbrücken, 2011); and Richard Harding and Sergio Solbes Ferri (eds), *The Contractor State and Its Implications, 1659–1815* (Las Palmas de Gran Canaria, 2012).

6   For American studies that concentrate almost exclusively on the American aspects of the war, see, for example, Willard M. Wallace, *Appeal to Arms: A Military History of the American Revolution* (New York, 1951); Christopher Ward, *The War of the Revolution*, ed. John R. Alden (2 vols, New York, 1952); Howard Peckham, *The War for Independence: A Military History* (Chicago, 1958); John R. Alden, *A History of the American Revolution* (London, 1969); Don Higginbotham, *The War of American Independence: Military Attitudes, Policies, and Practice, 1763–1789* (New York, 1971); Marshall Smelser, *The Winning of Independence* (New York, 1973); Robert Middlekauff, *The Glorious Cause: The American Revolution, 1763–1789* (New York, 1982); Harry M. Ward, *The American Revolution: Nationhood Achieved, 1763–1788* (New York, 1995); John Ferling, *Almost A Miracle: The American Victory in the War of Independence* (New York, 2007).

7   See, for example, Eric Robson, *The American Revolution in its Political and Military Aspects, 1763–1783* (London, 1955); Christopher Hibbert, *Redcoats and Rebels: The War for America, 1770–1781* (London, 1990); Jeremy Black, *War for America; The Fight for Independence, 1775–1783* (Stroud, 1991); Richard Middleton, *The War of American Independence, 1775–1783* (London, 2012).

8   Principally Piers Mackesy, *The War for America, 1775–1783* (London, 1964). See also N.A.M. Rodger, *The Insatiable Earl: A Life of John Montagu, 4th Earl of Sandwich* (London, 1993), Chapters 13–15; P.J. Marshall, *The Making and Unmaking of Empires: Britain, India, and America, c.1750–1783* (Oxford, 2005), Chapter 11; and Donald Stoker, Kenneth J. Hagen and Michael T. McMaster (eds), *Strategy in the American War of Independence: A Global Approach* (London, 2010).

9   Mackesy's *War for America* essentially adopts the perspective of the British ministers who were conducting the war; he is particularly positive about the role of Lord George Germain, who is presented rather more unflatteringly in other studies.

10   William Duane (ed.), *Extracts from the Diary of Christopher Marshall* (Albany, NY, 1877), p. 277.

11   See Stephen Conway, 'From Fellow-Nationals to Foreigners: British Perceptions of the Americans, circa 1739–1783', *William & Mary Quarterly*, 3rd series, lix (2002), pp. 65–100.

12 See, for example, James E. Bradley, 'The British Public and the American Revolution: Ideology, Interest, and Opinion', in H.T. Dickinson (ed.), *Britain and the American Revolution* (London, 1998), pp. 124–54; Eliga H. Gould, *The Persistence of Empire: British Political Culture in the Age of the American Revolution* (Chapel Hill, 2000), Chapter 5.

13 Charles F. Adams (ed.), *The Works of John Adams* (10 vols, Boston, 1850–6), x. pp. 63, 87.

14 For the estimate of one fifth, see Paul H. Smith, 'The American Loyalists: Notes on their Organization and Numerical Strength', *William & Mary Quarterly*, 3rd series, xxv (1968), pp. 259–77.

15 See Wayne E. Lee, *Barbarians and Brothers: Anglo–American Warfare, 1500–1865* (Oxford, 2011).

16 For more on this aspect of the struggle, a new book by Holger Hoock, of the University of Pittsburgh, provisionally entitled *The Scars of Independence*, is eagerly awaited.

Chapter One

1 For examples of histories of the Revolution starting in the 1760s, see Robert Middlekauff, *The Glorious Cause: The American Revolution, 1763–1789* (New York, 1982); R.W. Tucker and D.C. Hendrickson, *The Fall of the First British Empire: Origins of the War of American Independence* (Baltimore, 1982); Harry M. Ward, *The American Revolution: Nationhood Achieved, 1763–1788* (New York, 1995); Samuel B. Griffiths, *The War of American Independence: from 1760 to the Surrender at Yorktown* (Urbana, IL, 2002).

2 See, for example, Staughton Lynd, 'Who Should Rule at Home? Dutchess County, New York, in the American Revolution', *William & Mary Quarterly*, 3rd series, xviii (1961), pp. 330–59; Rowland Berthoff and John M. Murrin, 'Feudalism, Communalism, and the Yeoman Freeholder: The American Revolution Considered as a Social Accident', in Stephen G. Kurtz and James H. Hutson (eds), *Essays on the American Revolution* (Chapel Hill, 1973), pp. 256–88; Gary B. Nash, *The Urban Crucible: The Northern Seaports and the Origins of the American Revolution* (Cambridge, MA, 1979); Benjamin L. Carp, *Rebels Rising: Cities and the American Revolution* (New York, 2007).

3 See, for example, Jon Butler, *Becoming America: The Revolution before 1776* (Cambridge, MA, 2000), especially Chapter 1.

4 See, for example, Rhys Isaac, 'Evangelical Revolt: The Nature of the Baptists' Challenge to the Traditional Order in Virginia, 1765 to 1776', *William & Mary Quarterly*, 3rd series, xxxi (1974), pp. 345–68; Patricia

U. Bonomi, *Under the Cope of Heaven: Religion, Society, and Politics in Colonial America* (rev ed., New York, 2003).

5   Merrill Jensen (ed.), *English Historical Documents*, ix. *American Colonial Documents to 1776* (London, 1969), p. 716. For the colonists' relationship with the Crown, see Brendan McConville, *The King's Three Faces: The Rise and Fall of Royal America, 1688–1776* (Chapel Hill, 2006).

6   For a recent account of the origins of American resistance to parliamentary authority, see Craig B. Yirush, *Settlers, Liberty, and Empire: The Roots of Early American Political Theory, 1675–1775* (Cambridge, 2011).

7   Quoted in Robert M. Bliss, *Revolution and Empire: English Politics and the American Colonies in the Seventeenth Century* (Manchester, 1990), p. 19.

8   Ibid., pp. 42–3. See also W.A. Speck, 'The International and Imperial Context', in Jack P. Greene and J.R. Pole (eds), *Colonial British America: Essays in the New History of the Early Modern Era* (Baltimore, 1984), pp. 384–407, for a helpful periodization of imperial relations in the seventeenth and eighteenth centuries.

9   See Mary Lou Lustig, *The Imperial Executive in America: Sir Edmund Andros, 1637–1714* (Cranbury, NJ, 2002).

10   James A. Henretta, *'Salutary Neglect': Colonial Administration under the Duke of Newcastle* (Princeton, 1972); Jack P. Greene, *Peripheries and Center: Constitutional Development in the Extended Polities of the British Empire and the United States, 1607–1788* (Athens, GA, 1986), pp. 45–7.

11   See Jack P. Greene, 'An Uneasy Connection: An Analysis of the Preconditions of the American Revolution', in Kurtz and Hutson (eds), *Essays on the American Revolution*, pp. 32–80.

12   Robert C. Newbold, *The Albany Congress and Plan of Union of 1754* (New York, 1955). For a modern account, see Timothy J. Shannon, *Indians and Colonists at the Crossroads of Empire: The Albany Congress of 1754* (Ithaca, NY, 2000).

13   See, for example, Alan Rogers, *Empire and Liberty: American Resistance to British Authority, 1755–1763* (Berkeley, 1974), Chapter 6; Douglas Edward Leach, *Roots of Conflict: British Armed Forces and Colonial Americans, 1677–1763* (Chapel Hill, 1986), Chapter 6.

14   See Fred Anderson, *Crucible of War: The Seven Years' War and the Fate of Empire in British North America, 1754–1766* (New York, 2000), especially pp. 286–8 and pp. 412–14.

15   See P.J. Marshall, *The Making and Unmaking of Empires: Britain, India, and America, c.1750–1783* (Oxford, 2005), especially pp. 95–7.

16   Anderson, *Crucible of War*, p. 227.

17   Malcolm Freiberg (ed.), *Journals of the House of Representatives of Massachusetts*, xxxvii, Part i, *1760–1761* (Boston, 1965), p. 115.

18   See Fred Anderson, *A People's Army: Massachusetts Soldiers and Society in the Seven Years' War* (Chapel Hill, 1984), Chapter 2.

19   Nathan O. Hatch, 'The Origins of Civil Millennialism in America: New England Clergymen, War with France, and the Revolution', *William & Mary Quarterly*, 3rd series, xxxi (1974), pp. 407–30.

20   See, for example, University Library, Nottingham, Galway Collection, Monckton Papers, Ga M 23, 38, 62, letters to Robert Monckton from James Cuninghame, 24 June 1758, Isaac Barré, 9 April 1759 and Jeffrey Amherst, 24 July 1760; Centre for Kentish Studies, Maidstone, Amherst Papers, U 1350 C 84/2 Barré to William Amherst, 18 April 1758, and O 38/6, Jeffrey Amherst to Lord Barrington, 19 May 1760.

21   Edmund S. Morgan (ed.), *Prologue to Revolution: Documents on the Stamp Act Crisis, 1764–1766* (New York, 1959), p. 62.

22   See P.J. Marshall, 'The Thirteen Colonies and the Seven Years' War: the View from London', in Julie Flavell and Stephen Conway (eds), *Britain and America Go to War: The Impact of War and Warfare in Anglo–America, 1754–1815* (Gainesville, FL, 2004), pp. 82–4.

23   For a recent restatement of this old argument, see Linda Colley, *Britons: Forging the Nation, 1707–1837* (New Haven, 1992), p. 135.

24   Stephen Conway, *War, State, and Society in Mid-Eighteenth-Century Britain and Ireland* (Oxford, 2006), pp. 237–8.

25   Anthony Pagden, *Lords of All the World: Ideologies of Empire in Spain, Britain, and France, c.1500–c.1800* (New Haven, 1995), especially pp. 103–7; Bob Harris, '"American Idols": Empire, War, and the Middling Ranks in Mid-Eighteenth-Century Britain', *Past & Present*, no. 105 (1996), pp. 128–9.

26   Haines Hill, Berkshire, Colleton, Garth, and Godsal Family Papers, Box 23, transcripts of the Letter–books of Charles Garth, Garth to the Committee of Correspondence of the South Carolina assembly, 21 January 1764.

27   See John L. Bullion, '"The Ten Thousand in America": More Light on the Decision on the American Army, 1762–1763', *William & Mary Quarterly*, 3rd series, xliii (1986), pp. 646–57.

28   See especially Charles Ivar McGrath, *Ireland and the British Empire, 1688–1770* (London, 2012), Chapter 6.

29   See P.D.G. Thomas, *British Politics and the Stamp Act Crisis: The First Phase of the American Revolution, 1763–1767* (Oxford, 1975); John L. Bullion, *A Great and Necessary Measure: George Grenville and the Genesis of the Stamp Act, 1763–1765* (Princeton, 1982); Philip Lawson, *George Grenville: A Political Life* (Oxford, 1984).

30   For the consultation with colonial agents, see Morgan (ed.), *Prologue to Revolution*, pp. 27–8, 33–4.

31 P.D.G. Thomas (ed.), 'The Parliamentary Diaries of Nathaniel Ryder, 1764–7', Royal Historical Society, *Camden Miscellany*, xxiii (Camden 4th series, vii, London, 1969), p. 234.

32 Huntington Library, San Marino, California, Stowe Collection, Grenville Papers, Letter–book of Correspondence between Thomas Whately and John Temple, STG Box 13 (6), fos. 6–7.

33 Quoted in Stephen Conway, 'Britain and the Revolutionary Crisis, 1763–1791', in P.J. Marshall (ed.), *The Oxford History of the British Empire*, ii. *The Eighteenth Century* (Oxford, 1998), p. 328.

34 Morgan (ed.), *Prologue to Revolution*, p. 52.

35 Ibid., pp. 9, 14, 15, 17, 51, 56 and 61.

36 Thomas Whately, *The Regulations Lately Made concerning the Colonies and the Taxes Imposed on them Considered* (London, 1765); William Knox, *The Claim of the Colonies to an Exemption from Internal Taxes Imposed by Authority of Parliament, Examined* (London, 1765); Soame Jenyns, *The Objections to the Taxation of Our American Colonies by the Legislature of Great Britain briefly Consider'd* (London, 1765).

37 See Daniel Dulany, *Considerations on the Propriety of Imposing Taxes in the British Colonies, for the Purpose of Raising a Revenue, by Act of Parliament* (Annapolis, MD, 1765).

38 Jensen (ed.), *English Historical Documents*, ix. p. 678.

39 British Library (BL), London, Newcastle Papers, Add. MS 32, 973, fo. 343, Newcastle to the Archbishop of Canterbury, 2 February 1766 (copy).

40 See Paul Langford, 'The Rockingham Whigs and America, 1767–1773', in Anne Whiteman, J.S. Bromley and P.G. M. Dickson (eds), *Statesmen, Scholars, and Merchants: Essays in Eighteenth-Century History Presented to Dame Lucy Sutherland* (Oxford, 1973), p. 147.

41 Chatham's position was widely misunderstood; he was nowhere near as conciliatory as Americans imagined: see Thomas, *British Politics and the Stamp Act Crisis*, p. 292; and Marie Peters, 'The Myth of William Pitt, Earl of Chatham, Great Imperialist Part II: Chatham and Imperial Reorganization, 1763–78', *Journal of Imperial and Commonwealth History*, xxii (1994), pp. 397–9.

42 See P.D.G. Thomas, *The Townshend Duties Crisis: The Second Phase of the American Revolution, 1767–1773* (Oxford, 1987).

43 [John Dickinson,] *Letters from a Farmer in Pennsylvania* (Philadelphia, 1768), Letter III.

44 Morgan (ed.): *Prologue to Revolution*, pp. 145, 146.

45 See Richard Archer, *As If an Enemy's Country: The British Occupation of Boston and the Origins of the American Revolution* (Oxford, 2010), Chapters 10–11.

46 Leonard W. Labaree et al (eds), *The Papers of Benjamin Franklin* (38 vols to date, New Haven, 1959–), xviii. p. 3.

47 BL, Egerton MS 246, p. 6, parliamentary diary of Henry Cavendish, 26 April 1773.

48 Jensen (ed.), *English Historical Documents*, ix. p. 776.

49 For a recent account, see Benjamin L. Carp, *Defiance of the Patriots: The Boston Tea Party and the Making of America* (New Haven, 2010).

50 William Cobbett and John Wright (eds), *The Parliamentary History of England* (36 vols, London, 1806–20), xvii. p. 1164 (14 March 1774).

51 See Julie Flavell, 'British Perceptions of New England and the Decision for a Coercive Colonial Policy, 1774–1775', in Flavell and Conway (eds), *Britain and America Go to War*, pp. 95–115.

52 See Stephen Conway, 'The Consequences of the Conquest: Quebec and British Politics, 1760–1774', in Phillip Buckner and John G. Reid (eds), *Revisiting 1759: The Conquest of Canada in Historical Perspective* (Toronto, 2012), pp. 141–65.

53 W. Bernard Peach and D.O. Thomas (eds), *The Correspondence of Richard Price* (3 vols, Durham, NC, 1983–94), i. p. 189.

54 K.G. Davies (ed.), *Documents of the American Revolution, 1770–1783: Colonial Office Series* (21 vols, Shannon, 1972–81), viii. p. 186.

55 Jensen (ed.), *English Historical Documents*, ix. pp. 813–16.

56 See T.H. Breen, 'Where Have All the People Gone? Reflections on Popular Political Mobilization on the Eve of American Independence', in Roger Chickering and Stig Förster (eds), *War in an Age of Revolution, 1775–1815* (Cambridge, 2010), pp. 263–84.

57 Cobbett and Wright (eds), *Parliamentary History of England*, xviii. p. 97.

58 See, for example, R.C. Simmons and P.D.G. Thomas (eds), *Proceedings and Debates of the British Parliaments respecting North America, 1754–1783* (6 vols to date, Millward, NY, 1982–), ii. pp. 127, 340; iv. pp. 64, 76, 172; v. pp. 238, 295, for speeches in debates in the Lords and Commons in 1766, 1774 and 1775.

59 Ibid., ii. p. 282; iv. p. 209.

60 See Daniel A. Baugh, 'Maritime Strength and Atlantic Commerce: The Uses of "a grand marine empire"', in Lawrence Stone (ed.), *An Imperial State at War: Britain from 1689 to 1815* (London, 1994), pp. 185–223.

61 Ted Ruddock (ed.), *Travels in the Colonies in 1773–1775* (Athens, GA, 1993), p. 75.

62 Huntington Library, HM 818, Robert Honyman's Journal, p. 82.

63 See G.R. Barnes and J.H. Owen (eds), *The Private Papers of John, Earl of Sandwich* (4 vols, London, 1932–8), i. pp. 61–2, John Pitcairn to Sandwich, 4 March 1775.

64 Dartmouth to Gage, 27 January 1775, Davies (ed.), *Documents of the American Revolution*, ix. pp. 37–41.

65 Huntington Library, HM 66, 'Richard Pope's Book', 1775–7, p. 12.
66 City Archives, Sheffield, Rockingham MSS, R 150–2, Anon. to Dr Rogers, 23 April 1775.
67 Alnwick Castle, Northumberland, Percy Family Papers, vol L, Pt. A, fo. 53, Percy to Gen. Edward Harvey, 20 April 1775.

Chapter Two

1   Huntington Library, San Marino, CA, Loudoun Papers, LO 6483, James Abercrombie to Lord Loudoun, 4 May 1775.
2   See the account sent to their 'Friends and Fellow-Subjects' in Britain by the Massachusetts Provincial Congress, 26 April 1775, in Merrill Jensen (ed.), *English Historical Documents*, ix. *American Colonial Documents to 1776* (London, 1969), pp. 828–9. See also Troy Bickham, *Making Headlines: The American Revolution as Seen Through the British Press* (DeKalb, IL, 2009), pp. 71–2.
3   Centre for Kentish Studies, Maidstone, Amherst Papers, U 1350 O80/13, James Abercrombie to Lord Amherst, 20 June 1775.
4   City Archives, Sheffield, Spencer Stanhope of Cannon Hall Muniments, 60542/8, Francis Bushill Sill to John Spencer, 6 July 1775.
5   The National Archives of the United Kingdom (TNA), Kew, Colonial Office Papers, CO 5/92, fo. 187.
6   J.C. Fitzpatrick (ed.), *The Writings of George Washington* (39 vols, Washington, DC, 1931–44), iii. pp. 450–1.
7   Ballindalloch Castle, Grantown on Spey, Macpherson Grant Papers, Letter-book, Grant to Edward Harvey, 10 August 1775.
8   See, for example, William L. Clements Library, Ann Arbor, MI, Clinton Papers, James Robertson to Clinton, 13 January 1776. Robertson went on to be an advocate of much milder methods; that even he should recommend threatening to 'set free' the slaves and 'let loose' the Indians is a sign of his desperation.
9   Jensen (ed.), *English Historical Documents*, ix. p. 841.
10 Ibid., pp. 850–1.
11 For Barrington, see Shute Barrington, *The Political Life of William Wildman, Viscount Barrington* (London, 1814). See also the views of the adjutant-general, TNA, War Office Papers, WO 3/5, p. 37, and of a captain in the Boston garrison, Stephen Rumbold Lushington (ed.), *The Life and Services of General Lord Harris GCB, during his Campaigns in America, the West Indies, and India* (London, 1840), pp. 58–9.
12 K.G. Davies (ed.), *Documents of the American Revolution, 1770–1783: Colonial Office Series* (21 vols, Shannon, 1972–81), xi. p. 97.

13 British Library (BL), London, Martin Papers, Add. MS 41,361, fo. 289, Josiah Martin to Samuel Martin, 9 September 1775.

14 Longleat House, Wiltshire, Thynne Papers, Bath MSS, Official Correspondence, E5 B1, parcel N-Y, Rochford to Viscount Weymouth, 28 November 1775.

15 Staffordshire Record Office, Stafford, Dartmouth MSS, D(W) 1778/II/1523.

16 The debate within the French government is described in Jonathan R. Dull, *A Diplomatic History of the American Revolution* (New Haven, 1985), Chapter 7.

17 William L. Clements Library, Miscellaneous MSS (unbound), Montgomery to Perkins Magra, 2 July 1775.

18 See, for example, 'Journal of Ensign Nathaniel Morgan', *Connecticut Historical Society Collections*, vii (1899), p. 105; Richard B. Morris (ed.), *John Jay: The Making of a Revolutionary* (New York, 1975), p. 181.

19 See, for example, 'The Journal of William Humphrey', in Nathaniel N. Shipton and David Swain (eds), *Rhode Islanders Record of the Revolution* (Providence, 1984), p. 41.

20 Jensen (ed.), *English Historical Documents*, ix. p. 864.

21 'Lee Papers', *New-York Historical Society Collections*, v (1872), p. 18.

22 See John Shy, *A People Numerous and Armed: Reflections on the Military Struggle for American Independence* (New York, 1976), Chapter 6. For a recent reappraisal of the role of the militia, see Matthew C. Ward, 'The American Militias: "The Garnish of a Table"?', in Roger Chickering and Stig Förster (eds), *War in an Age of Revolution, 1775–1815* (Cambridge, 2010), pp. 159–75.

23 R.A. Bowler, *Logistics and the Failure of the British Army in North America* (Princeton, 1975), Chapters 3–4.

24 Public Record Office of Northern Ireland, Belfast, Hart Papers, D 3077/B/1/2, George Vaughan Hart to his father, 7 July 1776.

25 'Lee Papers', *New-York Historical Society Collections*, v (1872), p. 93.

26 BL, Haldimand Papers, Add. MS 21,680, fo. 122, Francis Hutcheson to Frederick Haldimand, 10 July 1776.

27 TNA, Loyalist Claims Commission, Audit Office Papers, AO 12/5, fo. 35.

28 Jensen (ed.), *English Historical Documents*, ix. p. 878.

29 See, for example, David Armitage, 'The Declaration of Independence and International Law', *William & Mary Quarterly*, 3rd series, lix (2002), pp. 39–64; Norman A. Graebner, Richard Dean Burns and Joseph M. Siracusa, *Foreign Affairs and the Founding Fathers: From Confederation to Constitution, 1776–1787* (Santa Barbara, CA, 2011), Chapter 1.

30 University Library, Nottingham, Mellish of Hodsock MSS, Me 171-110/4, Clinton to Charles Mellish, 25 September 1776.

31 William L. Clements Library, Clinton Papers, Howe to Clinton, 12 April 1776.

32 Leonard W. Labaree et al (eds), *The Papers of Benjamin Franklin* (38 vols to date, New Haven, 1959–), xxii. p. 575.

33 Somerset Record Office, Taunton, Strachey MSS, DD/SH, C.1165, box 34, draft of Strachey to — [26 August 1776].

34 Labaree et al (eds) *Franklin Papers*, xxii. pp. 604–5. For Adams's view, see Robert J. Taylor et al. (eds), *Papers of John Adams* (16 vols to date, Cambridge, MA, 1977–), v. p. 20.

35 Huntington Library, HM 615, Order-book of General Howe's army, After Orders, 13 September 1776.

36 See Ira D. Gruber, *The Howe Brothers and the American Revolution* (New York, 1972), especially p. 363.

37 Huntington Library, HM 39953, Israel Putnam's Orders, 14 December 1776.

38 Public Library, Boston, MA, Stanley Letters, MS Am. 228.4, Thomas Stanley to —, 23 December 1776.

39 W.E. Harcourt (ed.), *The Harcourt Papers* (14 vols, Oxford, 1880–1905), xi. p. 180, William Harcourt to Viscount Nuneham, 19 December 1776.

40 G.H. Ryden (ed.), *Letters to and from Caesar Rodney* (Philadelphia, 1933), p. 152.

41 New-York Historical Society, New York City, Order-book of the 17th Foot.

42 National Army Museum, Chelsea, Maitland Papers, 7902-12-47, Alexander Maitland to his father, 21 December 1776.

43 See David Hackett Fischer, *Washington's Crossing* (New York, 2004), for a vivid account of Washington's counterattack.

44 Fitzpatrick (ed.), *Writings of Washington*, vi. p. 398.

45 Centre for Kentish Studies, Amherst Papers, U 1350 O79/14, Robertson to Amherst, 7 January 1777.

46 Huntington Library, Loudoun Papers, LO 6556, David Cuninghame to Lord Loudoun, 2 May 1777.

47 National Archives of Scotland, Edinburgh, Gilchrist of Ospisdale Muniments, GD 153, box 1, bundle 4, William Sutherland to Dugald Gilchrist, 30 May 1777.

48 Ballindalloch Castle, Macpherson Grant Papers, bundle 2, Letter-book, Grant to —, 15 January 1777.

49 Bedfordshire Record Office, Bedford, Lucas of Wrest Park Collection, Robinson Papers, L 29/214, memo. 13 January 1777.

50 See, for example, 'Bamford's Diary: The Revolutionary Diary of a British Officer', *Maryland Historical Magazine*, xxvii (1932), p. 312.

51 Davies (ed.), *Documents of the American Revolution*, xii. pp. 265, 268.

52   Ibid., xiv. p. 66.

53   Edward Barrington de Fonblanque, *Political and Military Episodes in the Latter Half of the Eighteenth Century, derived from the Life and Correspondence of The Right Hon. John Burgoyne, General, Statesman, Dramatist* (London, 1876), pp. 232–3. For Knox on D'Oyly, see 'Knox MSS' in Historical Manuscripts Commission, *Report on Manuscripts in Various Collections* (8 vols., London, 1901–13), vi. p. 277.

54   On this episode, see Piers Mackesy, *The Coward of Minden: The Affair of Lord George Sackville* (London, 1979).

55   Library of Congress, Washington, DC, Miscellaneous Collections, Richard Fitzpatrick Papers, Fitzpatrick to his brother, 5 July 1777.

56   For conciliatory and hardline attitudes in the British military, see Stephen Conway, 'To Subdue America: British Army Officers and the Conduct of the Revolutionary War', *William & Mary Quarterly*, 3rd series, xliii (1986), pp. 381–407.

57   Jeanette D. Black and William Greene Roelker (eds), *A Rhode Island Chaplain in the Revolution* (Port Washington, NY, 1972), p. 53.

58   For an instance of Schuyler's negativity, see 'The Heath Papers', *Massachusetts Historical Society Collections*, 7th series, iv (1904), p. 135, Schuyler to William Heath, 28 July 1777.

59   S. Sydney Bradford (ed.), 'Lord Francis Napier's Journal', *Maryland Historical Magazine*, lvii (1962), pp. 324–5.

60   Sydney Jackman (ed.), *With Burgoyne from Quebec* (Toronto, 1963), p. 175.

61   William L. Clements Library, Clinton Papers, Vaughan to [Clinton], 26 October 1777.

62   National Library of Ireland, Dublin, Shannon Papers, MS 13,301.

63   Huntington Library, HM 25800, North to Lord Howe, 28 October 1777.

64   Edward H. Tatum (ed.), *The American Journal of Ambrose Serle* (San Marino, CA, 1940), p. 263.

65   Huntington Library, HM 20932, John Mervin Nooth to Henry Nooth, 22 May 1778.

66   'Journal of Oliver Boardman', *Connecticut Historical Society Collections*, vii (1899), p. 235.

67   See BL, Auckland Papers, Add. MS 34,420, fo. 352, for the subsequent recollection of William Knox, who claimed to have suggested the approach to the French.

Chapter Three

1   Germain's thinking on this issue is set out in a letter to Clinton: The National Archives of the United Kingdom (TNA), Kew, Colonial Office Papers, CO 5/96, fo. 25.

2   H.M. Scott, *British Foreign Policy in the Age of the American Revolution* (Oxford, 1990), pp. 268–9.

3   See, for example, *Morning Post, and Daily Advertiser*, 5 May 1778.

4   K.G. Davies (ed.), *Documents of the American Revolution, 1770–1783: Colonial Office Series* (21 vols, Shannon, 1972–81), xv. pp. 57–62.

5   Ibid., xv. pp. 73–6.

6   See William L. Clements Library, Ann Arbor, MI, Wedderburn Papers, a paper drawn up by Alexander Wedderburn, the British solicitor general, probably in January 1778, on the British position in the negotiations.

7   Robert A. Rutland (ed.), *The Papers of George Mason* (3 vols, Chapel Hill, 1970), i. p. 435.

8   Historical Manuscripts Commission (HMC), *The Manuscripts of the Earl of Carlisle* (London, 1897), p. 358.

9   See Jonathan R. Dull, *The French Navy And American Independence* (Princeton, 1975), pp. 107–11.

10 National Maritime Museum, Greenwich, Sandwich Papers, SAN/F/44/18, Sandwich's notes for cabinet, 4 April 1778.

11 National Archives of Scotland, Edinburgh, Logan Home of Edrom Muniments, GD 1/384/6/30.

12 University Library, Nottingham, Newcastle of Clumber MSS, NeC 2646.

13 'Revolutionary Letters Written to Colonel Timothy Pickering by George Williams of Salem', *Essex Insttute Historical Collections*, xliii (1907), p. 199.

14 Davies (ed.), *Documents of the American Revolution*, xv. p. 210.

15 Alexander William Crawford Lindsay, Lord Lindsay, *Lives of the Lindsays* (4 vols, Wigan, 1840), iii. p. 220.

16 Piers Mackesy, *The War for America, 1775–1783* (London, 1964), p. 232.

17 British Library (BL), London, India Office Records, Home Misc/142, p. 53, Hector Munro to Lord Weymouth, 27 October 1778.

18 Dull, *French Navy*, p. 133.

19 BL, Auckland Papers, Add. MS 34,416, fo. 246, Campbell to William Eden, 19 January 1779.

20 See, for example, William L. Clements Library, Clinton Papers, Sir George Collier to Clinton, [16 May 1779].

21 See Alexander A. Lawrence, *Storm over Savannah: The Story of Count d'Estaing and the Siege of the Town in 1779* (Athens, GA, 1951).

22 G.R. Barnes and J.H. Owen (eds), *The Private Papers of John, Earl of Sandwich* (4 vols, London, 1932–8), ii. p. 308.

23 For Clinton's attempts to provoke Washington into battle, see Davies (ed.), *Documents of the American Revolution*, xvii. p. 146.

24 Clinton's strengths and weaknesses are shrewdly considered in William B. Willcox, *Portrait of a General: Sir Henry Clinton in the War of Independence* (New York, 1964).

25 See W.S. Coker and R.R. Rea (eds), *Anglo–Spanish Confrontation on the Gulf Coast during the American Revolution* (Pensacola, 1982).

26 O.F. Christie (ed.), *The Diary of the Revd. William Jones, 1777–1821* (London, 1929), p. 58.

27 TNA, Colonial Office Papers, CO 137/75, fo. 31.

28 Ibid., CO 91/25, Eliott to Lord Weymouth, 25 August 1779.

29 For the Irish volunteers see especially Peter Smyth, 'The Volunteers and Parliament', in Thomas Bartlett and D.W. Hayton (eds), *Penal Era and Golden Age: Essays in Irish History, 1690–1800* (Belfast, 1979), pp. 113–36; and Vincent Morley, *Irish Opinion and the American Revolution, 1760–1783* (Cambridge, 2002), Chapters 3 and 4.

30 University Library, Hull, Hotham Papers, DD HO 4/20, Lord Buckinghamshire to Sir Charles Thompson, 12 October 1779.

31 TNA, State Papers Military, SP 41/33, fo. 20, Lord Edgcumbe to Lord Weymouth, 13 August 1779.

32 Wiltshire Record Office, Trowbridge, Savernake Estate Papers, MS 9, Matthew Bentham to Lord Ailesbury, 10 October 1779.

33 BL, Add. MS 46,473, fo. 86.

34 See A.T. Paterson, *The Other Armada: The Franco–Spanish Attempt to Invade Britain in 1779* (Manchester, 1960).

35 See Stephen Conway, *The British Isles and the War of American Independence* (Oxford, 2000), pp. 218–23, 233–8.

36 Birmingham City Archives, Galton Papers, 248/2.

37 Christopher Wyvill, *Political Papers* (6 vols, York, 1794–1802), iii. p. 236.

38 For the history of the French expeditionary troops, see Lee Kennett, *The French Forces in America, 1780–1783* (Westport, CT, 1977).

39 For Arnold and his defection, see Willard Sterne Randall, *Benedict Arnold: Patriot and Traitor* (New York, 1990).

40 National Library of Scotland, Edinburgh, Robertson–MacDonald Papers, MS 3945, fo. 61, Alexander MacDonald to his wife, 10 June 1780.

41 Jac Weller, 'The Irregular war in the South', *Military Affairs*, xxiv (1960), p. 133.

42 TNA, Cornwallis Papers, PRO 30/11/2, fo. 158, George Turnbull to Cornwallis, 15 June 1780.

43 Ibid., fo. 252, Lord Rawdon to Cornwallis, 7 July 1780.

44 Ibid., fo. 162, Turnbull to Cornwallis, 16 June 1780.

45 Davies (ed.), *Documents of the American Revolution*, xviii. p. 170.

46 BL, Journal of Alexander Chesney, Add. MS 32,627, fo. 17.

47   Library of Congress, Washington, DC, Greene Letter-book, I, to Robert Howe, 29 December 1780.

48   Mackesy, *War for America*, pp. 373–5.

49   National Archives of Scotland, Broughton and Cally Muniments, GD 10/1421/7/338.

50   TNA, Colonial Office Papers, CO 318/6, fo. 79.

51   BL, India Office Records, Munro Collection, MSS Eur. F 151/140, Thomas Munro to his father, 11 October 1780.

52   See Isabel de Madariaga, *Britain, Russia, and the Armed Neutrality of 1780: Sir James Harris's Mission to St Petersburg during the American Revolution* (New Haven, 1962).

53   See Scott, *British Foreign Policy*, pp. 307–9.

54   See, for example, Paul H. Smith et al (eds), *Letters of Delegates to Congress, 1774–1789* (26 vols, Washington, DC, 1976–2000), xvi. pp. 561, xvii. p. 279.

55   Richard B. Morris, *The Peacemakers: The Great Powers and American Independence* (New York, 1965), pp. 173–90.

56   See the contemporary material collected in N. Orwin Rush, *Spain's Final Triumph Over Great Britain in the Gulf of Mexico: The Battle of Pensacola, March 9 to May 8, 1781* (Talahassee, 1966).

57   See Lawrence E. Babits, *A Devil of a Whipping: The Battle of Cowpens* (Chapel Hill, 2001).

58   See Lawrence E. Babits and Joshua B. Howard, *Long, Obstinate, and Bloody: The Battle of Guilford Court House* (Chapel Hill, 2009).

59   HMC, *Report on the Laing Manuscripts* (2 vols, London, 1914–25), ii. p. 510.

60   Julian P. Boyd et al (eds), *The Papers of Thomas Jefferson* (19 vols, Princeton, 1950–74), v. p. 361.

61   John C. Dann (ed.), *The Revolution Remembered: Eyewitness Accounts of the War for Independence* (Chicago, 1980), pp. 220–1.

62   TNA, Cornwallis Papers, PRO 30/11/68, fo. 43, Clinton to Cornwallis, 11 July 1781.

63   See John D. Grainger, *The Battle of Yorktown, 1781: A Reassessment* (Woodbridge, 2005).

64   BL, Auckland Papers, Add. MS 34,418, fo. 213, Loughborough to William Eden, 13 December 1781.

65   West Yorkshire Archives Service, Leeds, Ramsden Papers, Rockingham Letters, vol 2c, William Weddell to his wife, 13 December 1781.

66   BL, India Office Records, Munro Collection, MSS Eur F 151/140, Thomas Munro to his father, 2 October 1782.

67   Ibid., India Office Records, Home Misc/160.

68   The true value of Jamaica to Britain has been much debated by historians: see, for example, R.B. Sheridan, 'The Wealth of Jamaica in the Eighteenth Century', *Economic History Review*, 2nd series, xviii (1965),

pp. 292–311; R.P. Thomas, 'The Sugar Colonies of the Old Empire: Profit or Loss for Great Britain?', *Economic History Review*, 2nd series, xxi (1968), pp. 30–45; Philip R.P. Coelho, 'The Profitability of Imperialism: The British Experience in the West Indies, 1768–1772', *Explorations in Economic History*, x (1973), pp. 253–80.

69 See Stephen Conway, '"A Joy Unknown for Years Past": The American War, Britishness and the Celebration of Rodney's Victory at the Saints', *History*, lxxxvi (2001), pp. 180–99.

70 Sir John Knox Laughton (ed.), *Letters and Papers of Charles, Lord Barham* (3 vols, London, 1907–11), i. p. 178.

71 Amandus Johnson (ed. and trans.), *The Naval Campaigns of Count de Grasse* (Philadelphia, 1942), p. 103.

72 BL, Add. 38,605, fo. 142.

73 Huntington Library, San Marino, CA, Extra Orderly Book, Boston and Gibraltar, 1775–1782, HM 52688, fo. 32.

74 John Drinkwater, *The History of the Late Siege of Gibraltar* (London, 1785), p. 291.

75 Minor operations continued: see, for example, TNA, Colonial Office Papers, CO 91/30, Eliott to Thomas Townshend, 15 January 1783.

76 BL, India Office Records, Diary of an unidentified officer, MSS Eur. C. 156a.

Chapter Four

1 For the British volunteers, see Stephen Conway, '"Like the Irish"? Volunteer Corps and Volunteering in Britain during the American War', in Julie Flavell and Stephen Conway (eds), *Britain and America Go to War: The Impact of War and Warfare in Anglo–America, 1754–1815* (Gainesville, 2004), pp. 143–69; for the Irish volunteers, see above, pp. 100–1.

2 For estimates of the number of slaves who fled from their owners in North America, see Casandra Pybus, 'Thomas Jefferson's Faulty Math: The Question of Slave Defections in the American Revolution', *William & Mary Quarterly*, 3rd series, lxiii (2005), pp. 244–64.

3 Leonard Lundin, *Cockpit of the Revolution: The War for Independence in New Jersey* (Princeton, 1940). The aptness of the phrase is considered in Mark Edward Lender, 'The "Cockpit" Reconsidered: Revolutionary New Jersey as a Military Theatre', in Barbara J. Mitnick (ed.), *New Jersey in the American Revolution* (New Brunswick, NJ, 2005), pp. 45–60.

4 Richard K. MacMaster (ed.), 'News of the Yorktown Campaign: The Journal of Dr Robert Honyman, April 17–November 25, 1781', *Virginia Magazine of History and Biography*, lxxix (1971), p. 394.

5 West Suffolk Record Office, Bury St Edmunds, Grafton Papers, Ac 423/191, O'Hara to the Duke of Grafton, 20 April 1781.

6 'Bamford's Diary: The Revolutionary Diary of a British Officer', *Maryland Historical Magazine*, xxvii (1932), p. 301.

7 The National Archives of the United Kingdom (TNA), Kew, Colonial Office Papers, CO 91/26, George Augustus Eliott to Lord Weymouth, 8 January 1780.

8 Centre for Buckinghamshire Studies, Aylesbury, Howard –Vyse Deposit, D/HV B10/8, 13.

9 British Library (BL), London, Egerton MS 2659, fo. 186.

10 New-York Historical Society, New York City, Joseph Reed Papers, Journal of John Miller, 25 September 1777.

11 TNA, Audit Office Papers, Loyalist Claims Commission, AO 12/50, fo. 78.

12 BL, Diary of Lieutenant William Digby of the 53rd Foot, Add. MS 32,413, fo. 64.

13 Ibid., Liverpool Papers, Add. 38,405, fo. 125, Sir Eyre Coote to Charles Jenkinson, 1 December 1780.

14 J.C. Fitzpatrick (ed.), *The Writings of George Washington* (39 vols, Washington, DC, 1931–44), xv. p. 189.

15 Their activities are vividly described in Wayne E. Lee, *Barbarians and Brothers: Anglo–American Warfare, 1500–1865* (Oxford, 2011), Chapter 8.

16 TNA, Cornwallis Papers, PRO 30/11/64, fo. 92.

17 Ibid., Colonial Office Papers, CO 5/95, fo. 39.

18 Ibid., CO 5/98, fo. 122.

19 E.L. Pierce (ed.), 'The Diary of John Rowe', *Massachusetts Historical Society Proceedings*, 2nd series, x (1895–6), p. 97.

20 John W. Jackson, *With the British Army in Philadelphia, 1777–1778* (San Rafael, CA, 1979), pp. 266–7.

21 TNA, Colonial Office Papers, CO 5/182, fo. 157–62.

22 Varnum Lansing Collins (ed.), *A Brief Narrative of the Ravages of the British and Hessians at Princeton in 1776–77* (Princeton, 1906), p. 13.

23 TNA, Audit Office Papers, Loyalist Claims Commission, AO 12/13, fo. 91.

24 Historical Society of Pennsylvania, Philadelphia, Chester County Miscellaneous Papers, Depredation Claims, account sworn by James Davis, elder of the church, 18 November 1782.

25 Ballindalloch Castle, Grantown on Spey, Macpherson Grant of Ballindalloch Papers, Bundle 393, 'Inventory of Articles found in the Possession of Josh Anderson Private Soldier in 15th Regiment of Foot'.

26 BL, Log-book of a member of Gen. Robert Boyd's staff, Add. MS 38,605, fo. 3.

27 Ibid., Haldimand Papers, Add. MS 21,760, fos. 78–9.

28 New York State Library, Albany, Israel Keith Papers, Israel Keith to Cyrus Keith, 4 January 1777.

29 R.K. Showman et al (eds), *The Papers of General Nathanael Greene* (13 vols, Chapel Hill, 1976–2005), i. p. 375.

30 TNA, War Office Papers, WO 71/82, pp. 412–25; William L. Clements Library, Great Britain Order-book, 1 October 1776.

31 Don Higginbotham (ed.), *The Papers of James Iredell* (2 vols, Raleigh, NC, 1976), ii. p. 225.

32 Elizabeth A. Fenn, *Pox Americana: The Great Smallpox Epidemic of 1775–82* (New York, 2001).

33 Donald Wallace White, *A Village at War: Chatham, New Jersey, and the American Revolution* (Rutherford, NJ, 1979), pp. 239–41 (Appendix B, table 9).

34 John Shy, *A People Numerous and Armed: Reflections on the Military Struggle for American Independence* (New York, 1976), p. 171.

35 Mary Beth Norton, *Liberty's Daughters: The Revolutionary Experience of American Women, 1750–1800* (Boston, 1980), p. 215.

36 William L. Clements Library, Dering Family Papers, vol I, Sarah Thomas to Sylvester Dering, 11 March 1779.

37 Ben Baack, 'Forging a Nation State: The Continental Congress and the Financing of the War of American Independence', *Economic History Review*, liv (2001), p. 654 (Table 1).

38 Ann Bezanson, *Prices and Inflation during the American Revolution: Pennsylvania, 1770–1790* (Philadelphia, 1951), p. 14.

39 Harry M. Ward, *The War for Independence and the Transformation of American Society* (London, 1999), p. 40.

40 James A. Henretta, *The Origins of American Capitalism: Collected Essays* (Boston, 1991), p. 241; Gordon S. Wood, *The Radicalism of the American Revolution* (New York, 1992), especially pp. 6–7, 248.

41 Bernard A. Uhlendorf (ed.), *Revolution in America: Confidential Letters and Journals, 1776–1784 of Adjutant–General Major Baurmeister of the Hessian Forces* (New Brunswick, NJ, 1957), p. 237.

42 K.G. Davies (ed.), *Documents of the American Revolution, 1770–1783: Colonial Office Series* (21 vols, Shannon, 1972-81), xviii. p. 171.

43 Howard C. Rice and Anne S.K. Brown (ed. and trans), *The American Campaigns of Rochambeau's Army* (2 vols, Princeton, 1972), i. p. 48.

44 T.I. Wharton (ed.), 'Memoir of William Rawle', *Memoirs of the Historical Society of Pennsylvania*, iv (1840), p. 43.

45 Royal Artillery Institution, Woolwich, MS 9, vol II, p. 117.

46 E. G. Schaukirk, 'Occupation of New York City by the British', *Pennsylvania Magazine of History and Biography*, x (1886), p. 423.

47 See, for example, TNA, War Office Papers, WO 60/32, 'Return of Wood to be furnished', 22–24 November 1781, and 'list of the Inhabitants Who has not furnished the Quantity of Wood', n.d.

48 Ibid., WO 71/90, pp. 410–16.

49 The name gained currency at least partly because the flies caused similar devastation to the Hessians: see Philip J. Pauly, 'Fighting the Hessian Fly: American and British responses to Insect Invasion, 1776–1789', *Environmental History*, vii (2002), pp. 485–507.

50 Alnwick Castle, Northumberland, Percy Papers, vol xlix, Part A, p. 13; TNA, Colonial Office Papers, CO 5/94, fo. 416, Address of the Inhabitants of Newport.

51 TNA, British Army Headquarters Papers, PRO 30/55/18, 2214 (6).

52 Royal Artillery Institution, MS 9, vol II, p. 117.

53 Jackson, *With the British Army in Philadelphia*, p. 83.

54 New-York Historical Society, Faulkner Papers, Day-book, 1774–88, and Account-book, 1773–90.

55 Historical Society of Pennsylvania, Clifford Papers, vol 5, Thomas Clifford Jr, to Thomas Franks, 27 December 1777.

56 Huntington Library, San Marino, CA, Stowe Collection, Brydges Papers, STB Box 26, John Pool to Anna Eliza Elletson, 27 March 1777. See also, for the impact of martial law, Pool to the Duchess of Chandos, 12 September 1779, Edward East to the Duchess of Chandos, 11 September 1779, 11 May 1782.

57 National Library of Wales, Aberystwyth, Nassau Senior Papers, E 36, Thomas Yea to Robert George Bruce, 24 December 1778.

58 Stephen Conway, *The British Isles and the War of American Independence* (Oxford, 2000), p. 70.

59 Ibid., pp. 233–8, for the campaign for 'economical reform'.

60 National Library of Scotland, Edinburgh, William Wilson Papers, MS 9672, Day-book, 1771–80.

61 Public Record Office of Northern Ireland, Belfast, Greer Papers, D 1044/552, 572.

62 TNA, War Office Papers, WO 1/1007, p. 789.

63 Ibid., WO 1/1004, p. 395.

64 Ibid., WO 1/1007, p. 259.

65 See Stephen Conway, 'Locality, Metropolis, and Nation: The Impact of the Military Camps in England during the American War', *History*, lxxxii (1997), pp. 547–62.

66 Kenneth Morgan (ed.), *An American Quaker in the British Isles: The Travel Journals of Jabez Maud Fisher* (Oxford, 1992), p. 229.

67 See James E. Bradley, *Popular Politics and the American Revolution in England* (Macon, GA, 1986), and *Religion, Revolution, and English Radicalism* (Cambridge, 1990), Chapter 9.

68 *Journals of the House of Commons*, xxxv. p. 405 (27 October 1775).

69 Conway, *British Isles and the War of American Independence*, pp. 131, 288.

70 For the Church of England, see Paul Langford, 'The English Clergy and the American Revolution', in Eckhart Hellmuth (ed.), *The Transformation of Political Culture: England and Germany in the Late Eighteenth Century* (Oxford, 1990), pp. 338–72.

71 City Archives, Sheffield, Rockingham MSS, R 1/1569.

72 For Presbyterian migration to North America see R.J. Dickson, *Ulster Emigration to Colonial America, 1718–1775*, 2nd ed (Omah, 1988).

73 Catherine Coogan Ward and Robert E. Ward (eds), *The Letters of Charles O'Conor of Belanagare* (2 vols, Ann Arbor, MI, 1980), ii. pp. 110, 114. See also, for the complexities of the situation, Vincent Morley, *Irish Opinion and the American Revolution, 1760–1783* (Cambridge, 2002).

74 See Mrs Gillespie Smyth (ed.), *Memoirs and Correspondence ... of Sir Robert Murray Keith* (2 vols, London, 1849), ii. pp. 60–1.

75 *Gentleman's Magazine*, xlv (1775), p. 396, and xlvi (1776), p. 228.

76 Bob Harris, *Politics and the Rise of the Press: Britain and France, 1620–1800* (London, 1996), p. 58.

77 Historical Manuscripts Commission (HMC), *The Manuscripts of the Earl of Dartmouth* (3 vols., London, 1887–96), iii. pp. 221–22.

78 Staffordshire Record Office, Stafford, Congreve Papers, D 1057/M/F/26.

79 Brian Fitzgerald (ed.), *Correspondence of Emily, Duchess of Leinster* (3 vols, Dublin, 1949–57), iii. p. 226.

80 Phyllis Hembry (ed.), *Calendar of Bradford-on-Avon Settlement Examinations and removal Orders, 1725–1798* (Wiltshire Records Society, xlvi, Trowbridge, 1990), p. 43.

81 Victor Enthoven, 'Dutch Maritime Strategy', in Donald Stoker, Kenneth J. Hagan and Michael T. McMaster (eds), *Strategy in the American War of Independence* (London, 2010), pp. 187, 189.

82 HMC, *Manuscripts of the Earl of Dartmouth*, iii. p. 222.

83 See Rafael Torres Sánchez, 'Monopoly or the Free Market: Two Ways of Tackling the Expenditure: The Expedition to Minorca (1781–1782)', in Stephen Conway and Rafael Torres Sánchez (ed.), *The Spending of States: Military Expenditure during the Long Eighteenth Century: Patterns, Organization, and Consequences, 1650–1815* (Saarbrücken, 2011), pp. 313–38.

84 Robert D. Harris, 'French Finances and the American War, 1777–1783', *Journal of Modern History*, xlviii (1976), p. 247.

85 For problems with the structure of French public debt, see James B. Collins, *The State in Early Modern France* (Cambridge, 1995), p. 236.

86 See Rafael Torres Sánchez, 'Public Finances and Tobacco in Spain for the American War of Independence', in H.V. Bowen and A. González

Enciso (eds), *Mobilising Resources for War: Britain and Spain at Work during the Early Modern Period* (Pamplona, 2006), pp. 191–224.

87 Enthoven, 'Dutch Maritime Strategy', especially Table 9.3 and Appendix 9.1.

88 José Jurado-Sánchez, 'The Spanish National Budget in a Century of War: The Importance of Financing the Army and Navy during the Eighteenth Century', in Rafael Torres Sánchez (ed.), *War, State, and Development: Fiscal-Military States in the Eighteenth Century* (Pamplona, 2007), p. 228 (Appendix).

89 BL, Miscellaneous Papers relating to the Spanish Navy, 1740–82, Add. MS 20,962, fo. 324.

90 Figures derived from Jonathan R. Dull, *The French Navy and American Independence* (Princeton, 1975), pp. 359–76.

91 Ibid., pp. 349, 359–76.

92 Agustín González Enciso, 'Buying Cannon Outside: When, Why, How Many? The Supplying of Foreign Iron Cannons for the Spanish Navy in the Eighteenth Century', in Richard Harding and Sergio Solbes Ferri (eds), *The Contractor State and Its Implications, 1659–1815* (Las Palmas de Gran Canaria, 2012), pp. 135–57.

93 Huntington Library, Intelligence, enclosed in Lord North to Admiral Lord Howe, 28 October 1777, HM 25799, pp. 3–5.

94 See, for example, BL, Bowood MSS, B1, fo. 15, Francis Baring to the Earl of Shelburne, 15 November 1782.

95 Dr Williams' Library, London, Wodrow–Kenrick Correspondence, MS 24157 (51).

96 M.L. Robertson, 'Scottish Commerce and the American War of Independence', *Economic History Review*, 2nd series, ix (1956–7), p. 123.

97 David J. Starkey, *British Privateering Enterprise in the Eighteenth Century* (Exeter, 1990), p. 217 (Table 23).

98 G.R. Barnes and J.H Owen (eds), *The Private Papers of John, Earl of Sandwich* (4 vols, Navy Records Society, London, 1932–8), iv. p. 148.

99 See above, p. 109.

100 C. Bruyn Andrews (ed.), *The Torrington Diaries* (4 vols, London, 1934–8), i. p. 94.

101 Leicestershire Record Office, Turville Constable Maxwell MSS, p. 1122.

Chapter Five

1 My account of the peacemaking draws heavily on C. R. Ritcheson, 'The Earl of Shelburne and Peace with America, 1782–1783', *International History Review*, v (1983), pp. 322–45; Jonathan R. Dull, *A Diplomatic History of the American Revolution* (New Haven,

1985), Chapters 17–20; H. M. Scott, *British Foreign Policy in the Age of the American Revolution* (Oxford, 1990), Chapter 12; and Andrew Stockley, *Britain and France at the Birth of America: The European Powers and the Peace Negotiations of 1782–1783* (Exeter, 2001).

2   See The National Archives of the United Kingdom (TNA), Foreign Office Papers, FO 27/2, Fox to Thomas Grenville, 26 May 1782.

3   See, for example, William L. Clements Library, Ann Arbor, MI, Shelburne Papers, Richard Oswald to Thomas Townshend, 11 October 1782.

4   Ibid., Oswald to Shelburne, 18 April 1782; Francis Wharton (ed.), *The Revolutionary Diplomatic Correspondence of the United States* (6 vols, Washington, DC, 1889), v. p. 538, Franklin to Shelburne, 18 April 1782.

5   TNA, Foreign Office Papers, FO 95/511, Fox's instructions to Grenville, 21 May 1782.

6   William L. Clements Library, Shelburne Papers, Franklin to Oswald, 26 November 1782.

7   Ibid., Oswald to Townshend, 15 November 1782.

8   Henri Doniol (ed.), *Histoire de la participation de la France à l'établissment des Etats-Unis d'Amérique: correspondence diplomatique et documents* (5 vols, Paris, 1886–99), v. p. 84.

9   Bedfordshire Record Office, Bedford, Lucas of Wrest Park Collection, Robinson Papers, L 30/14/307, Shelburne to the Earl of Grantham, September 1782.

10 See Charles Royster, *A Revolutionary People at War: The Continental Army and American Character, 1775–1783* (Chapel Hill, 1979).

11 Thomas W. Copeland et al (eds), *The Correspondence of Edmund Burke* (10 vols, Cambridge, 1958–78), iii. p. 294.

12 John Shy (ed.), *Winding Down: The Revolutionary War Letters of Lieutenant Benjamin Gilbert* (Ann Arbor, MI, 1989), p. 41.

13 Library of Congress, Washington, DC, Bland Papers, Bannister to [Theodorick Bland], 16 May 1781.

14 See above, p. 65.

15 Evelyn M. Acomb (ed. and trans), *The Revolutionary War Journal of Baron Ludwig von Closen* (Chapel Hill, 1958), p. 89.

16 See Troy Bickham, 'Sympathizing with Sedition? George Washington, the British Press, and British Attitudes during the American War of Independence', *William & Mary Quarterly*, 3rd series, lix (2002), pp. 101–22.

17 R.K. Showman et al (eds), *The Papers of General Nathanael Greene* (13 vols, Chapel Hill, 1976–2005), iv. p. 108.

18 Biographies of Washington are too numerous to list, but two recent additions to the genre present interesting perspectives: Ron Chernow,

Stephen Conway

Washington: A Life (London, 2010), and Stephen Brumwell, George Washington: Gentleman Warrior (London, 2012).

19 For Howe's involvement in training light infantry companies in 1774, see J.A. Houlding, Fit for Service: The Training of the British Army, 1715–1795 (Oxford, 1981), pp. 336–7.

20 The diary of Robert Honyman, a Virginian doctor, who saw British troops drilling in Boston just before the war, is clear on this point: Huntington Library, San Marino, CA, Robert Honyman's Journal, 1775, HM 818, p. 71.

21 Matthew H. Spring, With Zeal and With Bayonets Only: The British Army on Campaign in North America, 1775–1783 (Norman, OK, 2008), pp. 140–51.

22 See the stimulating essay by Julie Flavell, 'British Perceptions of New England and the Decision for a Coercive Colonial Policy, 1774–1775', in Julie Flavell and Stephen Conway (eds), Britain and America Go to War: The Impact of War and Warfare in Anglo–America, 1754–1815 (Gainesville, FL, 2004), pp. 95–115.

23 Alnwick Castle, Northumberland, Percy Family Papers, vol L, Pt. A, fo. 53, Earl Percy to Edward Harvey, 20 April 1775.

24 These timings are taken from Jonathan Scott, When the Waves Ruled Britannia: Geography and Political Identities, 1500–1800 (Cambridge, 2011), p. 74.

25 TNA, Colonial Office Papers, CO 5/94, fo. 311, Howe to Germain, 30 August 1777.

26 Ibid., Treasury Papers, T 64/108, fo. 73, Howe to John Robinson, 2 December 1776.

27 See R.A. Bowler, Logistics and the Failure of the British Army in North America (Princeton, 1975).

28 Acomb (ed. and trans), The Revolutionary Journal of Baron Ludwig von Closen, p. 75.

29 The political considerations that may have influenced Howe are assessed in Ira D. Gruber, The Howe Brothers and the American Revolution (Chapel Hill, 1972).

30 See Rodney Atwood, The Hessians: Mercenaries from Hessen–Kassel and the American Revolution (Cambridge, 1980), Chapter 9.

31 William L. Clements Library, Clinton Papers, memo of conversation, 7 February 1776.

32 BL, Haldimand Papers, Add. MS 21,760, fo. 32, John Butler to Mason Bolton, 8 July 1778.

33 See, for example, City Archives, Sheffield, Spencer Stanhope of Cannon Hall Muniments, 60542/10, Francis Bushill Sill to John Spencer, 19 September 1775.

34 Library of Congress, Horatio Gates Papers, folder 4, Gates to Burgoyne, 2 September 1777.

202

35 Charlotte S.J. Epping (ed. and trans), 'Journal of Du Roi the Elder', *German American Annals*, xiii (1911), p. 154.

36 See, for example, William L. Clements Library, Clinton Papers, James Robertson to Clinton, 13 January 1776.

37 See, for example, the speech of William Lyttelton, a former governor of South Carolina, 26 October 1775, in R.C. Simons and P.D.G. Thomas (eds), *Proceedings and Debates of the British Parliaments respecting North America, 1754–1783* (6 vols to date, Millward, NY, 1982 –), vi. p. 96.

38 For the relationship between slave uprising in the Caribbean and the events in North America, see Richard B. Sheridan, 'The Jamaica Slave Insurrection Scare of 1776 and the American Revolution', *Journal of Negro History*, lxi (1976), pp. 290–308.

39 See Philip D. Morgan and Andrew Jackson O'Shaughnessy, 'Arming Slaves in the American Revolution', in Christopher Leslie Brown and Philip D. Morgan (eds), *Arming Slaves: From Classical Times to the Modern Age* (New Haven, 2006), pp. 180–208.

40 Centre for Kentish Studies, Maidstone, Amherst Papers, U 1350 O79/13, Robertson to Amherst, 9 November 1776.

41 W.B. Weedon (ed.), 'Diary of Enos Hitchcock', *Rhode Island Historical Society Publications*, vii (1899), pp. 169–70.

42 See TNA, War Office Papers, WO 34/110, fo. 144, 'Remarks on some Improvements Proposed by an Officer to be made in the Plan of the American War', n.d. but probably 1778.

43 See John Shy, *A People Numerous and Armed: Reflections on the Military Struggle for American Independence* (New York, 1976), especially pp. 217–22.

44 See, for example, N.A.M. Rodger, 'The Continental Commitment in the Eighteenth Century', in Lawrence Freedman, Paul Hayes and Robert O'Neill (eds), *War, Strategy, and International Politics: Essays in Honour of Sir Michael Howard* (Oxford, 1992), pp. 39–55.

45 Percentages derived from Piers Mackesy, *The War for America* (London, 1964), pp. 524–5.

46 The British dilemma is succinctly analysed in William B. Willcox, 'British Strategy in America, 1778', *Journal of Modern History*, xix (1947), pp. 97–121.

47 For British responses to Rodney's victory, see Stephen Conway, '"A Joy Unknown for Years Past": The American War, Britishness and the Celebration of Rodney's Victory at the Saints', *History*, lxxxvi (2001), pp. 180–99.

48 As N.A.M. Rodger has noted, 'The Battle of the Saintes was the first and last major action ever fought by the principal British fleet outside European waters – indeed, it did not leave European waters again until 1944.' 'Seapower and Empire: Cause and Effect?', in Bob Moore

and Henk van Nierop (eds), *Colonial Empires Compared: Britain and the Netherlands, 1750–1850* (Aldershot, 2003), p. 107.

49 TNA, Colonial Office Papers, CO 91/25, Eliott to Viscount Weymouth, 25 August 1779.

50 See the figures in Jonathan R. Dull, *The French Navy and American Independence* (Princeton, 1975), pp. 359–76.

51 BL, Liverpool Papers, Add. MS 38,344, fo. 162.

52 Stephen Conway, *The British Isles and the War of American Independence* (Oxford, 2000), p. 54.

53 See, for example, the fears of the Rev. John Butler, Surrey Record Office, Guildford Muniment Room, Onslow MSS, 173/2/1/125, Butler to the Earl of Onslow, 6 October 1776.

54 John Brewer, *The Sinews of Power: War, Money, and the English State, 1688–1783* (London, 1989).

55 William Cobbett and John Wright (eds), *The Parliamentary History of England* (36 vols, London, 1806–20), xx. p. 57, xxi. p. 1330.

56 See Peter Mathias and Patrick O'Brien, 'Taxation in Britain and France, 1715–1810', *Journal of European Economic History*, v (1976), pp. 601–50.

57 See M.D. Kwass, *Privilege and the Politics of Taxation in Eighteenth-Century France: Liberté, égalité, fiscalité* (Cambridge, 2000).

58 For the British state's advantage in this respect, see Brewer, *Sinews of Power*, especially pp. 178–82.

59 For British consols, see C.E. Heim and P. Mirowski, 'Interest Rates and Crowding Out during Britain's Industrial Revolution', *Journal of Economic History*, xlvii (1987), especially p. 120.

60 Sir John Fortescue (ed.), *The Correspondence of King George the Third* (6 vols, London, 1927–8), v. p. 136.

Chapter Six – Epilogue

1 See Stephen Conway, *Britain, Ireland, and Continental Europe in the Eighteenth Century: Similarities, Connections, Identities* (Oxford, 2011), p. 94–7.

2 This view is supported in Brendan Simms, *Three Victories and Defeat: The Rise and Fall of the First British Empire, 1714–1783* (London, 2007), especially Chapters 22–3.

3 'The Present State of Europe Considered', *General Advertiser*, 26 November 1785.

4 Eliga H. Gould, 'A Virtual Nation: Greater Britain and the Imperial Legacy of the American Revolution', *American Historical Review*, civ (1999), pp. 476–89.

5   See P.J. Marshall, *Remaking the British Atlantic: The United States and Britain after Independence* (Oxford, 2012).

6   Sarah Pearsall, *Atlantic Families: Lives and Letters in the Later Eighteenth Century* (Oxford, 2008).

7   Sylvia R. Frey, *Water from the Rock: Black Resistance in a Revolutionary Age* (Princeton, 1991), pp. 193–6.

8   Maya Jasanoff, *Liberty's Exiles: American Loyalists in the Revolutionary World* (New York, 2011).

9   The terminology is disputed: see P.J. Marshall, 'Britain without America – A Second Empire?', in P.J. Marshall (ed.), *The Oxford History of the British Empire*, ii. *The Eighteenth Century* (Oxford, 1998), pp. 576–95.

10 See Simon Schama, *Patriots and Liberators: Revolution in the Netherlands, 1780–1813* (London, 1991).

11 Jacques A. Barbier and Herbert S. Klein, 'Revolutionary Wars and Public Finances: The Madrid Treasury, 1784–1807', *Journal of Economic History*, xli (1981), pp. 315–39.

12 Quoted in John Lynch, *Bourbon Spain, 1700–1808* (Oxford, 1989), p. 320.

13 J.H. Elliott, *Empires of the Atlantic World: Britain and Spain in America, 1492–1830* (New Haven, 2006), p. 355.

14 Quoted in Mario Rodriguez, 'The Impact of the American Revolution on the Spanish- and Potuguese-Speaking World', in Richard B. Morris (ed.), *The Impact of the American Revolution Abroad* (Washington, DC, 1976), p. 103.

15 Ibid., p. 115.

16 See Elliott, *Empires of the Atlantic World*, Chapters 11 and 12.

17 Paul Cheney, 'A False Dawn for Enlightenment Cosmopolitanism?. Franco–American Trade during the American War of Independence', *William & Mary Quarterly*, 3rd series, lxiii (2006), pp. 463–88.

18 See Laurent Dubois, *A Colony of Citizens: Revolution and Slave Emancipation in the French Caribbean, 1787–1804* (Chapel Hill, 2004).

19 Jonathan Boucher, *A View of the Causes and Consequences of the American Revolution: In Thirteen Discourses, Preached in North America between the Years 1763 and 1775* (London, 1797), vii.

20 A good example is the Swedish-born Axel Fersen, who seemed to despise everything he saw in America: see Katherine Prescott Wormeley (ed. and trans), *Diary and Correspondence of Count Axel Fersen* (London, 1902).

21 Forrest McDonald, 'The Relation of the French Peasant Veterans of the American Revolution to the Fall of Feudalism in France, 1789–1792', *Agricultural History*, xxv (1951), pp. 151–61.

22 See Claude Fohlen, 'The Impact of the American Revolution on France',

in Morris (ed.), *Impact of the American Revolution Abroad*, especially p. 27.

23 The classic exposition of the case for ideological transfer across the Atlantic is R. R. Palmer, *The Age of the Democratic Revolution: A Political History of Europe and America, 1760–1800* (2 vols, Princeton, 1959).

24 See, especially, Robert D. Harris, 'French Finances and the American War, 1777–1783', *Journal of Modern History*, xlviii (1976), pp. 233–58.

25 J.C. Fitzpatrick (ed.), *The Writings of George Washington* (39 vols, Washington, DC, 1931–44), xxviii. p. 500.

26 John R. McCusker and Russell R. Menard, *The Economy of British America, 1607–1789* (Chapel Hill, 1991), p. 374.

27 Harry M. Ward, *The War for Independence and the Transformation of American Society* (London, 1999), p. 47.

28 See Christopher Leslie Brown, *Moral Capital: Foundations of British Abolitionism* (Chapel Hill, 2006).

29 Richard Price, *Observations on the Importance of the American Revolution* (London, 1784), especially pp. 14–15.

Further Reading

The literature on the American Revolutionary War is vast. What follows represents a selection of particularly useful books, essays, and articles. Some have informed the arguments deployed in the current work; others present a very different picture to the one painted here. The list is confined to secondary sources; the endnotes give an indication of the range of primary materials – both archival and printed – available for scholars of the conflict.

Alden, John, *A History of the American Revolution* (London, 1969)

Armitage, David, 'The Declaration of Independence and International Law', *William & Mary Quarterly*, 3rd series, lix (2002)

Baack, Ben, 'Forging a Nation State: The Continental Congress and the Financing of the War of American Independence', *Economic History Review*, liv (2001)

Barbier, Jacques A., and Klein, Herbert S., 'Revolutionary Wars and Public Finances: The Madrid Treasury, 1784–1807', *Journal of Economic History*, xli (1981)

Bickham, Troy, *Making Headlines: The American Revolution as seen Through the British Press* (De Kalb, Ill., 2009)

Black, Jeremy, *War for America: The Fight for Independence, 1775–1783* (Stroud, 1991)

Bowler, R.A., *Logistics and the Failure of the British Army in North America* (Princeton, 1975)

Bradley, James E., *Popular Politics and the American Revolution in England* (Macon, Ga., 1986)

Brown, Christopher Leslie, *Moral Capital: The Foundations of British Abolitionism* (Chapel Hill, 2006)

Chickering, Roger, and Förster, Stig (eds.), *War in an Age of Revolution, 1775–1815* (Cambridge, 2010)

Coker, W.S., and Rea, R.R. (eds.), *Anglo–Spanish Confrontation on the Gulf Coast during the American Revolution* (Pensacola, 1982)

Conway, Stephen, *The British Isles and the War of American Independence* (Oxford, 2000)

Conway, Stephen, *The War of American Independence, 1775–1783* (London, 1995)

Dickinson, H.T. (ed.), *Britain and the American Revolution* (London, 1998)

Dull, Jonathan R., *A Diplomatic History of the American Revolution* (New Haven, 1985)

Dull, Jonathan R., *The French Navy and American Independence* (Princeton, 1975)

Enthoven, Victor, 'Dutch Maritime Strategy', in Donald Stoker, Kenneth J. Hagen, and Michael T. McMaster (eds.), *Strategy in the American War of Independence* (London, 2010)

Fenn, Elizabeth A., *Pox Americana: The Great Smallpox Epidemic of 1775–82* (New York, 2001)

Ferling, John, *Almost a Miracle: The American Victory in the War of Independence* (New York, 2007)

Fischer, David Hackett, *Washington's Crossing* (New York, 2004)

Flavell, Julie, and Conway, Stephen (eds.), *Britain and America Go to War: The Impact of War and Warfare in Anglo–America, 1754–1815* (Gainesville, 2004)

Gould, Eliga H., *The Persistence of Empire: British Political Culture in the Age of the American Revolution* (Chapel Hill, 2000)

Graebner, Norman A., Burns, Richard Dean, and Siracusa, Joseph M., *Foreign Affairs and the Founding Fathers: from Confederation to Constitution, 1776–1787* (Santa Barbara, Ca., 2011)

Griffiths, Samuel B., *The War of American Independence: from 1760 to the Surrender at Yorktown* (Urbana, Ill., 2002)

Gruber, Ira D., *The Howe Brothers and the American Revolution* (New York, 1972)

Harris, Robert D., 'French Finances and the American War, 1777–1783', *Journal of Modern History*, xlviii (1976)

Hibbert, Christopher, *Redcoats and Rebels: The War for America, 1770–1781* (London, 1990)

Higginbotham, Don, *The War of American Independence: Military Attitudes, Policies, and Practice, 1763–1789* (New York, 1971)

Jackson, John W., *With the British Army in Philadelphia, 1777–1778* (San Rafael, Ca., 1979)

Jasanoff, Maya, *Liberty's Exiles: American Loyalists in the Revolutionary World* (New York, 2011)

Kennett, Lee, *The French Forces in America, 1780–1783* (Westport, Conn., 1977)

Kurtz, Stephen G., and Hutson, James H. (eds.), *Essays on the American Revolution* (Chapel Hill, 1973)

Langford, Paul, 'The English Clergy and the American Revolution', in Eckhart Hellmuth (ed.), *The Transformation of Political Culture: England and Germany in the Late Eighteenth Century* (Oxford, 1990)

Lawrence, Alexander A., *Storm over Savannah: The Story of Count d'Estaing and the Siege of the Town in 1779* (Athens, Ga., 1951)

Mackesy, Piers, *The War for America, 1775–1783* (London, 1964)

Marshall, P.J., *The Making and Unmaking of Empires: Britain, India, and America, c.1750–1783* (Oxford, 2005)

Marshall, P.J., *Remaking the British Atlantic: The United States and Britain after Independence* (Oxford, 2012)

Middlekauff, Robert, *The Glorious Cause: The American Revolution, 1763–1789* (New York, 1982)

Middleton, Richard, *The War of American Independence, 1775–1783* (London, 2012)

Mitnick, Barbara J. (ed.), *New Jersey in the American Revolution* (New Brunswick, NJ, 2005)

Morley, Vincent, *Irish Opinion and the American Revolution, 1760–1783* (Cambridge, 2002)

Morris, Richard B. (ed.), *The Impact of the American Revolution Abroad* (Washington, DC, 1976)

Morris, Richard B., *The Peacemakers: The Great Powers and American Independence* (New York, 1965)

Norton, Mary Beth, *Liberty's Daughters: The Revolutionary Experience of American Women, 1750–1800* (Boston, 1980)

O'Shaughnessy, Andrew Jackson, *An Empire Divided: The British West Indies and the American Revolution* (Philadelphia, 2000)

Paterson, A.T., *The Other Armada: The Franco–Spanish Attempt to Invade Britain in 1779* (Manchester, 1960)

Peckham, Howard, *The War for Independence: A Military History* (Chicago, 1958)

Randall, Willard Sterne, *Benedict Arnold: Patriot and Traitor* (New York, 1990)

Robson, Eric, *The American Revolution in its Political and Military Aspects, 1763–1783* (London, 1955)

Shy, John, *A People Numerous and Armed: Reflections on the Military Struggle for American Independence* (New York, 1976)

Scott, H.S., *British Foreign Policy in the Age of the American Revolution* (Oxford, 1990)

Smelser, Marshall, *The Winning of Independence* (New York, 1973)

Torres Sánchez, Rafael, 'Public Finances and Tobacco in Spain for the American War of Independence', in H.V. Bowen and A. González Enciso (eds.), *Mobilising Resources for War: Britain and Spain at Work during the Early Modern Period* (Pamplona, 2006)

Torres Sánchez, Rafael, 'Monopoly or the Free Market: Two Ways of tackling the Expenditure: The Expedition to Minorca (1781–1782)', in Stephen Conway and Rafael Torres Sánchez (eds.), *The Spending of States: Military Expenditure during the Long Eighteenth Century: Patterns, Organization, and Consequences, 1650–1815* (Saarbrücken, 2011).

Wallace, Willard M., *Appeal to Arms: A Military History of the American Revolution* (New York, 1951)

Ward, Christopher, *The War of the Revolution*, ed. John Alden (2 vols., New York, 1952)

Ward, Harry M., *The American Revolution: Nationhood Achieved, 1763–1788* (New York, 1995)

Ward, Harry M., *The War for Independence and the Transformation of American Society* (London, 1999)

White, Donald Wallace, *A Village at War: Chatham, New Jersey, and the American Revolution* (Rutherford, NJ, 1979)

Willcox, William B., *Portrait of a General: Sir Henry Clinton in the War of Independence* (New York, 1964)

Index

Entries relate only to the text (not the notes). References to the belligerents – America, Britain, France, Spain and the Dutch – have been omitted on the grounds that they occur so frequently that to list them would be unhelpful.

A Short History of . . .

the American Civil War	Paul Anderson (Clemson University)
the American Revolutionary War	Stephen Conway (University College London)
Ancient Greece	P J Rhodes, FBA (University of Durham)
Ancient Rome	Andrew Wallace-Hadrill (University of Cambridge)
the Anglo-Saxons	Henrietta Leyser (University of Oxford)
the Byzantine Empire	Dionysios Stathakopoulos (King's College London)
the Celts	Alex Woolf (University of St Andrews)
the Crimean War	Trudi Tate (University of Cambridge)
the English Renaissance Drama	Helen Hackett (University College, London)
the English Revolution and the Civil Wars	David J Appleby (University of Nottingham)
the Etruscans	Corinna Riva (University College London)
Imperial Egypt	Robert Morkot (University of Exeter)
Italian Renaissance	Virginia Cox (New York University)
the Korean War	Allan R Millett (University of New Orleans)
Medieval English Mysticism	Vincent Gillespie (University of Oxford)
the Minoans	John Bennet (University of Sheffield)
the Mongols	George Lane (SOAS, University of London)
the Mughal Empire	Michael Fisher (Oberlin College)
Muslim Spain	Alex J Novikoff (Rhodes College, Memphis)
the New Testament	Halvor Moxnes (University of Oslo)
Nineteenth-Century Philosophy	Joel Rasmussen (University of Oxford)
the Normans	Leonie Hicks (University of Southampton)
the Phoenicians	Glenn E Markoe
the Reformation	Helen Parish (University of Reading)